BODIES IN MOTION

EVOLUTION AND EXPERIENCE IN MOTORCYCLING

For Max Beerms with
best wishes
08/23/08

BODIES IN MOTION

EVOLUTION AND EXPERIENCE IN MOTORCYCLING

BY

STEVEN L. THOMPSON

PUBLISHED BY

AERO DESIGN & MFG. CO., INC.

ISBN-13: 978-0-9819001-1-7
ISBN-10: 1-0-9819001-1-7

Copy editors: John Joss and Laning Pepper Thompson
Cover and book design: Benjamin Kaiser

PRINTED IN THE UNITED STATES OF AMERICA

First paperback edition

10 9 8 7 6 5 4 3 2 1

CONTENTS

FOREWORD

In this book, my friend Steve Thompson examines some of the most nuanced aspects of the rider-machine relationship. His research and analytics break new ground, and also confirm things I've long sensed about what is inside the experience and appeal of motorcycle riding. This work helped me disentangle some aspects of our psychobiological relationship to the physical sensations of riding from the complex mix of cultural and social elements which surround motorcycling and scootering. I hope you will find it similarly useful, enlightening and enjoyable.

Steve and I came to our common interests about the underlying connections riders have with motorcycling's sensory experiences via entirely separate routes. Before we met I'd just started a small business, the Aerostich company, to make protective textile coveralls to help people commute to work on motorcycles more safely and comfortably, while allowing riders to wear their regular clothing for convenience. And before Steve met me, he was working in literary writing, journalism, art, history and historical research. We were both experienced riding and racing motorcyclists (Steve as an international road-racer, and me at local amateur AMA Enduros). We each deeply incorporated riding into our different and distant lives.

Our paths began to converge while I was working on prototypes of the first Aerostich riding suit. I read an editorial titled "The Right Stuff For Summer" in *Cycle Guide* magazine. It was by someone named Steven L. Thompson, who'd suggested the need for an entirely new kind of riding gear that would be cooler, lighter and easier to wear than heavy leathers. Something that was designed specifically for the broiling, thunderstorm-prone summers common throughout most of America. This author even imagined the kind of person who might someday produce such a garment. It was exactly the garment I was making, and the person being described seemed to be me (!), so I promised myself that as soon as the first production Aerostich Roadcrafter suit was ready, I'd send it to him.

A year or so later, Steve had left *Cycle Guide* to become the East Coast editor of *Cycle World* magazine when he received that first suit to evaluate. He understood its intent immediately, but before he'd written a single word about it, he was on the telephone, explaining an unusual problem: "Can you send me another suit?", he began. "I need another one right away." After a brief pause, he continued: "My friend Bob Sinclair took mine. He's the president of Saab, the car company, and he's a dedicated everyday commuting rider. He saw it in my office yesterday and he had to have it. Now he's borrowed it, and he won't return it. He said you should send him a bill…which is why I need another suit to test." By the time Steve finished fully explaining the situation, he'd made a new friend, and the Aero Design & Manufacturing Company Inc., had sold its first Roadcrafter suit.

Soon after that, Steve wrote about some of his early experiences with the Roadcrafter, and about a disturbing cultural bigotry he'd unexpectedly ridden straight into. He already knew that whenever riders wore functionally appropriate gear which did not meet the pre-conceived expectations of non-riding people, the non-riders were less than understanding. He described once entering a dark roadside tavern on a hot day in the 1960s, wearing race-spec leathers, and how everyone in the place suddenly went silent and stared. So, when wearing his Aerostich suit, he rode to a motorcycle parts store and the 'expert' working at the counter disparagingly asked him why he was wearing the slightly sci-fi looking Roadcrafter suit on such a warm, clear day, it struck him as more than simple ignorance, especially coming from within the moto-world. This was an entirely unanticipated expression of bias, ostracization and prejudice.

Steve's editorial column about those experiences was titled "Dressing Up." In it, he expressed a conviction that function, not culture, ought matter most in the wearing of protective rider's gear. So why wasn't this obvious to all riders?

Riding was simply too important for anything less, because riding's sensations and benefits so completely transcend the styles and cultures of the day. That courageous perspective is what separated Steve from most other riders, and from other motorcycle magazine editors. Near the end of the editorial he wrote, "I realized that I was going to be at war with some basic American values for a long, long time." As I read those words, I knew I'd found someone who was asking the same kinds of questions about motorcycling, society, and culture that I was.

The Aerostich Roadcrafter suit's design embodied my first answers to those important questions, and this book contains some of Steve's. The central assumption behind the Roadcrafter is that everyday back-and-forth-to-work 'A-to-B' motorcycling is a social good—an activity that benefits everyone, not just the rider. I believe this is so because even the most mundane riding experience changes the rider in psycho-biological ways which ultimately are beneficial to everyone. In other words, motorcycle and scooter riding is one activity that helps people become more able to do many non-riding kinds of things better than they otherwise could, and these better-performing people are then better able to help make better communities, which directly benefits everybody. The specific causal mechanisms involved probably lie in both the episodes of transcendence that riding experiences provide, and with the more objective risk management affirmations that result from all motorcycling activity.

Transcendence, as I use it here, is a state of awareness in which the passage of time seems to slow and one feels more connected to some kind of universal consciousness. It's the sensation of being more in sync and merged into one's surroundings. In this state, one feels simultaneously very relaxed and very alert. This duality is not normally a part of our everyday lives, but it is such a satisfying feeling that many people seek the experience by practicing meditation, yoga, and similar kinds of activities. Motorcycle and scooter riding provides this same type of concurrent relaxed and alert engagement because the rider is unconsciously always busy, physically and mentally concentrating on guiding the machine, while simultaneously consciously experiencing the environment in ways which affect the overall nature of each ride. The result of such complex stimulation seems to be a type of transcendent experience which, at the conclusion of each ride, usually leaves the rider calmer, more focused and in a notably refreshed state.

Individuals who meditate regularly have recently been the subjects of controlled-study research using the latest brain-scanning technologies, and this testing has revealed how repeatedly achieving such a transcendent state helps the brain increase the skills involved in concentration and remembering, and provides one with a measurably stronger sense of well-being. These are cumulative and lasting physiological changes which seem to be the result of each kind of activity that produces episodes of transcendence, so this probably includes riding motorcycles and scooters. Unfortunately, it is not possible to do such brain-scanning while a test subject is riding, but as you'll see in *Bodies in Motion*, there are other ways to reach the objective of understanding how motorcycling and states of cognition interrelate.

Despite riding's many virtues and advantages, it is hard to justify, explain and rationalize motorcycling in the face of all counter-forces lined up against it. And this is specially so for utility and transportation riding. The mainstream population in most of the rich parts of the world doesn't buy transport-on-two-wheels, except for a tiny minority of stubborn, iconoclastic, skin-flinted, quixotic, romantic and idealistic types...to name them all. And although there is increasing interest in vehicles which offer reduced consumptive footprints and greater convenience and efficiency, encouraging the adoption of motorcycles and scooters is not being widely promoted. Instead, throughout most of the developed and congested parts of the world, people are eagerly awaiting the arrival of self-driving cars that will take them to their destinations automatically, while people in the still-developing world are just as eagerly looking forward to getting off their mopeds or bicycles and into cars. Neither group seems to appreciate that motorcycling is different from mere conveyances; that their inherent vulnerabilities and discomforts bring with them unequalled satisfaction and beneficial value when they are used for daily life, and not just recreation.

When automobiles are driven enthusiastically, or at higher speeds in adverse conditions, the experience of controlling the vehicle can sometimes be absorbing enough to produce episodic transcendence for the driver. But everyday driving rarely requires this supremely engaged level of concentration. Motorcycling is different. The old joke about the bacon-and-egg breakfast is that the chicken is "involved" but the pig is "committed." This fairly well describes the difference between the automobile driver and the motorcycle rider.

Motorcycles are inherently unstable and vulnerable to falling over, so the rider must actively and continuously commit to helping them function.

Similarly, many other kinesthetic and risk-management activities requiring participant "commitment" also seem to produce episodic transcendence experiences. The sports of skiing, skating, sailing, bicycling, skateboarding and surfing all provide many of the same psychobiological benefits as riding. Partly because of this, motorcycles in rich countries are usually both sold and understood as another of these leisure activities. But beyond that, riding offers a unique potential to provide the episodic-transcendence benefit as a built-in component of one's personal mobility activities. This holistic dualism is a little like how unprocessed foods which taste great are usually nutritionally very good for you. Here, within this healthy and synergistic combination of the intangible and the physical, exists an as-yet unverifiable, but potentially extremely important individual and societal benefit of motorcycling.

Unfortunately, and unlike most transcendence-providing "fun" activities, motorcycling brings with it the burden of enormous potential personal injury. No rider wants to be killed or injured, but it occasionally happens. This is a widely appreciated dread-risk fear, but as soon as a rider has learned how to control a motorcycle skillfully and safely, his/her calculus always changes. And when that happens, the efficiency and economy of even the simplest motorcycle or scooter is revelatory. A few days ago I made five different errand stops in two hours and always had a perfect place to park that was nearer each destination—and easier to get into and out of—than the spaces available for the cars. Everything was zip,

zip, zip.... And I am always bubbling happy to be getting so much stuff done so easily. It's like cheating! Afterward, when I reach 'point B', I always feel better and more renewed than I did before I left 'point A'. Always.

Because motorcycles and scooters have the potential to provide such a valuable personal-mobility option for many more individuals than the actual number of riders I observe, there clearly are some societal biases keeping the machines largely marginalized as recreational vehicles. The well-presented motorcycle accident and injury statistics are one powerful example of the influence of such a factor. In Vietnam today, about sixty-five percent of all motorized travel is via small, 150cc-and-under motorcycles. Here in the United States, less than one percent of our travel is by motorcycle, and the motorcycles we use are much larger. These two numbers represent the global extremes. In every culture the acceptance of riding's risks and vulnerabilities is viewed differently, by both the rider and the non-rider. This book is about some of the important universals beneath these differences.

From ancient, isolated hunter-gatherer cultures to our current world's complex matrix of interlocked civilizations, the cooperatively achieved mitigation of shared risk is one of humanity's central achievements. Successful accomplishment of those objectives, at every level, produces increased trust and this provides the foundations for the development of all types of faiths, which in turn is what allows us to hope. And it is that magic element which encourages us to seek out transcendence-generating activities. Every day I choose to encounter the world as a motorcycle or scooter rider, with only the intermediation of my gloves and riding gear, looking around nervously at all the other drivers, and the rain clouds in the sky, and the uncertain surfaces of the road ahead—and then still decide to continue making my own way though it all, to the best of my abilities, *that* is a great day. When we ride motorcycles, we decide to be idealists. We are deciding to celebrate, honor and assert the hopeful awareness within ourselves which creates our uniquely human center of humbleness, perspective, place-in-the-world and self-confidence.

Here in America, as elsewhere, those who are not personally interested in experiencing and accepting motorcycling's vulnerabilities and discomforts can provide all kinds of insults and ostracizations toward those who are. And here, it is easy to say riding is "too dangerous" because local personal-mobility experiences almost always involve automobiles, not motorcycles and scooters. In Vietnam, and throughout most of the developing world, this same concern may not nearly be as easily expressed, because the majority, or some large percentage, are on two wheels. Cooperatively mitigating shared risk is how many of our universal social behaviors evolved, so the outward appearance of violating or flaunting this part of the social construct is usually viewed as a problem. In the United States, it is rarely a simple or easy decision to be the singular motorcycle rider commuting to and from work, alone among thousands of cars.

Riding's strongest disincentives—discomfort, increased vulnerability and social estrangement—are all related. The socio-cultural search for the opposites of these three elements is what drives ever-expanding markets for all technologies, including everything from cosmetics and fashions, to cellular telephones and passive-safety systems in automobiles. The lessening of risk and discomfort is almost always an integral part of the promise of successful manufactured artifacts, from safety razors to suspension bridges, and is inseparably connected to our evolved natures, our social behaviors, and with the goals of civilization itself.

In personal transportation, the continually improving convenience, reliability and safety of cars and the infrastructure they demand, represents a civilization-wide outsourcing of various risk management responsibilities from individual drivers to a broad variety of interconnected stakeholders. Our deepest impulses powerfully justify and support these kinds of responsibility transfers. To many individuals, and in many contexts, motorcycle riding is a repudiation of this norm because it involves the active assumption of risk management through the rider's individually acquired knowledge and skills. Car drivers ask themselves and riders, "Why?"

The less we know about anything, the more fearful of it we become. As automotive technologies continue to improve, ever-larger numbers of people become further insulated and isolated from experiencing the vulnerabilities and discomforts of automobility that were once commonplace, and were, to some extent, shared with motorcyclists. In improving automobiles to eliminate their vulnerabilities and discomforts, manufacturers inevitably also eliminated some—perhaps most—of the visceral and kinesthetic experiences which best help prepare individuals to counter some of the socially isolating and estranging affects of modern life. Motorcycle riding, by more directly and intimately reconnecting us with the surrounding indifferent world, and with each other, helps us better understand and face the always uncertain future.

And this is one way we become better able to support and contribute to the lives of others.

It should be self-evident that, regardless of motorcycling's many powerful individual and societal benefits, not everyone should ride. If anyone reading this book comes to the conclusion that either Steve or I feel that motorcycle riding is some kind of societal magic potion, or a transportation panacea, he or she has misunderstood what is being presented here. Riding is only for those who decide to give it a try. My sister Ellen and her husband, Jeff, began to ride in their mid-fifties, as did my cousin Joel. During her learning process, Ellen emailed me about motorcycling's risks as she saw them, writing that, "It rained last night and the roads are a bit damp still. I keep thinking about cousin Joel's recent spill (and sorry, but a broken collarbone/clavicle are not what I consider minor, but that's just me!), and the story in the beginning of your catalog by Rand Rasmussen—one minute you're up, the next second, without warning, you're down. EEEK! I am very cautious, to the point of excess, so far, and hope to become more comfortable with time and miles. I have been meaning to ask you if you ever fell, because I don't remember visiting you in the hospital or anything, or even you mentioning it."

To this I replied, "Rand Rasmussen's story was the truth about motorcycling. There is a high element of uncertainty involved, even for an experienced rider. God only lets us know what we need to know. We never get to see it all. So we stumble faithfully forward, from one thing to the next, doing the best we can. In a funny way, motorcycling helps people learn this. Riding makes a point about the uncertainty of life in a cool way. And so far, over the forty years since I began, I've never been hospitalized due to riding."

Statistics sometimes present riding in the United States as being about six to eight times riskier, per mile traveled, than driving. The exact percentage involved seems to vary greatly, depending on how the motorcycle accident data are collected and manipulated. For example, adjusting for accident causal contributors significantly changes many things. Excess speed and rider impairment are responsible for about half of the difference between car and motorcycle crash rates. Wearing a helmet and protective clothing, riding regularly, and even the size, color and style of the machine—all influence one's vulnerability. So does completing rider skills training. After factoring in more items like these, the risks of motorcycling across most traffic environments may actually be much more closely comparable to the risks of traveling by automobile. Unfortunately, that's not what most people believe.

Motorcycles and scooters will always be inherently more vulnerable, but they are not inevitably always riskier. The odds of experiencing any kind of motor vehicle accident lessen slightly every year. There are fewer annual accidents per driver, per rider, per vehicle, per mile of road, and per mile driven, than ever. But don't try using this fact to justify riding to any one who doesn't ride. They are only concerned about the future likelihood of accidents and injuries happening to them, and the relative numbers. The problem is that although less than two percent of all active American riders are injured each year in some way as a result of some kind of motorcycling or scootering accident, this is still far higher than the percentage of automobile drivers who are injured each year.

We endlessly remodel our individual lives in countless ways to better accommodate an ever-changing mix of circumstantial realities. In rich countries, riding-as-transportation may be slightly more appealing during periods of political upheaval and economic hardship, and riding-as-entertainment may be dominant during times of peace, stability and prosperity. But riding always remains. In locations where roads are highly congested and automobiles dominate traffic, riding may be more risky since the rider is a member of a very small road-going minority. But when the ratio of cars to bikes changes, things get a lot better for the rider in terms of the way the surrounding traffic behaves. Thus, if the number of motorcyclists and scooterers in the United States were to increase even slightly, congestion would ease a bit, and riding itself would become statistically safer and easier.

Democracy coupled with universal citizen education and political equality theoretically leads to equal rights, but sometimes a minority—comprised in this case of motorcyclists—deserves more than a level playing field. The theory of 'social justice' is that overall social progress can be hastened when governments do things which incentivize beneficial activities and provide special privileges for the disadvantaged. Riders, particularly those who motorcycle for utility transportation reasons, should receive the benefits of both. Although motorcyclists are not being denied equal rights under the law, sometimes regulations and legal practices, whether intentional or not, effectively make motorcycling both less attractive and more dangerous. Because riding may in the long run turn out to be an individually and societally desirable activity, I believe the relevant laws, regulations and policies should actively protect and encourage it.

To specifically address the increased burdens of vulnerability that come with motorcycling's vehicular minimalism, one such helpful bias might, for example, involve mandating stiffer vehicle-code violation penalties for accidents involving instances when the driver of a larger vehicle is found responsible for negligently causing harm to any more vulnerable person, including those who are walking, skating, bicycling or motorcycle riding. Traveling across the state of Michigan, one sees signs at every road construction zone which read, "Kill a highway worker, automatic $12,000 fine and one year in jail." Simple and effective. Similar future signage might be seen in all states, rewritten as: "Kill a highway worker, motorcyclist, bicyclist or pedestrian and the fine is $12,000 plus a year in jail." Even though the chances of this actually happening seem unlikely, for obvious reasons falling outside the scope of this book, that does not make the ideas themselves any less worthy of our consideration, discussion or implementation.

Riders already enjoy High Occupancy Vehicle lane access on limited-access federal highways. The principles underlying this extra privilege came directly from positive historical experiences, and from the extensive legal precedents for government regulation of automobility. And there are many other ways to further extend such regulatory biases. Motorcycles and scooters are a distinctive vehicle type and a specially licensed vehicle class, so implementing sheltered, discounted or free parking might be even easier than providing loading zones for licensed commercial trucks. And since multiple motorcycles are able to use a single space, if such an incentive became law, the aggregate number of spaces available for everyone driving cars should slightly increase. In related areas, if riders could somehow be exempted from bridge and road tolls, and given increased, carefully defined lane-sharing and 'filtering' privileges, urban road congestion levels might be slightly reduced for everyone who drives. Interestingly, lane sharing is already permitted (or tolerated) across most of the motorized world.

The United States could also easily increase the percentage of its population that starts on motorcycles and scooters, as done in Europe and most of Asia, which have rider entry programs that directly influence the ways in which these vehicles are perceived. My friend Jim summarized the typical approach in an email: "Having been brought up in East Africa and Europe," he wrote, "my solution is based on the European model. Here are the basic tenets: A) Permit 50cc motorcycle licensing at age 13 with speed restrictions, B) Motorcycle and scooter learner permits at 15 1/2—with restrictions on night riding, freeway travel and passengers, C) Raise the driving age for a car to 18—no exceptions, and D) Professional training for everyone which would include street operations." I wouldn't bet that such changes will be made here in the United States anytime soon, or without large compromises and adjustments. But these are well-proven, effective methods of increasing riding populations. Significantly more motorcycles and scooters are part of the traffic mix across all of Europe and Asia, with far less accidents occurring per rider mile in all of these areas.

For many individuals, riding involves acquiring the 'best' machine possible and riding it so as to have the 'best' experiences imaginable. People pay big money for coolness, particularly for purified epic coolness that is untainted by any other considerations. But the ways we compete for personal advantage are continually changing because of new, ever-developing external factors. Moto-fashions, both material and behavioral, alter like all fashions in response to changing environmental, cultural, economic and social externalities. Key parts of our sociobiological connections with most advancing technologies, and with automobility in all of its forms—including motorcycles and scooters—are pragmatic, opportunistic and fluid. What is cool for one generation may turn out to be the opposite for the next. Only, as you'll read here, are our evolutionarily derived underlying psychobiological imperatives relatively timeless.

The Aerostich company's mission statement is: "To profitably provide products that encourage the adoption of motorcycles," and publishing this book falls well within that business goal. Our immediate commercial opportunities are very closely related to the number of people who choose to ride, so a large part of my motive for publishing the ideas that follow has been selfish. But beyond this, and an important part of who I am, is one of Aerostich's central marketing narratives. We try to present ideas which encourage our customers to think about their lives and mobility choices in ways which are not part of mainstream societal and cultural programming. This value comes straight from my life's most influential experiences. I've never felt, and won't ever feel, that there are too many cars. Or that automobiles are not useful, fun, interesting, functional, and wonderful machines. Cars and trucks are all of those things, and much more. But for me, riding motorcycles and scooters is usually (though not always) better.

My years of riding have been a transformational, and in some ways radicalizing, experience. A committed rider might be either a tough-looking, old-school, greasy, chopper-riding badass—or a milquetoast, clean-cut, dedicated scooter rider. Or anything in between. The underlying reasons they each ride are, in part, as similar as their external appearances are different, though they might not know it, and it is that deeper and more important commonality all riders share that this book, in part, investigates.

I learned about *Bodies in Motion* while Steve was writing an early draft. Later, after the first draft of the manuscript was submitted, I learned that the University of California Press, which had commissioned Steve to write the book, underwent staff changes that effectively resulted in their decision not to publish the book. At that point, I asked for a chance to read the manuscript. As soon as I'd finished reading, I requested the opportunity to publish the book because it will help everyone better understand how and why motorcycling is important, and why riding has such a powerful influence on us.

I hope every reader enjoys this book as much as I did, and learns as much from it as I did, not least because it clarifies the many ways in which riding is a "social good." In any case, emerging trends are likely to support the greater acceptance of motorcycle and scooter riding in utility roles. Like Steve, I hope that as more of us learn more about our external and internal environments, substantial changes will occur in how we design and use our machines of mobility, and that riding will steadily become easier, safer and more popular. Until then, whenever I'm in doubt, I choose to ride.

—Andy Goldfine, June 2008

INTRODUCTION

Why to Ask Why

When I began planning this book in 1996, I intended it to be a social history of American motorcycling. In pursuit of this study, I expected to find documents in the relevant archives that would provide useful primary-source material created by motorcyclists throughout the last century. I knew that these documents would help me identify who they were, their attitudes about motorcycle-related matters, what they rode, why they'd chosen what to ride, and when. Because I also wanted to find answers to what I considered a more important question—why they had chosen to ride at all, if they had alternatives—I expected the documentary evidence to be often far from ideal for that purpose. I did not, however, expect to unearth what I actually discovered in the archives.

What I found was exemplified by my day of sifting through an archival box in the collections of the Smithsonian National Museum of American History in Washington, D.C. Poring through the diaries, letters, magazines, advertisements and other ephemera, I realized that I had seen all this before. As editorial director of *Cycle Guide* magazine and editor-at-large of *Cycle World* magazine, I had read many letters from fellow motorcyclists and listened to many more accounts of what motorcyclists cared most about in various venues around the world that echoed all our predecessors' themes. Even the terms used throughout the century by motorcyclists to describe what riding motorcycles gave them were often the same, and could be grouped into what I came to call the Three Fs of Motorcycling: Fun, Freedom, and Flying on the ground.

There was, in short, nothing new to me in this archival collection, as there was similarly nothing new in any of those I'd examined so far. Because of the diversity of the archives I'd examined, this had significant implications, among them, that in the event no Mother Lode of previously unseen and unstudied primary-source material could be found, I would not be able to provide 'documentary' answers to the most important question animating the book: the 'why' question. A rigorous social history could still be written using other historiographic methodologies, of course, most of which are quantitative. I'd expected to do statistical analysis for this book as a means of framing the important documentary evidence, not as a replacement for it. Rather than do that, and thus, in effect, to use archival material to produce a book not all that useful except, perhaps to scholars, I called a time-out and considered what the situation meant.

It became clear then that I'd attempted too much with a historian's approach—not surprising given that I'd been educated as a historian. But once I freed myself from the historian's disciplinary harness, I realized that my search for deeper understanding of what motivates motorcyclists to ride and keep riding required an exploration not primarily of history, but of the behavioral sciences, in which great progress has been made in the last few decades. What, I wondered, could contemporary science illuminate about why a given individual might be not merely attracted to, but virtually addicted to motorcycles and motorcycling, while another might be either indifferent to motorcycles or openly hostile to them? This is not a trivial matter, as I had discovered in the summer of 1965, when I was a 17-year-old who had been riding since November, 1963.

That summer seemed to be particularly hot in the little town of Fair Oaks, California to which my father had retired from the U.S. Air Force in 1962 following his career flying bombers. I had a summer job working in a laundry near the intersection of Winding Way and Fair Oaks Boulevard and I rode to work on a motorcycle, as I had ridden to school for the previous year. My first choice of a vehicle had been a car of any kind, but my father had what I later learned was an unusual view among his generational contemporaries about kids and cars. Cars, he declared, were for adults, while teenaged boys should ride bicycles or motorcycles until they matured enough to understand the responsibilities that driving a car demanded. I found out long afterward that this view was shaped in part by his having been a child of the Depression. He had ridden bicycles and motorcycles while growing up, but had not owned a car until he was commissioned in the U.S. Army Air Corps during World War II. My mother, who had also ridden bicycles, motorbikes and horses while growing up in Texas, likewise considered that providing a car for a high-school kid was an almost scandalous idea when I first proposed the notion in mid-1963. Though my high school was only five miles or so from our home and I could and did ride my bicycle to school, I did not like doing so, for I was not a strong bicyclist, having been afflicted by polio as an infant. So when my father agreed to buy me a used 1963 Yamaha YG-1, powered by an 80cc two-stroke single, I was reasonably happy. A year and a half later, I was riding a bigger motorcycle, having discovered that I absolutely loved riding motorbikes. My father had traded in the little single for a twin-cylinder, 250cc Yamaha YDS-2. This was my daily driver, my mount for commuting to my job and, on that sweltering summer day in '65, the means by which I would take my lunch break to go to the nearby A&W hamburger joint about half a mile away.

I left the laundry's cool interior, strapped on my English pudding-basin helmet and kick-started the Yamaha. It needed only a little choke and I accelerated quickly out of the gravel parking lot onto Fair Oaks Boulevard, heading up the little hill behind the laundry. At the top of the hill was a 90-degree turn, not particularly challenging except when, as on that day, the temperatures were near the triple digits. Under those conditions, I knew, the turn could be treacherous because of the oil, water and other glop dumped on the road by cars and trucks.

My mind on the Papa Burger and the cold root beer awaiting me just down the road, I downshifted the Yamaha and leaned it into the corner, gaze fixed on the burger joint in the distance. It should have been fixed on the slippery pavement directly ahead of me, because a heartbeat later the front wheel seemed to jerk out from under me and I was slammed into the hot, grimy asphalt. The bike somersaulted over me and I was flipped over and over again, my helmet whacking the road repeatedly until the Yamaha and I finally stopped sliding and came to rest.

Stunned, I realized that I was lying against the gas-station curbing on the inside of the corner, the bike on its side a few feet away, rear wheel spinning and engine sputtering until it died. My ears ringing, I levered myself up onto my elbows, which had been flayed as I'd flopped along the road. The bike had fared worse: its fuel tank was dented badly, probably where my left knee had been driven into it, to judge by the pain. The seat beading was ripped, the handlebar was bent, the shift lever twisted back on itself, the chromed headlight rim dented and scraped, the headlight lens and mirror smashed.

I noticed that a big white '64 Oldsmobile sedan had stopped just across from where the bike and I had come to rest. The driver's-side window went down, and I saw that the driver was a white-haired lady wearing winged pink sunglasses and a scowl. For a second, we looked at one another. Then she said, her voice as hard as the pavement under me: "Young man, you've gotten glass all *over* the road." Then her window went back up and she drove away.

A few seconds later, the gas station attendant ran up and helped me to my feet. I was able to get the bike back into shape good enough to get back to the laundry. It turned out that I'd suffered only minor damage, though the Yamaha would need extensive repairs. After that crash it was never quite the same. Neither was I, but for a different reason.

Until the lady in the Olds had surveyed the scene of my unfortunate get-off and told me, in effect, what a mess I had made—rather than asking me if I were okay—I had never given much thought to how other people might view motorcycles and motorcyclists. In part this was a cultural phenomenon and, though I did not think of it in those terms, I understood it after the incident on the way to the A&W. I had been raised in a wholly different world from most Americans, having been born into the Air Force and grown up on Air Force bases during the height of the Cold War. In that world, the quest for speed with any vehicle was a positive social phenomenon. General Curtis E. LeMay, for example, who loved fast cars all his life, had authorized sports-car racing on Strategic Air Command bases during his time as Commander in Chief of SAC. LeMay also rode a motor scooter around the flight line and established auto-hobby shops on SAC bases, equipped with tools and supplies, so that SAC personnel could work on their own cars, as he did. [1]

Many Air Force people, no doubt, did not share my parents' views about the motorcycle's positive value, but I never encountered them or their views while growing up. Thus the old lady in the Olds had a profound effect on me, by directing

[1] In May, 1990, I was able to interview Gen. LeMay about the SAC-Sports Car Club of America racing he'd authorized; the result was "Racers on the Runway," *Car and Driver*, April, 1992, pp. 153-162.

my teenaged thoughts to trying to understand why she had acted as she had. As my father pointed out, many people in such situations act oddly, so perhaps she did not know what to say and simply blurted out a rather unsympathetic response. Perhaps. But her cold stare and tone of voice suggested otherwise. As I continued to ride motorcycles I continued to encounter, ever more frequently as the 1960s progressed, more and more people who did not just dislike motorcycles and motorcyclists, but hated and sometimes feared them.

The obvious question, to me, was *why*? In the ensuing decades, I continued to ride and race, and because I was deeply involved in editorial work centered often on motorcycles, I also continued to explore the 'why' question. I did so in part because, like most motorcyclists, I was frequently asked by others, in one form or another: "Why on earth do you ride those things? They're *so* dangerous!" This question was often asked by people who would never dream of asking such a heavily loaded question of me regarding any other behavior. The unsubtly hidden assumption was thus that it was they who were normal, I who was not. Why and how could this be, for me and my motorcycling colleagues and friends?

About the same time as my youthful musings, the intellectual class grew increasingly interested in motorcycling. Many explorations of the cultural and social aspects of motorcycling appeared subsequently in scholarly journals, newspapers, magazines, books, film, on TV and later, online. In most of those, it seemed, the theory was that we who rode motorcycles did so because we wanted to establish cultural identity through them. Likewise, the pundits proposed that those who disliked or feared motorcycles and motorcyclists did so because of portrayals of us in movies like "The Wild One," reflecting the outlaw-biker image gloried in by motorcycle gangs in the real world. In these notions about social and cultural cause and effect, the images of motorcycling and motorcyclists were more powerful in attracting or repelling people than motorcycles as 'mere' machines.

I could understand the appeal of this line of thought, but a problem remains with this explanation of why some of us are addicted to motorcycling, no matter what may happen to us socially or physically because of them, while others remain hostile. The problem is that motorcycling is inherently and intensely physical. Just getting from one place to another by motorcycle is a physical experience, and many people worldwide use motorcycles for that basic task. Absent the physical aspects of motorcycling, nothing would be left. If it could not move under its own power guided by a human, a motorcycle would be just another mechanical device, a mere appliance—stylized, maybe, with paint and chrome, but no more commanding an emotional response than, say, a portable generator or a refrigerator.

With a clear understanding of this physicality, in contrast to those who assert that we ride for social reasons, over the years I became more and more certain that we ride primarily for physical—or more precisely, psychobiological—reasons, and that the bike's social aspects are artifacts of its physicality. In other words, I think that it is the actual and perceived nature of the motorcycle in motion, and the bodies thus in motion on it, which drive the social dimensions of the motorcycle developed over the last century.

This might not seem like a particularly controversial concept, but the current conventional view of 'why' among many liberal-arts and social-sciences academics and their popular-culture followers is considerably different. In their view, all significant behaviors are culturally constructed. That is, the culture into which we are born and by which we are indoctrinated creates behavioral templates into which we try to fit ourselves. Choice of transportation mode in this view of how human societies work is, therefore, for those with the physical and financial means, overwhelmingly a culturally-constructed decision.

For true believers in this assessment of humanity in what historian James J. Flink famously called 'The Automobile Age,'[2] motorcyclists choose to become motorcycle riders because they are trying to express some social value; they want to be perceived as rebels, as macho, as *this* or as *that*, depending on who is doing the theorizing. Automobile drivers, by these standards, behave as they do for the same reasons, choosing to drive instead of to ride because of a similar set of culturally constructed identity templates. And so on, with all behaviors involving powered, privately owned and controlled machines.

My own experiences growing up in a culture that approved, in the main, of any motorized device (and the faster the better) certainly gave me a culturally constructed basis for liking, or at least not disliking, the idea of motorcycling, so that it is not difficult to imagine that I was fitting myself into a behavioral template when I started riding motorcycles. After all, my father directed me to motorcycles in the first place.

[2] In his book of the same name, published by MIT Press, 1988, 1990.

However, the theory that culture alone determines what we do in an automotive society collides with and cannot overcome this fact: All transportation machines produce stimuli that feed into the people who use them, some obvious and consciously observed, but many affecting us in ways of which we are consciously unaware. In motorcycling, the stimuli are intense and the demands on the operator much greater than on the automobile driver. Thus, even if one wants to ride, one must be able to meet those demands, only then to enjoy or at least not be overly stressed by what the ride feeds into one, to sustain interest and involvement at the operational level.[3] Motorcycles, in this sense, are *not* just automobiles with two wheels.

A career spent writing about automobiles, motorcycles and aircraft has taught me about what those vehicles do in the physical sense that clarifies not only how they are similar but, more importantly, how they differ in what they do *to*, not just *for*, their operators and passengers.[4] These experiences are the foundation of my belief that, to understand better why people choose to ride motorcycles when alternative modes of transportation are available, purely or even primarily cultural and social causes cannot capture the whole truth. Thus, in the context of 'why,' my book project that had begun as an exploration of the social history of American motorcycling became an exploration of the motorcycling experience itself, and what it does both for and to the rider.

---

[3] The same is of course true of piloting aircraft, and to a lesser degree of nautical craft (at least in calm waters).

[4] A misspent youth found me working as senior editor of *Competition Press & Autoweek*, editor-in-chief of *Road Test*, executive editor of *Car and Driver,* and executive editor of *AOPA Pilot*, as well as in my roles for *Cycle Guide* and *Cycle World*.

Bodies in Motion is the result. It is best understood as an essay about what I've found in my research into the nature of humans-as-riders, and the stimuli that motorcycling delivers, willy-nilly, to the riders, coupled with what I think the research results might mean. It is written both for motorcyclists and non-motorcyclists, so that longtime riders will inevitably find some material familiar, though I have tried to ensure that, when covering conceptual ground common to all riders, the context is analyzed to highlight aspects of the commonalities that are usually overlooked or misunderstood. Likewise, though motorcycle lore is dense with jargon, I've tried to explain terms and ideas that often baffle non-riders or neophytes. Further to aid understanding, words and phrases with single quotes are either neologisms or common but 'coined' words, while words and phrases with double quotes are actual textual quotations.

The research reviewed in the following pages is of two kinds, as indicated by the subtitle of the book: *Evolution and Experience in Motorcycling*. Following where the research for this book led, I concluded, as have many others, that evolution has played a critical role in shaping what we do and why, and for determining what we enjoy and do not enjoy while in motion. Evolution, in the form of genetically transmitted traits, has also been convincingly shown to determine, in large part, who might seek the stimuli generated by motorcycles and motorcycling and who might be likely to avoid those sensations.

Though evolutionary theory about human origins is far from settled and agreed upon, compelling evidence exists for thinking that the experiences our species' ancestors had

for millennia in the trees imprinted upon us a set of preferences for our behavior where motion-based fun is concerned.
Motorcycles, I propose, capture more of those preferences
than any other mode of automobility. (As I will use the term
in this book, 'automobility' refers not just to the 'auto-mobile'
vehicles and the systems that sustain them, but also to the
social and cultural consequences of our use of the vehicles.)

On motorcycles, we put our bodies in motion in obvious
and not-so-obvious ways. One way, particularly important
to understanding why some think motorcycling is fun and
others do not, is the motion, perceived as vibration, generated
not only by the machine's passage through the air and over
the ground, but by the engine. Motorcycle lore is loaded with
beliefs about how this or that engine produces, through the
vibration it feeds into the rider, different emotional states.
Experimental research to verify or debunk that belief was
not available when I was doing the research for this book and
might not be for a long time. But the assumption that different motorcycle engines produce vibration different enough to
be at least potentially influential in creating an emotional state
is itself subject to experimental analysis. Even before I began
to research the question in the human-factors literature, I had
reason to believe that the major motorcycle manufacturers
had done studies on vibration levels in each of their own
machines; however, open-literature searches disclosed nothing useful for my purposes.

I did not have the resources to pay an engineering
research company for the study I needed, but through a series
of fortunate events I was able to commission an experiment
by Stanford University engineering graduate students to

determine how certain well-known motorcycles differed in what their engines delivered to their riders. The research and its results appear in summary form in Chapter Three, and in more detailed form in a Vibration Study Appendix. This study of the vibration 'signatures' showed that the motorcycles did indeed differ significantly in the 'vibes' they delivered to their riders. This might not seem important to a non-rider, but the results showed unequivocally that different 'strokes,' as it were, really were delivered by each bike, which there-fore would appeal—in themselves and apart from anything else—to 'different folks,' as popular wisdom has long held.

Bodies in Motion thus explores what evolutionary science, psychology, human-factors research and engineering research can tell us about why some people seek certain kinds of automotive-activity experiences and others do not. The reason to be concerned about this is more important than just what it might mean to a motorcyclist trying to figure out which bike to choose or trying to explain to someone why he or she chose to ride instead of, or in addition to, driving a car. The overwhelming importance of automobility to our way of life means that human nature, as science can show it to be, is vital to our continuing attempts to cope with the costs that automobility has thrust upon us, along with its benefits.

In the United States, a nation founded on the belief that people can regulate their own affairs, properly conceived regulation of our automotive lives demands that our elected representatives and the agencies in the executive branch of government regulate wisely. The prerequisite for wisdom being knowledge unsullied by fallacies, understanding ourselves as we really are when our machines transform us from walkers to drivers or riders should be a priority goal. It is too much to hope that *Bodies in Motion* might directly aid in reaching that objective, but perhaps not too much to hope that it might encourage others to continue research into the influences of our machines of mobility on us, thereby ultimately to help shape society to fit us, and not the other way around.

CHAPTER ONE

SPEED IN THE GENES

The search for answers as to why some of us like to put our bodies in motion any way we can, while others do not, begins not on the ground but in the trees. Though few of us ever wonder why, most people like trees. If asked, most of us would probably answer that we like trees because, well, just because they make us feel good, even if all we do is look at them (as opposed, say, to climbing them or otherwise reveling in them far above the ground, as some do). This makes sense because, not so long ago in evolutionary time, they were home to our direct ancestors.

Until fairly recently, the consensus among paleoanthropologists was that we became human after we 'came down from the trees'—when we started walking upright and surviving mainly on the ground. But fossil evidence that continues to be discovered has led to a broadening base of support for evolutionary theories that locate our species' defining evolutionary changes in the arboreal environment itself. In these scenarios, the Environments of Evolutionary Adaptedness, or EEAs, in which we became fully bipedal and anatomically human, not only began in the trees but continued there for a long time.[5] How long is still unknown, though one thing is clear: We and trees are joined in ways few of us realize.

Among those who concentrate on understanding as much as can be known scientifically about our evolutionary history, what happened between two and four million years ago in the trees somewhere, possibly in Africa, is crucial. Then, many evolutionary biologists think, the configuration of our uniquely human form evolved. This was followed, apparently, about two million years ago with a major increase in our brain size. Since then, humanity has experienced adaptations influencing body size, skin color, disease resistance, and other environmentally 'useful' changes, but our fundamental morphology and biology seems to have remained mostly unchanged. Nobody knows how much our psychological attributes have changed, exactly, but it's a fairly safe bet that, in the words of evolutionary psychologists Leda Cosmides and John Tooby of the University of California's Center for Evolutionary Psychology: "Our modern skulls house a stone-

---

[5] See, for example, Russell H.Tuttle et al. "Heel, Squat, Stand, Stride: Function and Evolution of Hominoid Feet" in *Primate Locomotion: Recent Advances* (435-448).

age mind." Elaborating, they add, "The environment that humans—and, therefore, human *minds*—evolved in was very different from our modern environment. Our ancestors spent well over 99% of our species' evolutionary history living in hunter-gatherer societies. That means that our forebearers lived in small, nomadic bands of a few dozen individuals who got all of their food each day by gathering plants or by hunting animals. Each of our ancestors was, in effect, on a camping trip that lasted an entire lifetime, and this way of life endured for most of the last 10 million years."[6]

It is easy to misunderstand the implications of our evolutionary history. It does not mean that most of us can scamper up a tree like monkeys. It means that we have the genetic material within us to learn to climb trees, not as well as monkeys, but *better* than they can. The reason is the human brain, which—some theories posit—developed as it has in part because our direct ancestors' bodies are thought by some to have been so big, relative to the tree limbs and branches that defined their habitat at the time.

In the trees, size does matter. The costs of a mistake in movement are potentially high for an animal living primarily in the trees at any height; a fall can mean death, or a wound so serious that it leads sooner or later to death. The requirement and the subsequent ability not only to predict the movement of the environment—tree limbs and branches—but also to forecast the most effective path toward a food source or away from a predator led to the selection of individuals who could, increasingly, best perform those kinds of mental functions. They were further selected through what we now

[6] Cosmides and Tooby, *Evolutionary Psychology: A Primer* (online).

call situational awareness; assimilating, judging and reacting to our environments effectively, assessing in milliseconds the ability of a particular tree limb to sustain weight, and seizing the moment as well as the limb, typifying the innumerable survival tests. Researchers Daniel Povinelli and John Cant propose that the resulting changes to the brains continued to favor more and more self-awareness and consciousness, until the human mind was born.[7]

Though that proposal is still considered controversial, the importance of locomotion in the arboreal environment as a crucial factor in the evolution of the human form and behavior is widely accepted. The upshot is that there is good reason to think that the adaptations to our bodies and minds, molded by millions of years living in and near trees of certain kinds, are still the primary behavioral guidance systems for how we interact with the world.

We enjoy activities that make this obvious, once you think about it, and many involve motion of some kind. As kids, most of us like being swung through the air, one way or another; on a playground swing, on a merry-go-round, on 'monkey bars,' in innumerable ways that so clearly relate to what our ancestors would have experienced growing up in the long-ago forests. We also like strictly terrestrial motion too, of course: walking, running, swimming, hunting, fishing and the other activities that typified what Cosmides and Tooby call our hunter-gatherer ancestors' "camping trip that lasted an entire lifetime." In that almost incom-

---

[7] Povinelli and Cant, "Arboreal Clambering and the Evolution of Self-Conception" in *The Quarterly Review of Biology*, Vol. 70, No. 4 (Dec., 1995), pp. 393-421.

prehensibly long period, our ancestors were 'on walkabout' all over the world.

Among much else, one immensely important consequence of our past is that we're now stuck in traffic jams—or zooming along the highway after the jams finally break up—with what is almost exactly the same set of pre-programmed enjoyments that our ancestors developed, bit by bit, in response to the demands of living in the trees.

Our evolutionary inheritance has also, of course, left us with some other artifacts. For example, figuring out how to deal with our appetites, which so often and so easily seem to urge us to eat what is not necessary in quantities that are not healthy, to figuring out why so many males, young and old, find it so easy to pick and start a fight over what seem to be trivial issues. But just as our psychobiological inheritance produces problems for us, I am persuaded that our evolutionary history—properly understood—probably contains clues to the answers we need as to why we do much of what we do that seemingly makes no sense. Those answers include important but not usually recognized reasons for what has happened to us as individuals and as societies since the advent of mechanically powered, individually controlled vehicles in the last decades of the 19th century.

Obviously, to anyone who takes the time to think about it, the changes have been profound. To examine the changes, it is better to begin not with the statistics about how everyone's use of automobiles of all types (a motorcycle is in this sense an 'auto-mobile' vehicle) has changed the world, but to begin instead with a careful look at what any vehicle does *to*, and not just *because of*, its operator and passengers.

The primary 'product' delivered by any form of vehicle is transportation. Whether it is animal-powered, human-powered, wind-powered or self-propelled, it takes us from one place to another. In so doing, it also delivers something else: motion, of varying kinds, depending on the vehicle and how and where it is used. If the motion is too unsuited to us, we cannot and will not use the vehicle. But what does 'unsuited' mean? We can learn to accept a wide range of motions, from sailboats rolling, yawing and pitching badly in rough seas to camels giving us a ride we only seek when we have no other choice. People who no longer need to use animals trained for human use as conveyances may often ignore the reality that faces trainers, but there is nothing 'natural' about 'breaking' a horse to a saddle. Horses did not appear in humankind's campgrounds and ask to be 'broken' and shackled to millennia of usually hard lives. In short, though horses and people do bond, we remain separate species, except in myth. A centaur is as much a human invention as a Buick Century.

Unlike the centaur, however, a Buick is both real and engineered by humans to provide as much of what we want with as little of what we do not want. When it delivers the former, we often describe the results as pleasurable. The car gives us a 'good ride.' We use it not only to get from place to place but to make the process stimulating in various ways that operate on our bodies, unconsciously (or, to be more precise, pre-cognitively), to create sensations we enjoy. The machine thus becomes a 'stimulus-delivery device' as well as a 'transportation-delivery device,' though we rarely think of it that way. In fact, we notice the stimuli generated by our machines primarily when they are unpleasant. Too much heat, too much noise, too much of something else. We seek comfort, notice its absence and try to create it wherever and however we can.

In this sense—comfort—it is reasonable to think that our closest bipedal ancestors had to be comfortable in the tree-world if they were to survive and reproduce. Thus they had to master certain kinds of movement. They moved by various means through the foliage and branches that were the furniture of their lives, sometimes perching on their haunches atop a big branch, resting a back or a buttock against the tree trunk where it joined the branch, sometimes clambering through a tangled mass of branches and smaller limbs, standing more upright, grasping this or that branch above and balancing on the branch below. Sometimes they used their hands' remarkable 'power grip' to hold onto a branch from below, hanging from it, moving from one spot to another by brachiation, made possible only by the complex architecture of their wrists and by the useful opposable thumb. Over the millennia, as their bodies adapted to the environment, their behavior adapted similarly. Pleasure was one such adaptation. All the kinds of motion necessary to live and survive in the trees that were adaptive must eventually have become either non-painful or, more likely, pleasurable.

Pleasure, like pain, exists only as a complex array of biochemical activities in the brain and nervous system. What is known about its mechanisms today indicates that it derives primarily from neurotransmitter action in the synaptic gaps between neurons. From the evolutionary perspective, then, the links between external stimuli and the chemistry of pleasure or pain are important. They are the means by which a complex organism is directed to or away from some activities, including those that involve what used to be called the primal drives, as well as what biologists call 'hedonic' or enjoyable behavior. In the arboreal environment, some activities had, necessarily, to become pleasurable, among them those involving motion of the sorts demanded by successfully pursuing mates, food, shelter and so forth. We see this in our nonhuman primate relatives as they swing from branches, leap from tree to tree and otherwise cavort above the ground. It is hard not to conclude that they are sometimes having fun up there.

Knowing that we are descended directly from ancestors who lived in trees and had fun in them, it is far from a logical or evolutionary leap to conclude that the kinds of fun we have in motion are strongly connected to our arboreal past. Hence amusement parks and, in a sense rarely recognized, hence too all automotive devices—especially motorcycles.

Motorcycles produce a wider range of motions that mimic the ones central to our collective evolution in the trees than any other ground-bound personal transportation devices. By leaning to turn, they allow us to experience something like what our ancestors would have felt in grabbing a vine hanging from an overhead branch or a trunk far above, which they would then use to leave one branch for another branch or tree, sometimes by sequentially grabbing interspersed vines and branches. What is important about such experiences is that a large number of people seek them out, and always have, while some people do not enjoy such motions in any form and a few in any population avoid them entirely. The reasons seem to be determined as much by genetic inheritance as do any other of our sensation-seeking traits. Those traits have interested us for millennia, either to seek or to control, but only since the last half of the 20th century have they been subject to serious scientific study. What has been learned adds enormously to our understanding of how the traits express themselves throughout our populations, and it has been shown that more than half the tendency to seek sensations of certain kinds is heritable, meaning transmitted genetically.

There is obviously a relatively stable platform of 'normal' sensations associated with daily life everywhere, not 'sought' but simply present as a consequence of the environment. Thus, in the arboreal world, our ancestors did not seek the sensations of swinging from vines or other brachiating motion so much as find them normal and therefore non-stressful. Similarly, to function in our automotive environment, our ancestors' descendants cannot find the motions associated with driving a car (or if one is a motorcyclist, riding a motorcycle) stressful or unpleasant, even if one might not seek out or think of the motions as 'pleasure.'

But some people deliberately seek out such experiences, and for them those experiences are pleasurable. These would be people who score high on sensation-seeking scales. For them, the psychobiological payback of a ride or a drive can be the equivalent of a drug, and for the same reasons: A chemical transaction occurs in their brains, activated by the physical sensations of the motions created by driving or riding, producing an emotional state of pleasure. Culture can lead someone to try out the stimuli that generate the pleasurable responses, but only individual genetic heritage can transform the stimuli instantly into pleasure, rather than into stress and discomfort.

The power of pleasure-seeking can hardly be overstated, especially in societies swamped by such seeking in the form of so-called recreational drugs. Research experiments performed on laboratory animals have consistently shown how an animal will sacrifice all else to engage in the behavior that generates the most intense pleasures. It is no surprise that so many people will likewise seek substances or activities that create states of super-pleasure. In Woody Allen's 1973 movie, "Sleeper," for example, the futuristic scenario at the heart of the plot proposed that sexual intercourse, which many people experience as the most intense pleasure in their lives, would have been replaced as an 'activity' by using an 'Orgasmatron,' a device similar to a phone booth into which both parties would step and in which both would experience, by means not explained in the film, orgasms without physical interaction. Though used as a gag, the Orgasmatron is no different in principle from any artificial stimulant, external to the body or internal to it, that we make or use to generate pleasure for ourselves.

We do not think of our automobiles as Orgasmatrons, not least because their transportation and social functions are the ones to which we most consciously attend. Transportation by a personal device is essential throughout most of the United States, so whether or not any vehicle is fun, it is necessary. Nevertheless, for millions of people in America and elsewhere, vehicles of all sorts—especially motorcycles—are operated routinely as automotive Orgasmatrons, delivering not sexual pleasure but motion-based pleasures. Though few people clearly recognize it, this is the basis of such vehicles' ability to 'addict' so many so powerfully to automobility.

If one grows up in an automotive world, the physical experiences of automobility define a significant part of the growth process. That does not just mean that an individual is 'used to' cars and trucks. It means that his or her physical environment is literally defined by movement felt but not usually noticed. This occurs even before birth, as the mother uses her own vehicles or public transportation. How, precisely, these vehicular experiences may influence the developing fetus in her womb is unknown. What is known is that, both before and after a child is born, that infant is embedded in an automotive world whose defining characteristics generate the expectations, in terms of experiences, of the maturing child.

It is likely, given how and why we construct our automobiles, that the pre-natal experiences of most children born into automobility are not particularly troublesome for mother or child. Automotive engineers have worked hard since the dawn of the automotive age to make the vehicles comfortable for users, because of obvious marketplace concerns as well as increasingly stringent governmental regulations. Even so, no matter how comfy or luxurious an automotive interior may seem, it differs crucially from a living room: It moves, sometimes very quickly.

Our arboreal and terrestrial ancestors understood speed because in any contest for survival the fighter pilot's favorite aphorism applies: "Speed is life." Unable physiologically to match the speed that other species' evolution provided them, we developed technological ways to enhance our own and have never stopped developing them. When we put our own bodies in motion, we discovered pleasures unlike any other, though for those who did not find it exhilarating, its allure has always seemed unfathomable. T. E. Lawrence ("Lawrence of Arabia") knew this well, since his preference for fast Brough Superior motorcycles was as baffling to many people in the England of the 1920s and early 1930s as his decision to change his name, enlist in the Royal Air Force and serve as a low-ranking enlisted man, rather than a high-ranking officer, to which his education and wartime Army career entitled him. His choice of a motorcycle rather than a car seemed especially puzzling, since a motorcycle was the antithesis of the gentleman's conveyance in the last days of the British Empire, in which the word 'gentleman' had class-based significance. In 1933, as part of a biography he was writing on Lawrence, Basil Liddell Hart wrote to Lawrence, and asked him: "Can you explain the appeal that speed on a motorcycle has for you?" Liddell Hart noted, as a memorandum to himself: "Though he [Lawrence] had often discussed various aspects of this appeal, I wanted to see if he could throw a fuller light on it." [8]

Lawrence replied, "To explain the lure of speed you'd have to explain human nature; but it is easier understood than explained. All men in all ages have beggared themselves for fast horses or camels or ships or cars or bikes or airplanes; all men have strained themselves dry to run or walk or swim faster. Speed is the second-oldest animal craving in our nature, and our generation is fortunate in being able to indulge it more cheaply and generally than our ancestors. Every natural man cultivates the speed that appeals to him. I have a motor-bike income." [9]

[8] Liddell Hart, *T.E. Lawrence to His Biographers Robert Graves and Liddell Hart* (New York: Doubleday, 1963), p. 160; letter sent to TEL 11 August 1933.

[9] Ibid., p. 161 (TEL replied by letter to BLH n 14 August 1933).

By 1933, two years before he died from a motorcycle accident on his Brough Superior SS100, Lawrence had often been asked about his fondness for speed on motorcycles. In 1930, another friend, the author Robert Graves, had suggested to Lawrence that he write a book about speed. Graves noted: "The idea appealed to him. He said that speed, and especially the conquest of the air, was the greatest achievement of civilisation, and was one of the few subjects now left to write about."[10] Lawrence subsequently declined the invitation, telling Graves that "The itch to write died in me many years ago and I do not think it will revive." [11]

Lawrence's itch to ride, however, died only when he did, and he savored speed on his motorcycle literally to the end. To Graves he had written of experiences common among motorcyclists everywhere. "The greatest pleasure of my recent life has been speed on the roads. But I am not a racing man. It was my satisfaction to purr along gently between 60 and 70 mph and drink in the air and the general view. I lose detail at even moderate speeds, but gain comprehension. When I used to cross Salisbury Plain at 50 or so, I'd feel the earth moulding herself under me. It was *me* piling up this hill, hollowing this valley, stretching out this level place; almost the earth came alive, heaving and tossing on each side like a sea. That is a thing the slow coach will never feel. It is the reward of Speed." [12]

It was also, though Lawrence did not point it out, the reward of acceleration, for then, as now, motorcycles delivered the best bang for the buck in automotive acceleration.

[10] Ibid., p. 166.

[11] Ibid.

[12] Ibid., pp. 52-53 (TEL's letter to RG dated 26 June 1927).

At the time he wrote to Liddell Hart about the joys of speed, Lawrence's Brough Superior was the latest model, producing "57 hp and doing maximum 97 mph."[13] The bike weighed about 500 lbs., which meant that the unladen power-to-weight ratio was better than 1:9. By comparison, the same year—1933—the notorious outlaw John Dillinger chose the new Hudson Essex Terraplane at least in part because it had, the company claimed, the highest power-to-weight ratio of any production car in the world. The lightest Terraplane weighed just over 2000 lbs. and was powered by a six-cylinder, 70hp engine. Though every horsepower had to drag around 29 lbs., the car still set records for the flying mile at 85.8 mph and ran through the standing mile at 68 mph.[14] The Terraplane was 'hot' by the standards of the day. But anyone who wanted speed and acceleration on the road, and who was not a millionaire, bought a motorcycle.[15]

The difference between speed and acceleration is immensely important. People often mistake one for the other; they will say someone went fast when what they really meant was that he accelerated quickly. The difference in behavioral terms is not trivial, since our bodies respond differently to each kind of motion. Acceleration is change in velocity over time and has directionality, which is why it's defined as a 'vector quantity.' Velocity itself is not just speed, but speed to or from someplace, so it, too, is a vector quantity. Speed

[13]   Ibid., p. 71; BLH talk with TEL 28 May 1933; quote from BLH.

[14]   These data are frequently cited by Hudson marque historians and automotive journalists; see, for example, Bill Vance's *Canadian Driver* online story, "Terraplane" online at: *http://www.canadiandriver.com/articles/bv/terraplane.htm*.

[15]   Although automotive technology has vastly improved the highest of high-performance cars' acceleration and speed, the same is true today.

is 'scalar,' meaning that it has dimensional characteristics but not directionality. (Further confusing high-school physics students, all three quantities can have 'instantaneous' or 'average' values.)

We feel acceleration's effects immediately when we are the objects being accelerated (or decelerated), as G-forces. Sometimes, for example, when we accelerate from a stop sign in a minivan with sleeping children in the back seats, we try to minimize the G-forces by accelerating slowly; that is, we increase our velocity by smaller increments over time than we might if we were trying to enter a fast-moving traffic stream from a standstill. We set our comfort levels for acceleration through a number of decisions, some conscious, others unconscious but no less significant. We also seek, or accept as comfortable, different acceleration rates in different environments and for different purposes.

A desired velocity can be attained either by accelerating quickly or slowly, depending on the time and distance available to reach that velocity. Once the acceleration rate has stabilized and the power train is providing only enough thrust to sustain the target velocity, we cannot 'feel' the speed at all if we are inside a car's environmentally-controlled cabin. We infer it from audible and visible signals from inside and outside the vehicle, but until and unless we change direction—incurring another acceleration in some plane—we can feel as though we were motionless, seated in a chair at home, watching a particularly convincing movie projected around us and using an equally convincing soundtrack to mimic the wind noise, tire noise and other mechanical noises.

How do we decide what levels of acceleration or speed to seek or to accept? Most of us can get used to a wide range, but some will be more comfortable with more intense acceleration and speed than others. What we experience growing up, in an automotive culture, obviously has a lot to do with our self-imposed limits. But the limits established by our evolutionary heritage operate below the socio-cultural radar, as it were, to establish even more stringent limits for us. These are the ones that set not only the range of physiological tolerances beyond which our biological equipment just cannot work, but also the psychological range. Because of how evolution works—conservatively—it's a safe bet that those tolerances were set in large part by the demands of life in the ancestral trees, where everyone had to accept accelerations of certain types, intensities and durations as part of the arboreal-environment 'package.' [16]

That package demanded that our ancestors develop, by evolution, traits that enabled them to shove away from a tree, for instance, holding a vine or a branch in one hand and, maybe, an infant clutched to a breast in the other, and clamber, swing or jump to another spot, en route to another position of choice or necessity. Sometimes the move had to be made almost instantly, as when a predator threatened offspring or a cherished friend or relative. Being able to do that included a predisposition to find whatever physical effects were embed-

[16] The reason this is a safe bet is that our species' post-'camping-trip' experiences in the agrarian age (beginning roughly 10,000 years ago) have not demanded—until what I call the Automotive Transformation—'resetting' the arboreal-environment spectrum of 'normal' accelerations to accommodate more intense forces. It could be argued that the period from the Neolithic Agrarian Revolution to the Automotive Transformation might well have reset the spectrum for lower intensities, but the evidence for this is not available in the fossil or historical record.

ded in the ensuing leap or swing or step into space as perfectly normal. And for some, perhaps most, of our ancestors, the sensations thereby delivered often must have been what we'd call fun.

Millions of years later, the consequences for us, direct descendants of tree-dwellers who could and did have fun in the trees also include looking for similar kinds of fun wherever we can find it. The list of the things we have built to do that in one form or another is long, and extends up the complexity scale from ropes hung on tree limbs to playground swings, monkey bars, and a host of ever-more breath-taking amusement park rides.

The key point is that our automotive devices have been created to fit the physical and psychological needs and wants of a species that has evolved over millions of years in a wholly different environment from today's, one for which it seems to have been anatomically and psychologically well adapted. Our subsequent genetic evolution seems to have slowed dramatically as we have shaped the environment to suit ourselves instead of it shaping us through adaptive selection of biological traits.[17] However, some evolutionary scientists have proposed recently that our genetic evolution has been replaced by cultural evolution. The most famous proponent

---

[17] Recent comparative DNA studies, made possible because of the 'decoding' of the human genome, have led some evolutionary biologists to conclude that selection pressures have continued to evolve differences in humanity. Attention in research has been focused on single-nucleotide polymorphisms (SNPs), which can be determined through 'haplotype' comparisons. Weiss and Mann (*Human Biology and Behavior*) define haplotypes as "combinations of genetic traits that can be inherited as a block due to their presence on the same chromosome" (p. 641.) For more detail, see, for example, "A Haplotype Map of the Human Genome," in *Nature,* Vol. 437, pp. 1299-1320 (27 October 2005), online at: *http://www.nature. com/nature/journal/v437/n7063/full/nature04226.html*.

of this concept is the biologist Richard Dawkins, who first argued in 1976 that, just as genes are the essential units of biological evolution, 'memes' embodying beliefs, ideas and behaviors are transmitted from one generation to the next and are the units of cultural evolution.[18]

Whether or not subsequent research and experimentation verifies Dawkins' and others' memetic evolutionary theories, we remain as much physical and emotional creatures as mental or spiritual ones, whose pleasures remain rooted in our genetic inheritance. Memetic or cultural evolution does, however, modify the means by which our pleasures may be expressed or enjoyed, inevitably, through the social environment in which we live. Even so, in the case of automobility, it can be argued that biological evolution literally drives cultural evolution. This is because our need for mobility and our desires for certain kinds of sensory stimuli created a 'behavioral template.' Artists, engineers and others involved with making and selling vehicles must closely attend to this template if they wish to succeed in the economic environment that has replaced hunting and gathering: the marketplace.

Since all who enter the marketplace want to succeed, their products, when successful, tell us a lot about what we value. That we value the sensory experiences delivered with the personal transportation in our vehicles, especially motorcycles, is therefore made clear in the marketplaces where we buy and sell them. To understand exactly how the sensations we seek for pleasure and the vehicles we buy in our quest for pleasure actually work, we must delve deeply into the machines themselves, as well as into the hybrid entity created

[18] Richard Dawkins, *The Selfish Gene* (Oxford Univ. Press, 1976)

when human and machine are brought together. Or, as the cultural evolutionists might put it, we need to examine what happens, and why, when genetic and memetic evolution meet on a motorcycle seat.

CHAPTER TWO

GO FAST,
LOOK GOOD,
FEEL GREAT

Like sex, motorcycle riding is a lot more fun to do than to analyze. Under the microscope, everything we do for fun eventually winds up being just a bunch of chemical reactions, at least if we follow the trail of evidence about why we do what we do through the layers of interrelated causes and effects. This is more difficult than it may at first appear, because it means asking questions about behavior that seems normal on its face. It requires us to adopt the outlook of Bill Cosby's Temple University philosophy-major girlfriend, who, he says, used to ask questions like "Why is there air?"[19] In their primer for studying evolutionary psychology, Leda Cosmides and John Tooby cite the "twisted outlook" of cartoonist Gary Larson as a necessary way to combat the "instinct blindness" that makes any study of "natural competences"[20] so difficult. If a single Larson cartoon could summarize the enterprise, it would be the classic in which a cow in a fenced field, flanked by two other cows grazing nearby, is looking up with an angry expression. "Hey, wait a minute!" she exclaims. "This is grass! We've been eating grass!"

The way people react to this question can tell you a lot about their own assumptions. If they laugh, giggle or even smile, it is a good bet that they have a nicely tuned sense of the ridiculous and can extrapolate from the startled and angry cow's realization that what seems normal is just normal to someone because…well, why? Cows eat grass. They are 'designed' that way, and it does not matter whether you think they are equipped with their unique bovine way of life by God or evolution; they still eat grass and evidently like it. So when, in an "Aha!" moment, we put what she is doing into the context of the strange, we see how much of our own lives is ruled by the 'natural competences' with which we are equipped. Among them, the idea of fun itself—that it is a good rather than a bad thing to seek wherever we can find

[19] In "The $75 Car" section of his standup comedy routine, recorded in 1964 at the Flamingo Hotel in Las Vegas and released by Warner Bros. in 1965 on the LP album, *Bill Cosby/ Why is There Air?*

[20] *Evolutionary Psychology*, 1997.

it and will seek it in any way we can—includes putting our bodies in motion on motorcycles.

To get beyond instinct blindness, we must examine the systems that make fun possible before we can even reach the "Aha!" That means we must understand, at a minimum, something of our own and the motorcycle's anatomy and physiology, as well as the nature of the phenomena we encounter when straddling the bike. Even before we start the engine, we are in a psychobiological state of 'arousal.' That does not mean sexual arousal, but arousal of the autonomic nervous system that controls the heart, the lungs and all the systems configured by evolution to enable fight or flight.

Arousal tenses muscles, speeds up heart rate and breathing, releases endorphins and clotting agents into the bloodstream and triggers brain mechanisms that heighten the ability to focus on the task literally at hand. Which is a good thing, since aboard a motorcycle, you are about to light off a powerful engine and use it to launch yourself through space, often surrounded by other vehicles, any one of which can kill or maim you. Psychologist Peter Gray summarizes what has been learned by experiments about arousal states this way: "The usual finding is that high arousal is beneficial for tasks that require a good deal of physical energy, or where performance of the task is instinctive or very well practiced, but is often harmful for tasks that call for novel (unpracticed) movements, creativity, or careful judgment." [21]

Neophytes obviously encounter the highest arousal states, since the whole affair is 'novel' and the movements necessary to make the bike do what the new rider wants it to

[21] *Psychology* (New York: Worth, 1991), p. 227.

do are far from instinctive. New riders must learn the array of actions and effects that will soon become familiar and that will result in the optimal arousal state. Though psychologists disagree about how to define that 'optimal' state, for a motorcyclist the definition is simple: the optimal arousal state is the one that makes a ride fun.

This definition seems so obvious that it is just plain silly. But it is not, because the relationship between arousal and emotion is not well understood. 'Fun' is not an emotion but a summary and judgment we make of an activity that we find enjoyable in certain ways, even if it exhausts us mentally or physically. Thus can a motorcyclist plunge into a rainstorm on a dark, cold night, ride for two hours, and consider it fun. What can possibly make it so? The cultural view is that it derives from a sense of achievement, knowledge that one is doing what others cannot or will not, and conscious awareness of connections to nature that are unavailable to those who dare not. This might well be so; but behind these satisfactions are the physical stimuli that create the optimal level of system arousal, and the psychophysical responses to those stimuli. The same conditions that make the ride fun for one rider can make it terrifying for others, especially neophytes. Likewise, the rider's own physical and mental state obviously affect the fun-factor of the ride. But the primary fun generator, operating for all who seek moto-motion under any circumstances, is the set of stimuli acting on the rider that can vary in intensity, but not in type.

Stimuli (plural) and stimulus (singular) play such an important role in everything related to motorcycles in motion that it is worth considering carefully what the word 'stimulus' means or does not mean. It has nuances that are emphasized according to who is using the word. To a historian or a classicist, depending on the context, the Latin word could be a masculine-gender noun that Caesar and other Roman soldiers used as a technical term for a certain kind of stake in the ground meant to slow an enemy advance, or it could be a metaphoric 'stake,' used to goad or to create an incentive. To psychologist Peter Gray, it is "A well-defined element of the environment that can potentially act on an individual's nervous system and thereby influence the individual's behavior."[22] Biology-textbook authors Karen Arms and Pamela Camp narrow the definition by calling it "Energy (chemical, electrical, thermal, light, mechanical, etc.) in the external or internal environment of an organism, to which the organism may respond."[23] Another set of biology-text authors—William T. Keeton, James L. Gould and Carol Grant Gould—distill the definition to nine words: "Any environmental factor that is detected by a receptor."[24] But that is deceptively simple, because a 'receptor' itself must then be defined precisely: "In cell biology, often the exposed part of a membrane protein, that binds a substance but does not catalyze a reaction in the chemical it binds; the membrane protein frequently has another region that, a result of the binding, undergoes an allosteric change and so becomes catalytically active." ('Allosteric' refers to an enzyme "that can exist in two or more conformations,"[25] and

---

[22]   Ibid., G-20.

[23]   Arms and Camp, *Biology: A Journey Into Life* (W. B. Saunders: New York, 1988), G-12.

[24]   Keeton, Gould and Gould, *Biological Science (Fifth Edition)* (W.W. Norton: New York, 1993), A32.

[25]   Ibid., A17

an enzyme is itself "a compound, usually a protein, that acts as a catalyst."[26])

Biological scientists know the secret world of sensors. For the rest of us, a little sensor-summarizing is useful because it is the engineering of the sensors that determines what 'gear' we are in, so to speak, when they 'shift' their states. Sensory receptors come as a wide range of highly specialized cells in five categories. Photoreceptors respond to light energy; chemoreceptors to the chemistry that defines substances; thermoreceptors detect and respond to temperature changes, free nerve endings respond to cell-tissue damage and mechanoreceptors are stimulated by pressure or fluid movements.

Whatever the sensory organ—eyes, ears, nose, skin, tongue, vestibular system—the basic means by which the sensory information is detected and sent to the part of the brain that is adapted and specialized to translate the signal into a 'sensation' is the same. A change in some external or internal environmental condition affects an array of receptors that responds with a chemical reaction that itself activates nerve cells. Those cells fire an electrical impulse through the nerves to the appropriate part of the brain which then, via a phenomenon called 'projection' created in the cerebral cortex, enables us to perceive the location and intensity of the stimuli.

That perceptive process means that what you feel is not happening at the point of impact, as it were; it is happening in various areas of the brain, nearly simultaneously and so quickly that the time lag between stimulus, perception and projection of the response to the stimulus is literally imper-

[26] Ibid., A22.

ceptible to us, though it can be measured. The purpose of the system in humans is the same as in other organisms: It enables us to perceive and to respond, either to our internal world or to the external world. That is necessary, of course, for us to survive, reproduce and have fun.

The sensory system with which we are equipped includes much more than the so-called primary senses centered in the head. Those senses are intended to guide the attention and enable the brain thus to guide the body that sustains the brain to or away from some action. For the body to do that, it must be balanced appropriately; that is, it must know both where it is in space and how its own parts are located in relation to each other. Only those people with certain kinds of injuries or disorders have to think about this; the rest of us do it automatically. Or rather, the specialized cybernetic systems evolved over millennia do it for us.

The key is 'proprioception,' which some biologists and physiologists summarize simply as 'joint sense' but which comes from two Latin words: *proprius,* meaning 'own' or 'particular' and the verb *recipere,* to take back or receive. Proprioception is the process by which specialized cells in the muscles continuously update the brain about the position and movement of the body. The proprioceptor cells, in concert with the cells that tell the brain about the condition of the skin and visceral organs, comprise the somatosensory system—*somato* coming from the Greek word *soma,* or body. The somatosensors include specialized thermoreceptors (temperature), free nerve endings (pain) and mechanoreceptors (touch and pressure).

This incredibly complex system comprises receptor cells, nerve cells that pass their data in the form of electrical impulses to areas of the brain that process and integrate the signals to give us involuntary-reflex movement (such as the knee-jerk reaction triggered by the physician's little rubber hammer just below the patella) or voluntary movement. The system also keeps everything in static and dynamic equilibrium, which is why we can straddle something that won't stay upright by itself, grab a couple of handgrips, wriggle our butts on the seat, ride away from a stop and keep the thing upright until the end of the ride. Because the system that gives us that capability is the basis of what differentiates types, directions and intensities of perceived somatic motion, it is important to understand how it works.

Static and dynamic equilibrium are sensed by two complementary and adjacent organ groups in our inner ears. They are usually called the vestibular system because they are attached to or inside the vestibule, a bony chamber connecting the orientation organs to the cochlea. Three semicircular canals and two expanded chambers—the utricle and saccule—contain the mechanoreceptors that signal changes in head position. The semicircular canals are oriented at right angles to one another, in three axes. At the base of each fluid-filled canal is an enlarged section that contains a clump of hair cells moved by a gelatinous mass whenever the head is moved. The semicircular canals are specialized to aid in dynamic equilibrium and are our primary means (apart from vision) of detecting and responding to angular acceleration. The utricle and saccule are chambers inside the vestibule lying at right angles to each other, containing more hair cells that

respond to the motion of the jelly-like fluid. The sensitivity
of the motion is enhanced by calcium-carbonate crystalline
structures called *otoliths* (from the Greek word *ot*, or ear, and
lith, stone). These crystals, though microscopic, are relatively
heavy, and lie in a layer atop the gelatinous mass so that any
movement, no matter how tiny, will activate the hair-cell
mechanoreceptors, enabling the brain to control our muscu-
lature to ensure static equilibrium. The otolith organs are our
primary mechanisms for detecting linear (fore and aft or side
to side) accelerations, as well as gravity.

In evolutionary terms, the main purpose of all the
motion-detection sensors is to enable a 'stabilized retinal
image.' Physicians Louis D. Eldridge and Susan E. Northrup,
in their chapter about the effects of acceleration in the *United
States Air Force Flight Surgeon's Guide*, put it this way:

> The primary reflex for stabilizing the retinal
> image in humans is the vestibulo-ocular reflex.
> This reflex can be demonstrated by holding one's
> finger about half a meter in front of one's face and
> moving it back and forth. If the rate of motion
> is increased, a point is reached where the image
> of the finger becomes blurred. If one then holds
> one's finger still and moves one's head back and
> forth at the same frequency the image stays in
> focus. This example demonstrates that the vestib-
> ulo-ocular reflex is more powerful at stabilizing
> retinal images than are the optokinetic reflexes
> used for tracking objects. As demonstrated in this
> example, the vestibulo-ocular reflex is very good

at compensating for rapid, high-frequency movements of the head.[27]

What that means is that our built-in systems enable each of us to focus better on something when our body is swinging, twisting, bouncing or swaying than when the object we are focused on is itself moving too quickly. Doctors Eldridge and Northrup, speaking to the specialized needs of Air Force flight surgeons, make this clear: "The important concept to grasp is that these perceptual organs have a 'design' frequency response. The accelerative forces encountered in flight often provide stimuli outside the design envelope of these organs, and as a result, illusions, or misperceptions, occur that can lead to spatial disorientation." [28]

Any one of us who as a kid got going really fast on the playground merry-go-round discovered this the hard way. We would gleefully spin and spin, whooping and taunting the other kids who, perhaps being more sensible or experienced, had gotten off before we could reach nearly escape velocity with the platform, until we too finally jumped off and tried to stand. The world kept whirling, we got dizzy and, depending on the kid, nausea and maybe an upchuck might have ensued, followed by stern lectures from annoyed parents. We had produced "stimuli outside the design envelope" of our organs of spatial orientation.

While it is easy to induce the illusions that can cause serious problems for a pilot in flight, it is more difficult to

[27] Eldridge and Northrup, *United States Air Force Flight Surgeon's Guide*: Chapter 4 (Sensory Effects of Acceleration: Basic Neurophysiology), online (retrieved 20 August 2002); *http://wwwsam.brooks.af.mil/af/files/fsguide/HTML/Chapter_04.html.*

[28] Ibid.

induce them on a motorcycle, at least for most people. This is because the range of motions and the intensity of the accelerations we encounter on a bike glued to the ground more or less firmly by gravity do not exceed the 'design envelope' of our biological mechanisms of automatic dynamic and static equilibrium, assuming that our brains are unaddled by alcohol or drugs and can respond to the stimuli and sensory data appropriately. The motorcycle, in other words, delivers a stimulus-package—the moto-package—that is closer than the jet fighter's to the evolutionary benchmarks set in place in the Environments of Evolutionary Adaptedness millions of years ago.

Take the riding position. A motorcycle can be seen—if you squint at it just right, anyway—as a collection of branches from the extinct African moto-tree. You sit athwart the main branch, the one that is broad and deep; your hands and feet control the bike's systems through transverse branches—handlebars and footpegs—upon which your limbs rest. By comparison, a car creates an environment never seen in the natural world: a chair stuck in a moving box controlled by a steering wheel (a branch bent into a circle, at best) and pedals, with a hand-operated gear selector and assorted other buttons, switches and knobs. You can drive a car successfully via hand controls if you are paralyzed below the waist—many paraplegics do—but it is much harder (though not impossible) to do the same on a 'solo' motorcycle.

Likewise, except for hang-gliders and some early ultra-light aircraft, all fixed- or rotary-wing airplanes these days place the pilot in a posture analogous to the automobile driver's. Moreover, since the success of any automotive passive-safety system requires the car's occupants to be as immobile as possible, like fighter pilots, today's automobilists are strapped in so tightly that the body-position changes not only possible but necessary for a motorcyclist in many conditions are almost impossible for them.

The motorcyclist, unlike the automobilist, is out in the weather atop a contraption that will eventually fall over if he or she does not positively control it. We must provide steering input continuously to keep the machine aligned, with our evolutionary gift of built-in dynamic balancing systems operating in the background, as it were, while we focus on things like the old lady in the Oldsmobile across the road who looks as if she is about to turn left in front of us without signaling. When we want to turn to avoid her, we must lean the bike into the direction of the turn and keep supplying subtle steering inputs through the handlebars. This is because motorcycles turn primarily by means of 'camber thrust.'

In turning a motorcycle, as with a car, the act generates centrifugal force. This force—from the Latin for "center-fleeing"—is a felt but fictitious force in scientific terms, and can be calculated as the product of vehicle mass times acceleration divided by the radius of the turn. As every high-school physics student learns, centrifugal force is equal in magnitude but opposite in direction to the centripetal, or center-seeking force that is required for any object to continue turning. In automobiles, which are self-balanced, the centripetal force is maintained by turning the steered wheels into the turn at angles greater than the desired turn radius. Because the car or truck is relatively stable, the tires can be held more or less upright and generate cornering power through slip angles.

Slip angle is the angle between the direction of the tire and the tangent to the curve the tire is following, and rarely exceeds 15 degrees (until loss of control, that is).[29]

Motorcycles and bicycles, in contrast, are not self-balanced, being single-track vehicles (a car is a double-track vehicle, as is a wagon, train or horse carriage). The motorcycle must lean into the turn. In doing this, the motorcyclist uses the weight of the machine and rider to counteract—or balance—the centrifugal force, both operating through the combined bike-rider center of gravity.

Lean angle necessary for the bike to negotiate a corner depends on the speed the bike is traveling and the turn radius the rider wants to sustain. Due to the many variables present in any cornering situation, the lean angle of the wheel must be adjusted continuously by the rider through handlebar pressures to achieve the desired track. The drag force of the road surface, the size and construction of the tires and aerodynamic effects such as side winds all play a role in how the rider does that.

In this process, as with initiating the turn, to turn left—a turn in which the wheels will be leaned left, or into the turn—the rider first turns the front wheel slightly in the opposite direction. This is 'countersteering' and motorcyclists learn as neophytes the countersteering mantra: push left to go left, push right to go right. Meaning that one pushes on the left hand grip to induce the wheel to turn away from the desired direction to turn into it. In leaning, the motorcycle

---

[29] Usually ignored by physics textbooks, the means by which motorcycles turn can be researched online in great detail; a good source is *http://tonyfoale.com*, wherein Tony Foale—a highly regarded motorcycle designer—explains cornering and tire functions very well.

inevitably leans the rider too, generating acceleration forces in the sensory organs, just as straight-line acceleration does. As noted previously, whatever else their shortcomings— weather protection, passive safety, etc.—motorcycles can accelerate more quickly to street-legal speeds than most cars, even today.

Any motorcycle ride, then, is a sequence of accelerations, as is any car trip. But what differentiates the bike ride from the car drive is that the bike's accelerations are greater in intensity and different in perceived axis. The automobile is a stable platform, like any quadruped—one reason why the comparison of a motorcyclist to an equestrian is not appropriate. A horse and car will stay upright at rest without action by the driver/rider, but the motorcycle will topple over at rest and at any point thereafter (eventually) unless the operator provides input. Likewise, when the automobile turns, its wider tires and steering geometry, in concert with the suspension, work to keep the platform horizontal, though most vehicles without computer-controlled active suspensions actually lean away from the direction of the turn. Cars with old shocks and softer springs are particularly prone to do this, whereas sports and racing cars can corner almost 'flat.'

In hard cornering—the kind enthusiast drivers love to experience in their sports cars—the car's occupants are sometimes subjected to high G-force loads. Under these conditions, it can feel as though the forces are trying to fling you out the door, just as you felt when you were a kid on the merry-go-round. Formula One and Indy cars can generate more than five lateral and four vertical Gs, because their combination of mechanical and aerodynamic devices keep the cars glued to the track as much as possible. Their high power-to-weight ratios and powerful brakes subject the drivers to similar fore-and-aft G-forces.

The effects of such sustained high G-force loads can be dangerous, which is why an Indy car race at Texas Motor Speedway scheduled to begin on April 29, 2001 was called off only hours before the start. In the pre-race meeting, the medical director of the organizing body surveyed the drivers and found that 21 of the 25 had experienced the onset of potentially lethal G-force effects, including vision problems and dizziness, known precursors of 'G-LOC' or G-force-induced loss of consciousness. Clearly, these are outside the 'design envelope' of the human vestibular and cardiovascular system. The drivers had never experienced anything like these forces before; they were the consequence of the steep banking of the speedway and the very high speeds the cars could achieve and sustain.[30]

For passengers in a sports car driven too fast on a twisting road, as for the G-force-whacked Indy car drivers under conditions like those in Texas, accelerations involved with cornering are no fun. Yet for motorcyclists, the forces experienced in turning-by-leaning are perceived not just as part of the fun of riding but central to it. Likewise, for the sports-car driver, if not the passenger, flinging the car around curves at high speeds is also central to the fun of a sports car; the more quickly the car answers the control commands of the driver, the more fun the car is thought to be. What makes these kinds of acceleration fun? How do forces applied to us in certain

---

[30] An excellent review and analysis of the events at TMS and their causes is available online, by Martin Voshell; *csel.eng.ohio-state.edu/voshell/gforce.pdf*.

ways produce pleasure while others do not? Why is the act of balancing a motorcycle in a turn so enjoyable to so many, no matter how fast they are going as they make the turn?

Motorcyclists themselves have tried to understand this since there have been motorcycles, just as bicyclists did for the two decades or so before the appearance of motorbikes as commodities rather than oddities. The same words crop up in their testimony, whether at the dawn of the 20th or the 21st century. Freedom and flying on the ground top the list. But what, exactly, is more 'free' about riding a device that won't stay upright by itself without the operator, and which, though narrower by far than cars or most three wheelers, is far less easy to fling about on the road without fear of crashing than a car? Motorcyclists believe that freedom from being enclosed, as in a car—or 'cage' as cars are now routinely called by some—leads to freedom in other ways. For example, priest and professor of history John M. Staudenmaier, S.J., replied to my question of why he chooses to ride a motorcycle instead of a car whenever he can this way:

> On my bike, the relationship between my tiny human self and the immense world around me is unmistakable. I dip down and across a gully and feel the air change from hot and dry toward cool and damp, and back again as I climb the other side. I watch storm clouds with particular attention and, in the process, notice subtle changes in the light as it is endlessly repainted by clouds and passing time. Road surfaces matter to me, oil patches, bits of loose gravel, potholes; so does

traffic and other people's road behavior. Biking is much more like the rest of my life than driving. In my life, with its loves and vulnerabilities and interruptions and occasionally well planned achievements, I get in trouble when I fantasize myself as a massive figure within a small frame of reference. I do better when I imagine myself as a durable real, attentive and supple traveler who needs the cooperation of the large universe of which I am a part. Biking, I suppose, especially because it is so fun, helps me to like being small in a large domain. It is one of my favorite ways to make myself present to God.[31]

Father John is more eloquent than most in his descriptions of the appeal of motorcycling, but it is important that he cites many of the same sensations and associated emotions that T. E. Lawrence did. So do many motorcyclists when asked why they are so seemingly addicted to riding and, though I have never seen nor heard another reference to Father John's experience of being "small in a large domain" and thereby closer to God, I am sure he speaks for many. However, even so philosophical a thinker as Fr. John understands the centrality of fun to the motorcycle's appeal and the kind of fun he describes is the cumulative effect of the physical sensations of riding. The motorcycle as Orgasmatron only works because of this physicality; were it not so, only those forced to ride by circumstance would do so.

---

[31] Personal correspondence with the author, 14 May 1997.

Motorcycling as a package of sensations is clearly a more 'natural' activity than driving a car, in the sense not only of one's being immersed in Nature but also in the sense that one must use all one's natural biological equipment to make the motorcycle work. Take, for example, the method of turning a motorcycle and the forces we encounter thereby. Not only do we lean into a turn when we are running hard and quickly on our own feet, for the same reasons as we do on a bike—to balance the body against the centrifugal force—but we also have, in our species' behavioral repertoire, millennia of arboreal locomotion by means of vines and whatever else our ancestors could use to get from here to there. Just because our daily lives in an industrial society do not require us to use the traits that enabled such movements does not mean they are not still available to us. Yet if we are serious about finding the roots of motorized fun, how exactly does a particular kind of force we encounter become enjoyable? What happens at the molecular level, the chemistry-set level to which I referred at the start of this chapter, to convert a turn into a grin?

Unfortunately, in spite of the recent advances in psychobiology—in which behavior is studied by attempting to understand the bio-chemistry of mental processes that produce it—the short answer seems to be that nobody knows for sure. As a physician friend who was a leading researcher in psychobiology at the National Institute of Mental Health told me, anyone who figures out how all our emotions are generated, and why, will become very wealthy very quickly. Drugs, of course, have been a way to produce pleasure for humans since there have been written records to tell us about them, but pleasure *per se* is not necessarily 'fun.' Pleasure is a state that can be induced by any number of external stimuli, most of which will trigger the release of endorphins, the truncated form of the phrase 'endogenous morphines.' These opiates and the mechanisms by which they generate pleasure for us are reasonably well understood, as is the operation of neurotransmitters, which work at the synaptic gaps of neurons. But fun, as noted previously, is a summary judgment we make about an activity, and the precise means by which an activity can create an emotional state have yet to be fully understood.

Candace B. Pert, Professor of Physiology and Biophysics at Georgetown University Medical Center, writes in her book, *Molecules of Emotion: Why You Feel the Way You Feel*, that "Unfortunately, *emotion* is another of those words mainstream science likes to spit out at the very first taste."[32] Her research led her to propose that emotions of greater sophistication than fear and rage are primarily the function of what she calls a 'second nervous system' that operates by means of chemicals called neuropeptides and their receptors throughout the body. These comprise part of an information network, as she puts it, that links body and mind seamlessly to create the 'bodymind.' In her view, "Emotional states or moods are produced by the various neuropeptide ligands [substances that bind to specific receptors on a cell surface] and what we experience as an emotion or a feeling is also a mechanism for activating a particular neuronal circuit—*simultaneously throughout the brain and body* [orig. emphasis]—which generates a behavior involving the

[32] Pert, *Molecules of Emotion: Why You Feel The Way You Feel* (Scribner: New York, 1997), p.178.

whole creature, with all the necessary physiological changes that behavior would require." [33]

If she is right, it leads immediately to the question Pert herself asks: "Is there one kind of peptide that is specific to each emotion? Perhaps. I believe so." She adds: "But we have a way to go to work this out."[34] This is the crux of the search for the fun factors in motion at the biochemical level. Until research is completed on how a given external stimulus or 'package' of stimuli can create an emotional state reliably, the precise ways in which the discrete stimulus elements of the moto-package work to make a certain kind of motion either sought or avoided cannot be identified. To date, as far as I am aware, that research has not been done, so we are left to speculate about why some kinds of motion are fun (for some) and others not.

The acceleration question is a good example. In a car being driven at high speed around a sharp curve, we are sub-jected to lateral acceleration and held in place in a box, so that we feel the force as an often uncomfortable shove to the out-side of the turn. This is a sideways push, which we encounter as if we were on a chair fixed to a spinning merry-go-round, facing not in toward the center or out toward the rim, but sitting perpendicular to the circle's radius looking either into the direction of the spin or away from it. Though we would initially feel what we would translate as longitudinal accelera-tion as the merry-go-round spun up to high speed, once it got there we would be pushed to the outside by centrifugal force that would become increasingly uncomfortable with each

[33] Ibid., p.145

[34] Ibid.

increase in rpm of the merry-go-round. Outside the fun-fair milieu, in which participants place themselves deliberately in situations where they are stressed in all three axes in order to produce prodigious amounts of shriek-inducing adrenalin and derive innocent joy from overcoming their discomfort or fear, I have never met anyone who finds this kind of lateral acceleration 'fun,' though drivers encounter the same G-force-loading as passengers. What's fun about it for the driver is the concentration and mastery of skill needed to maintain controlled high speed around the turn. The physical experience of the driver thus centers on the control feedback, not the acceleration effects, as I discovered early in my work as a road-test editor.

In that role, to find the maximum sustainable lateral acceleration of each car or truck we would test, we drove the vehicle as quickly as possible around a circular skid pad, following a painted line. The objective was to do whatever it took with steering or throttle control to get the vehicle into a steady state—or as close as we could come to it—to find its limits. The higher the lateral acceleration number, the more bragging rights the car had among enthusiasts. Though the criticism was often made that we were testing the tires more than the chassis, suspension or power-train quality, the skid-pad test, in conjunction with a slalom, delivered a useful measure by which we could compare certain important handling qualities. To get reliable numbers, we would often spend all day at the track with as many test cars as we could, to minimize the time and money spent to gather the test data. Each test driver thus made many circuits of the skid pad on test days, sometimes with high-performance or racing cars, generating more than one G lateral acceleration. Though this is nothing compared to the forces Indy-car drivers face on their high-speed oval tracks, after a day or more of such testing our bodies were clearly affected. Moreover, however eager a new editorial staffer might be at first to jump into cars to test lateral acceleration, it was not long before he or she also realized that it was hard physical work in which the only fun was in the control itself, not the experience the control of the car delivered.

To see how we instinctively avoid experiencing lateral acceleration of the kind typical of skid-pad tests, one need only watch automobile drivers to observe how they respond to freeway or Interstate highway off-ramps or similarly long and tight turns. Almost everyone who has not been trained out of the behavior leans his or her head and upper body into the turn, especially when driving a car with 'soft' suspension. The passengers lean similarly when they can, because it lessens the discomfort of the lateral acceleration, as if they were making the turn on a motorcycle.

Leaning into a turn is indisputably more natural to us than the way we are forced to endure lateral acceleration in a car or truck. Airlines realized early in commercial aviation that passengers were most comfortable in turns that produced the sensation of one G, their vestibular systems being tricked by the physics of flight into thinking that the floor of the airplane was 'down' at all times. Sudden increase or decrease of this G-force load factor, from turbulence or from the pilot's steepening or easing the turn, results in unhappy passengers whose arousal states are often already high, despite the airlines' best efforts to assure them that flying seven miles high in an aluminum tube is as safe as or safer than crossing the street.

Being strapped into an airplane seat in a heightened arousal state is particularly distressing because of the inability to use the psychobiological advantages that state confers to affect anything about the flight. The flight crew, even to some extent the cabin crew, are busy doing something. Not so the hapless passengers, among whom may be people on the edge of panic because their arousal mechanisms make them want to flee the airplane as quickly as possible. Similarly, the driver of a car also finds himself or herself put into an arousal state by things beyond his or her control, such as pileups on the road or mistakes by fellow drivers. However, the artificial environment of the automobile so effectively insulates the occupant and reduces his or her role to remaining seated and doing little, physically, that the veteran driver is not usually in a state of high arousal. It might well be comfortable to sit in a plush chair moving down the road at more than 100 feet per second, using only one's hands and the right and occasionally the left foot to control the machine's progress, but for many drivers, it is not usually conducive to alertness.

The motorcyclist, like the bicyclist, is in a different situation entirely. The rider must continually anticipate and react to the road conditions while balancing the bike. Though some sophisticated touring motorcycles have created as comfortable an interface for the rider as is possible to imagine on a motorcycle, the machine remains a single-track two-wheeler that needs 'minding,' as the British say, at all times. Thus riding a bicycle or a motorcycle is like walking: we must use all our body's systems to do it, but after we learn how in early childhood we normally do it without thought, balancing more or less perfectly for the rest of our lives. When exercise physiologists and other physicians prescribe plain old walking as a way to achieve both physical and mental health, they are asking us to do what our bodies, thanks to evolution, 'want' to do.

The same applies to riding a bicycle or a motorcycle, the latter easier for people lacking the physical stamina or other traits needed to make a bicycle ride fun. Bodies not suffering from disabilities enjoy being used to balance and walk, so any locomotion that involves or demands the use of our arms, legs, hands and feet is more inherently satisfying to us than just sitting immobile in a car. Even so, it must be acknowledged that one reason the automobile has been so successful is that it delivers both personal transportation and 'personal space' in relative comfort for millions. Their idea of vehicular fun is not to fling the vehicle around turns or accelerate so hard to legal speeds that the passengers are pinned to their seats, heads against the headrests. Instead, those drivers want peace and quiet, disturbed only by the kind of audio information or entertainment they like. The arousal-as-enjoyment process is not on their agendas.

These drivers are also not, in general, as alert as the motorcyclists around them. Riders' arousal states are high because of the constant need to stabilize the bike, a need that cannot be met without continuous concentration and body movements. The hands always have something to do, even if the rider sets the cruise control and steers lightly with one hand. But it is precisely because this 'Interstate' mode requires so little actual braking and shifting and throttle control—using all one's equipment, so to speak—that many motorcyclists do anything they can to avoid multi-lane, restricted-access roads on which riding is referred to by them as the self-explanatory 'droning.' Instead, they seek riding environments that demand their constant attention and use of controls, no matter what kind of bike they ride. This continuous use of the body and mind—necessary to 'stay ahead of the bike'—may not be exactly analogous to walking or running, but it is as close as we can come in an automotive culture. When we ride a motorcycle, assuming that we seek and thus enjoy the sensations associated with the activity, we put our bodies in motion and sustain that motion in ways much more like those that formed our 'design envelope.' It is easy to see why, if you consider walking or clambering around in a tree. Especially in the latter case, heightened arousal is vital since it puts all our systems in high gear, as it were.

This sharpens our ability to concentrate and focus on our next move or how we will use it to connect with some other faraway branch or vine that can get us to the food or the family or the sheltering umbrella of leaves for protection against the sun or the storm. Because the arboreal environment is dynamic, not static, the capabilities of focus, concentration and a finely-tuned sense of balance were primary requirements for surviving. Those who lived long enough to mate and thus pass along their genes clearly had the capabilities needed for the 'bodymind' to function well and happily in that environment, so the ensuing adaptations were passed down to us. Because there was no natural-world selection pressure for our ancestors to accommodate to high lateral acceleration other than the angular motion of climbing, swinging or just hanging out in the tree-home, it is reasonable to propose that we do not 'like' skid-pad Gs as much as leaned-over Gs, for evolutionary and not cultural reasons.

Interestingly, though, in this lateral-acceleration context, there is one kind of sideways motion that many race-car drivers and other enthusiast drivers savor. That is the 'power-oversteer' mode of cornering in which the car tracks around the curve with the nose aimed sharply into the corner and the tail 'hung out,' as the car is balanced between spinning out and slowing down. This is easiest to achieve with a stiff chassis and suspension, a highly responsive and powerful engine driving the rear wheels, and sensitive steering. On any dirt-track oval throughout America on any given race day, you can see how the racers pitch their cars into this position just before they enter and maintain control through a turn by feeding power to the rear wheels judiciously, feeling for the breakaway point by 'the seat of their pants.' Likewise, 'drifting,' in which highly-tuned cars are put into much the same nose-in/tail-out position as dirt-track race cars, but on pavement, for style-comparison points, is also fun for the drivers. Why? Perhaps because by turning the car more steeply into the turn, the driver has changed substantially the axis through which the centrifugal force is working on him or her, bringing it closer to the longitudinal and further from the lateral. And longitudinal acceleration, like angular motion, is one that many people seek, in vehicles and elsewhere, at least up to certain limits.

Motorcycles provide the best bang for the acceleration buck in this sense, but in this arena, cars are no less and possibly more fun for untold numbers of drivers and even passengers. It is no secret to worried parents of newly licensed teenaged drivers—especially boys—that getting the car to provide 'lunge,' in the form of quick acceleration from a stop, is common. Nowadays, most middle-class American dads themselves grew up in an automotive culture in which burning rubber to signify power and skill, as well as to launch the car as quickly as possible, was commonplace. In this way, drag racing is not just a contest but also a means of legitimizing—even when done on the street, illegally—the delivery of a big dose of lunge.

The fact that our innate acceleration-detection systems are specialized to provide us with precise information about different kinds of acceleration must be significant in explaining why linear or longitudinal lunge is considered so much fun by so many, while lateral, whole-body acceleration is not. But until the neurochemical bases for motion stimuli as emotion generators are themselves understood, tracking the data pathway from the organ that detects motion and dispatches information about it to and throughout the 'bodymind' is the closest we can come to mapping the way in which leaning into a turn generates a grin.

The same is true of the other sensations that define the moto-package. The rider is immersed in the environment, subject to the whims of weather as no car driver is, even in a convertible. As everyone who rides notices, the odors, sights and sounds encountered on a motorcycle are more intense than those the people in cars experience. Being 'out in it' is one reason, of course, but the other is the rider's psychobiological arousal state compared with the driver's. Through the process of sensor-cell adaptation, the sensory systems that create the state gradually reduce their intensity for most riders, assuming the environment remains at the same threat level, but even in the least-aroused condition the rider's need to balance and control the bike actively keeps the senses on a heightened state of alert. It is only during long stints in the saddle that engine and road vibration, fatigue and the effects of battling wind and weather, not to mention traffic, reduce, through physical and mental exhaustion, the rider's ability to focus and control effectively. It is peculiar to the effect of the combined stimuli on some riders that even when wet, cold, dirty and exhausted after long stints in the saddle, they still think that what they've been doing is fun.

Other riders, of course, think they are crazy. Though you can find plenty of riders who like to do it all, from trials riding to road racing or touring or just cruising, you can find just as many more riders who like one style of motorcycle and the riding it makes possible. Because each type creates a different and unique riding environment, it also creates a different kind of fun, which attracts its own set of sensation seekers. We may not understand moto-fun at the molecular level yet, but millions of motorcyclists do not care. They'd rather ride than wonder why, though what they ride, and where, gives us some useful clues as to why.

CHAPTER THREE

DIFFERENT STROKES FOR DIFFERENT FOLKS

We are taught early in our lives that the book is not the cover, but we never lose our tendency to make snap judgments about character based on first impressions. There is a strong evolutionary basis for this, determined largely by the dominance of vision in our repertoire of sensors. Other animals depend on other sensory inputs to judge the most basic questions in any encounter with strangers: is this thing in front of me (a) a threat? (b) not a threat? (c) if not a threat, is it food? or (d) if not food, what is it?

Humans have depended on vision to perform such discrimination for eons. We use our brains to modify what we see, how we see it and how we interpret what we see. Yet the dominance of our visual sense has a cascade of consequences, among them assessments of other things, places and people based often on how they look. This includes motorcycles, and as will be shown in detail, the way a motorcycle looks is vitally important to its social and cultural role. However, it is just as incorrect to judge a motorcycle solely by the way it looks as it is to judge a person by looks alone. The core of human personality is the animating spirit or soul that, though influenced by the body, far transcends it in creating the personality. Likewise, the animating spirit in a motorcycle, analogous in some ways to a soul, is its engine. In a motorcycle as in a human, the animating force is all-important in its personality. As the soul makes the person, the motor makes the cycle.

The engine's primacy in the moto-package is one reason why motorcyclists have demanded so consistently that the engines in their motorcycles be visible. Full or nearly full enclosure of the engine by bodywork, as with cars since the beginning, is culturally accepted only in certain configurations: touring bikes, sport bikes, scooters and, of course, road-racing motorcycles that are the style models for sport bikes. Even in those machines, whenever possible, designers are careful to enable certain elements of the engines to show through the bodywork, understanding how important it is for riders to signal their values by displaying the 'personality and performance generator' at the heart of their motorcycles. Much more is behind this than the amount of power or torque provided by the engine. The entire character of the ride is determined by engine type, state of tune and overall power delivery. These literally characterize the engine, determining how it sounds, feels and responds to the rider's control through the throttle. Rider response to the engine's character is the single most important determinant in the rider's choice of what to ride, when and where. The 'feel' of the engine is therefore at the heart of the motorcycling experience.

Throughout the last century, though various engine designs have been bolted into motorcycle frames, certain configurations and types of engine have become associated with certain kinds of motorcycles. Taking the notion of cultural evolution seriously, one might discern in this effect the operation of a 'meme' for each mode of motorcycling in play, as each generation of riders adopts or discards engine-chassis-personality combinations, one at a time. The marketplace is the Environment of Evolutionary Adaptedness in which this selection occurs, as ruthlessly as in the Darwinian world of natural selection.

Charles Darwin's theory of natural selection cannot, of course, be directly applied to the marketplace, but even a cursory review of the way the markets have 'selected' motorcycle types shows that some have survived and been developed in ways others haven't. The survivors embodied traits more valued than others, and some traits obviously involve the social and cultural usefulness of the rider-machine combination. What drives that socio-cultural role is the cumulative effect of highly individual psychobiological reactions to the stimuli delivered by the unique characteristics of each type of engine-chassis combination. These stimuli operate at several levels simultaneously, influencing the rider's arousal state and thus his or her emotional state. The primary generator of the stimuli is the engine.

Most motorcyclists know more about engines than most automobile drivers, and probably always have. Motorcycling culture does not reward obvious ignorance of the basics of engine terminology, design and function, though any motor-cycle dealer will tell you just how few customers know as much as they think they know about their machines. Even so, motorcyclists quickly learn the basics of engine architecture in their first years of riding. They know that the characteristics that define their engines are the number and arrangement of cylinders in the engine, the bore, stroke and swept capacity of the pistons in the cylinders, and the means by which the air-fuel mixture is brought into and expelled from the com-bustion chamber. These have been the defining elements of all internal combustion engines since the type began to dominate as a power unit in the late 19th century. Motorcyclists learn early to speak casually of singles, twins, triples, fours, fives and sixes, adding modifiers as needed: rotary-valve, reed-valve or piston-port two-stoke, single or double overhead cam, side or overhead valve, desmodromic, vertical, horizontal, opposed, transverse, or longitudinal four-stroke.

It often strikes non-riders as absurd to speak of an engine's personality, but it makes more sense after long exposure to different kinds of powerplants. Engines have traits that let us categorize them by displaced cylinder volume, by how the cylinders are arranged on the crankcase and by their 'breathing' systems (how the combustible mixture is fed into the cylinder and expelled after combustion). Further characteristics are defined by engine flywheel weight—a heavy or light flywheel imparts a feel, reflected in how rapidly the engine responds to the throttle. Heavier flywheels tend to deliver slower throttle response, lighter flywheels tend to enable a quicker response. Flywheel weight, alone, can profoundly influence an engine's character.

Inside the motorhead world, these artifacts of the engine's architecture are routinely discussed as if they were obvious to everyone. The social task of the moto-neophyte in trying to gain acceptance into the group depends largely on the ease and accuracy with which he or she can command the terminology to make a point about how this or that bike or engine feels or responds. What seems to be a trivial pursuit to the person utterly uninterested in the details of how engines work is actually immensely important to the denizens of the moto-world. For good reason; the devils and the gods lie in the details of everything important in life, including life spent riding a motorcycle within, at most, two feet of a powerful engine. Learning as much as one can about the various kinds and quirks of engines thus has much more than just social value; what is not known can cost one dearly.

It is not surprising, then, that moto-lore is rich with storytelling about the various characters of engine types. As much as animal vocalizations in a jungle, the exhaust-pipe 'voices' of each type are significant to bike identity and thus preferred rider image. Small-displacement two-stroke twins, for example, emit characteristic high-pitched sounds as unlike the 'potato-potato' rumble of a big Harley-Davidson V-twin as an eagle's cry is from a lion's growl. Riders who favor one type over the other thus select not only a particular power-delivery system with specific and quantifiable differences in performance, but also radically different stimulus packages that come with each engine configuration. The quantifiable differences are those that describe the power and torque output of the engines, as well as their fuel efficiency, while the stimulus packages are defined in how the power is transmitted to the rear wheel, how it sounds, and what happens to the bike/rider as a consequence of how the inevitable engine vibration is attenuated by the motorcycle's frame and human-machine interface components.

Vibration is a sensed quality we notice most when it exceeds our comfort levels, wherever and whenever we encounter it. Those levels can be reset to some extent, but the built-in limits imposed by our biology cannot be exceeded without incurring potentially damaging effects. Like all other biological tolerances, our tolerances for mechanical vibration are set by our evolution. It is no exaggeration to say that vibration in the form of speech—we vibrate our vocal cords by forcing air past them and tensing them in certain ways, then shaping the resulting sound waves by moving our tongues, lips, the oral cavity and the pharynx—is the basis of all that we have become since language developed.

It is likewise no exaggeration to say that vibration is an enormously important component of the stimulus package that characterizes and differentiates each motorcycle type and model. This is manifest in the engine's sound signature—sound is of course created by vibration—and in how that mechanical vibration is transmitted to the rider. That vibration is primarily generated by the engine, though some results from the machine's passage over the terrain under the wheels and by its passage through the air. Road-generated vibration was of great concern in the early years of motorcycling, as it had been among bicyclists until the advent of pneumatic tires and wire-spoked wheels. This concern reflected the low power and mass of the early engines as much as the undeveloped state of the roads and suspensions. Soon, as engine power and size increased, the vibratory modes of the various configurations became apparent and encoded in moto-lore.

The study of human response to mechanical vibration in vehicles goes back at least to the early 1930s, and the potentially damaging effects of localized mechanical vibration to the pioneering work of Alice Hamilton in the first decades of the 20th century. Dr. Hamilton investigated the health problems of stonecutters and other workers in Indiana who were using air hammers, and reported her findings in a 1918 U.S. Department of Labor report. The workers were suffering from what would soon be called white-finger disorder, which can create irreversible 'blanching' of the fingers, as the capillaries in the fingers are 'shut down.' This vasoconstriction is widespread among users of all kinds of hand tools and Vibration White Finger is high on the list of industrial maladies that have prompted governments to set standards for exposure to local vibration of certain frequencies, force and duration.

Motorcycle handlebars have long been known to transmit vibration from the engine, the road, and the combined effects of the chassis and powerplant. As long ago as 1914,

the popular British publication *Motor Cycling* was advising its
Motor Cycling Manual readers that "The only objection that
can be raised against 7/8 in. [diameter] bars is that they are
more likely to transmit vibration, being less rigid than those
of larger section."[35] That the vibration of the machines then
was severe is inferred easily from the first chapter, where, in
classically boosterish fashion, the first sentence proclaims:
"The wonderful popularity of the motorcycle is largely, perhaps entirely, the result of its rapid development....Whereas a
few years ago the motorcycle was a mount for the young and
athletic and required a fondness of things mechanical if much
pleasure was to be obtained from it, we find today the fair
sex, the middle-aged and the elderly all participating in the
pastime as the result of the development of machines suitable
to their individual requirements."[36] Six paragraphs later, the
"development" is confidently announced to have reached a
state in which "detail work all round has been perfected" and
"carriers no longer rattle to pieces...."[37] This must have made
the contemporary motorcyclist smile and wonder when,
exactly, that state of perfection would actually come to pass,
since things on motorcycles continued to "rattle to pieces"
among 1914's motorcycle crop, as they did throughout the
entire century to come. Motorcycles deliver vibration; it is
part of the package, one that is—perhaps amazingly, to non-
riders—actively sought by riders.

[35] *Motorcycling Manual: All About Motorcycles in Simple Language* (Temple Press: London, 1914), p.164.

[36] Ibid., p.1.

[37] Ibid., p. 2.

Considering the intensity with which automotive engineers work to remove noise, vibration and harshness (NVH) from automobiles, the affection many riders develop for certain kinds of moto-vibes must baffle them, as it must the legion of ergonomists, occupational physicians and others whose lifework focuses on minimizing human exposure to mechanical vibration. Perhaps a hint of why is contained in the comments made by Michael J. Griffin, of the Institute of Sound and Vibration Research in England, in his exhaustive and definitive work, the *Handbook of Human Vibration*. Prof. Griffin's nearly 1000-page book is the standard reference work, in which every aspect of the human response to vibration is examined and explained thoroughly. In his discussion of the model for the exact mechanism by which Vibration White Finger may develop (there is still no universal consensus), Griffin cites the evidence from other research on how blood chemistry changes with vibration. He notes that:

> Among other blood constituents to have attracted attention are epinephrine (i.e., adrenalin) and norepinephrine (i.e., noradrenalin, secreted by the adrenal glands on the kidneys). These are catecholamine hormones; epinephrine is capable of causing either vasodilation or vasoconstriction, while norepinephrine primarily produces vasoconstriction. Drugs impeding the action of norepinephrine (e.g., reserpine [...] and nifedipine [...]) have been reported to have beneficial effects on peripheral circulation in persons adversely affected by hand-transmitted vibration

[....]. Abnormal concentrations of epinephrine, norepinephrine and other hormones secreted by the adrenal medulla and adrenal cortex have been variously reported in the blood or urine of persons exposed to hand-transmitted vibration [....]. Laboratory studies with animals show that whole-body vibration can cause adrenal changes [...] although the effects may be less with local vibration [....]. Some authors conclude that such findings arise from the action of vibration as a non-specific stress; others state that they show how vibration induces disorders in body-hormone regulation. The matter is of interest because it concerns not only the cause and treatment of finger blanching but also the possibility that local vibration more generally affects, for example, the autonomic nervous system.[38]

The importance of such blood chemistry to mood is clear, and thus so is the potential for vibration to influence mood, for better or worse. For this reason alone, motorcyclists have a keen interest in the effects of vibration that is transmitted through any of the places where body contacts machine. The principal human-machine-interface areas are the handlebars, footpegs or foot-boards, the seat and fuel tank or other bodywork where the knees or thighs touch it. Too much vibration at any contact point renders the ride something less than fun and maybe physically and psychologically dangerous, as the

[38] Griffin, *Handbook of Human Vibration* (Academic Press: San Diego, 1990), p. 582.

extensive human-factors literature pertaining to the known vibration-induced illnesses and maladies attests.

Because the character of the ride depends so much on the character of the engine, a rider's trajectory through the motorcycle marketplace is as much a search for the right 'fit' between a vibration mode and motorcycle model/type as it is a search for a certain kind of quantifiable performance. This is never, or rarely, acknowledged except in the negative sense, when someone will reply to a question about what happened to his/her previous bike by saying something like: "Well, I got tired of the thing shaking out my fillings after an hour in the saddle."

The difficulty of matching a rider to a ride-vibe package is exacerbated by the individual, subjective response to vibration. Just as music (vibrations made with instruments for pleasure) is personal, so too is moto-music. Moreover, real confusion can occur for a rider who likes a particular sound—say, the spine-chilling wail of a high-rpm, highly-tuned, multi-cylinder sport bike engine—but dislikes the feel the bike imparts to the chassis, and thence to the rider. In this example, the feel is often reported as a high-frequency buzz that strikes many riders as either annoying or debilitating. Someone in that conundrum usually buys and sells a series of bikes looking for the right mix, though few acknowledge or even perceive that their search is driven by such a fundamental psychobiological response to the potent engine stimuli. Since the motorcycling experience is a compendium of feelings, often intense, each triggered by sensory stimuli, the effect of engine vibration on how a rider feels is important. What is not obvious is how various engine types compare in what they deliver to riders. Like so much in motorcycling, the absence of scientific data creates a vacuum filled immediately with lore.

Riders who evaluate motorcycles for a living learn to be cautious in extrapolating how any given engine type will feel to others, though they succumb too often to generalizations that help categorize experience, even as they distort it. In truth, each motorcycle has its own feel; the same engine placed in two substantially different frames can result in a significantly different subjective experience for the same rider. The physics of materials determines this, as does rider posture, since extensive research has shown that the single most significant change a human can make to the way in which the body is being vibrated while seated is to change his or her posture.[39] The human body's transmission of vibration fed into it at any given point is not uniform; each appendage, each organ, each body component reacts differently to the frequency, force and duration of any vibration, which is one reason why it is so difficult for researchers to issue definitive cause-effect summaries of vibration, especially regarding emotional states that might be induced or influenced by vibration.

---

[39] Prof. Griffin makes this clear: "Posture can have a large influence on the amount of vibration transmitted to a seated person and determine the extent of any detrimental effects. In the region of a body resonance a small alteration in position or muscle tension may help to reduce vibration severity. The effects of postural changes increase with increasing frequency; minor variations in the orientation of the lower back and the angle of the head can cause substantial changes in the vibration transmitted up the spine to the head. A change in body position which alters the contact with a vibrating surface, such as a backrest, also modifies the effects of the vibration." Ibid., p. 31

Obviously, when we expose ourselves to mechanically-produced vibration, we experience effects that potentially can far exceed the limits set by the design envelope of our evolution. The individual motorcyclist usually knows only the lore that pertains to the vast engineering knowledge now available, as well as what he or she likes or dislikes about any particular engine type, based on personal experience. With extensive experience, it is possible to form opinions, but without more objective data, the vibration signature of any engine-chassis combination is impossible to describe accurately. Motorcycle testers exhaust their vocabularies quickly in trying to describe what they feel during a test session, a problem made harder by the fact that the changing rpm range of the engine in any ride, as well as the changing environmental conditions, changes the vibro-package the rider feels. Likewise, each rider's physiognomy transmits or attenuates the vibration differently; a small-framed person with a 30-inch inseam, a 30-inch reach, a weight of 120 pounds, and gracile bones will respond entirely differently to the same set of vibrations as someone who weighs 200 pounds, has a 34-inch inseam, a 34-inch reach, and large, heavy skeletal structure. One person's buzzing nightmare of a ride can thus be another person's Orgasmatronic delight.

Given the significance of vibration, it would be reasonable to expect that some kind of standard method of testing and reporting it would have been developed over the last century, so that prospective buyers could compare graphs of a given bike's vibration signature as easily as they can compare its other performance data. As with so much in the moto-world, what seems reasonable often does not exist. Whatever the causes, the effects include the fact that people often buy motorcycles without knowing how they will respond to each vibration mode until it is perceived, on the road, track or trail. This is just part of the deal, as it has always been, and though it's less a problem when dealers allow extensive test rides, those rides are not possible everywhere. So a motorcycle buyer often has no actual experience of the machine until he or she has bought it. This is one reason so many bikes show up on the used market so quickly, as riders discover that the seating position that felt fine on the showroom floor is no good on the road after the first half hour, or that the slight buzz in the handgrips that could be felt as the bike was revved while immobile has become unbearable on the Interstate at speed.

This concern for vibration can thus seem puzzling, if one has never felt it. The closest many non-riders come to experiencing such vibration is likely to be in the handlebar of a lawn mower, a snow-blower, a personal watercraft or some other small-engined machine. But none of those can compare with the experience of riding all day on a motorcycle, let alone riding one, day after day, cross-country. One becomes intimate with the vibes delivered by any motorcycle under those circumstances, and vibration quality becomes anything but incidental to ride quality.

To determine, and then to illustrate the differences between exemplars of various engine configurations for this book, I commissioned a study of motorcycle vibration by Stanford University's Smart Product Design Lab. I envisaged a real-world test of motorcycles, using accelerometers to record the vibration 'signatures' of ten bikes at the primary human-machine interface points: the seat, the handlebars and the footpegs. At the time I decided this study was needed, a search of the open literature disclosed no similar tests. Researchers who had studied motorcycle vibration had done so to identify particular problems, such as those that can trigger Vibration White Finger, whereas I wanted to have comparative data to determine exactly how much the bikes differed or were similar in the vibration they delivered to their riders.

Stanford engineering graduate students designed the experiment, built the testing apparatus and conducted the tests. Because my goal was to provide snapshots of the vibration produced on all the bikes in three different running environments—at stationary idle, at a steady 60 mph indicated, and in acceleration from stop to whatever speed was attainable in ten seconds—it was agreed that the road-test approach was suitable for the experiment. This approach accepts the inevitably wide range of variables that can affect any test performed on a vehicle in the real world, whereas the laboratory approach minimizes the variables. While the latter can provide data more suitable for some purposes, it does not reflect how people actually encounter the world. Thus, though researchers strongly prefer to minimize the variables, we agreed to instrument the motorcycles on a given day at a given place and run them through the test sequences that way, returning only if the data were unusable or wildly out of the expected range.

The test apparatus was designed to be portable and adaptable to the motorcycles selected. Though 10 motorcycles were originally slated for the experiment, one was unavailable, so we were left with nine; all were excellent examples of machines I knew from experience had significantly different perceived vibration characteristics. Moreover, each motorcycle also had a substantial body of moto-lore attached, which held, commonly, that bike character reflected not just engine power and torque but the vibrational personality of the powerplant. The tested bikes were:

—1994 BMW K1100LT (1092cc longitudinal, four-stroke, in-line four)

—1974 BMW R90S (898cc longitudinal, four-stroke opposed twin)

—1969 BSA Rocket 3 (740cc transverse[40], four-stroke in-line vertical triple)

—1998 Ducati ST2 (944cc transverse, 90-degree, four-stroke V-twin)

—2000 Harley-Davidson Fat Boy (1449cc, transverse, 45-degree four-stroke V-twin)

—1978 Honda CBX (1047cc transverse, four-stroke, in-line vertical six)

—1987 Honda VFR700F2 (700cc transverse, four-stroke, V-four)

---

[40] "Ttransverse" refers to the orientation of the engine's crankshaft, and means that it lies transversely *across* the longitudinal axis of the motorcycle (that is, its fore-and-aft axis), whereas "longitudinal" refers to a crankshaft aligned *with* the fore-and-aft axis.

—1968 Triumph TR6C (649cc transverse, four-stroke vertical twin)

—1959 Velocette Venom (499cc transverse, four-stroke vertical single)

Each motorcycle was instrumented to measure vibration at the left footpeg, the left handgrip and the seat. The engineers used three-axis accelerometers to record acceleration forces in a 20G range (-10G to +10G) over a frequency bandwidth from 0.3 Hz to 10 kHz. These accelerometers were data-linked to a Toshiba notebook computer purchased and configured specifically for these tests, carried by the test rider on his back during each run. The rider used a push-button switch mounted on the handlebar to begin each recording session. Data were gathered to enable comparison of spectra from several time sequences, so that representative information could be extracted from the record. The final data displayed shows the stationary-idle results from a one-second segment, the steady-state 60 mph likewise from a one-second segment and the 10-second acceleration period (though, as with the other records, more data were captured than displayed, to ensure consistent and reliable input). All the tests took place on the same day, in the same location using the same stretch of road. From beginning to end, the tests required about six hours.

The results of our tests, like all vibration testing, are not easily distilled for display. This is largely because vibration is itself not easily defined, at least not if precision is required. Most people probably think that vibration is just shaking or wobbling or some such thing. But a scientist or engineer needs something more specific, such as Prof. Griffin's definition: "The variation with time of the magnitude of a quantity descriptive of the motion or position of a mechanical system, when the magnitude is alternately greater and smaller than some average value."[41] Vibration has amplitude, direction, and duration, and when that vibration is complex—as in vehicles—each defining value varies in ways that can be significant, yet not appreciated as such if the right quantity is not used for measurement. This is one reason, among several, that engineers prefer to isolate as many variables as possible in studying vibration and thus dislike the road-test approach, which yields only comparative data that might or might not be predictive for accurate generalizations. For my purposes, however, the goal was to gather comparative data, since, as noted above, I was searching for quantifiable differences that might help us understand the basis of the extensive motorcycle lore about how a given kind of vibration might induce a particular psychobiological state.

The full results are displayed in the Vibration Study Appendix, in which more detail about the test equipment, procedures, and motorcycles prefaces the three different types of graphs that summarize the results. The first type of graph is the "G_{rms}" comparison, which uses the bar-chart technique to allow a viewer to see, at a glance, how much average force the transducers recorded at each test station and in each test mode. "G_{rms}" means 'root-mean-square acceleration,' and is a standard method of measuring and comparing oscillatory signals, especially those with an average value of zero. For

[41] Griffin, *Handbook of Human Vibration*, P. 859.

those with a good grounding in the physics of vibration, this is explanation enough, but of course for those who are not engineers or physicists, a bit more information is required to understand what the bar-graph displays. G_{rms} displayed this way is usually defined more precisely as the square root of the area under the Acceleration (or Power) Spectral Density trace, plotted against the frequency curve derived from the accelerometer tests. Engineers studying vibration routinely use ASD graphs, and although those could be derived from our test data, it was decided by the test team that showing the vibration 'trace' in which the plus-and-minus values of the vibration force are plotted as a function of time (not frequency) would be more indicative of the ride and engine characteristics for non-engineers. These spectra show the vibration's force and duration, and the frequency is 'in' the spectra, but in order to be displayed, it must be extracted by means of a mathematical operation called a Fast Fourier Transform (FFT).

Close study of the vibration-trace spectra, FFT charts, and G_{rms} charts is necessary for a real understanding of what the transducers detected at the human-machine interfaces on our motorcycles. Because there were nine motorcycles, each tested at three points, in three axes, in three different modes, the displays run to many pages in the Appendix. However, comparing the overall G_{rms} results is a convenient way to illustrate the substantial differences in the 'vibro-packages' of the tested motorcycles, so those charts are reproduced on the following pages.[42]

[42] For more detail about G_{rms} and Fast Fourier Transforms, many good tutorials are available online; see, for example, NASA's Ryan Simmons' at: _http://femci.gsfc. nasa.gov/random/randomgrms.html_ for G_{rms}, and Wikipedia's explanation of FFTs: _http://en.wikipedia.org/wiki/Fast_Fourier_transform_.

OVERALL MOTORCYCLE COMPARISON
Idle Handlebar Vibration — Root Mean Square (RMS)

x-Axis

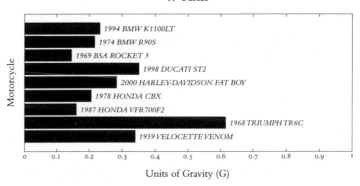

y-Axis

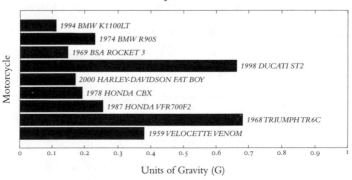

z-Axis

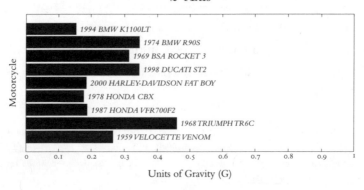

OVERALL MOTORCYCLE COMPARISON
Idle Seat Vibration — Root Mean Square (RMS)

x-Axis

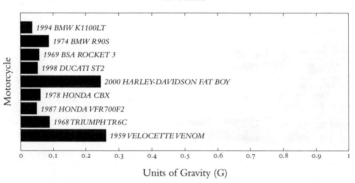

y-Axis

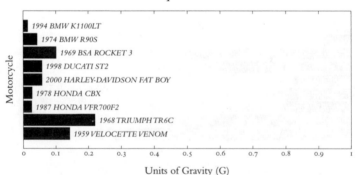

z-Axis

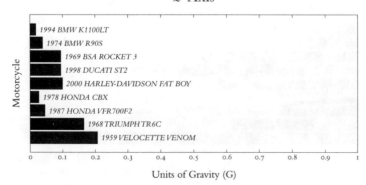

OVERALL MOTORCYCLE COMPARISON
Idle Footpeg Vibration — Root Mean Square (RMS)

x-Axis

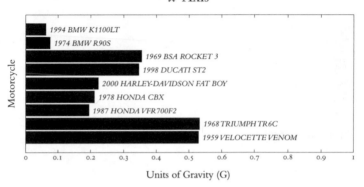

Units of Gravity (G)

y-Axis

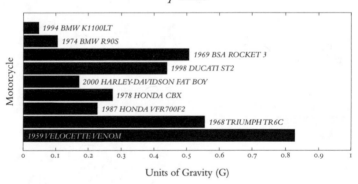

Units of Gravity (G)

z-Axis

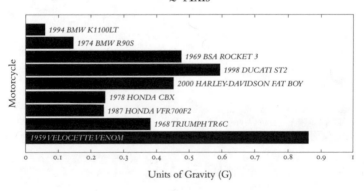

Units of Gravity (G)

OVERALL MOTORCYCLE COMPARISON

Acceleration Handlebar Vibration — Root Mean Square (RMS)

x-Axis

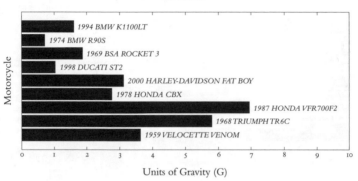

Units of Gravity (G)

y-Axis

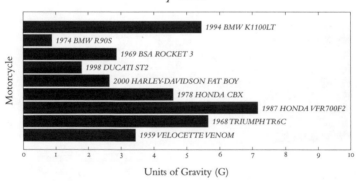

Units of Gravity (G)

z-Axis

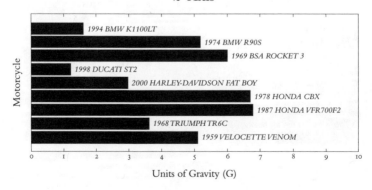

Units of Gravity (G)

OVERALL MOTORCYCLE COMPARISON

Acceleration Seat Vibration — Root Mean Square (RMS)

x-Axis

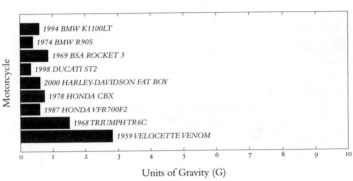

Units of Gravity (G)

y-Axis

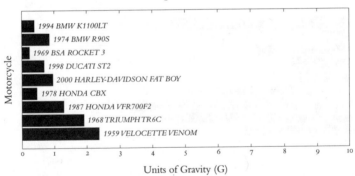

Units of Gravity (G)

z-Axis

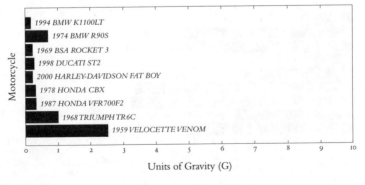

Units of Gravity (G)

OVERALL MOTORCYCLE COMPARISON

Acceleration Footpeg Vibration — Root Mean Square (RMS)

x-Axis

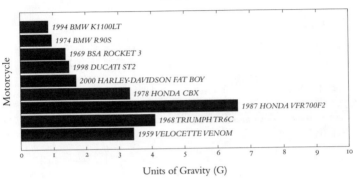

Units of Gravity (G)

y-Axis

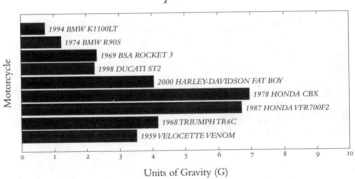

Units of Gravity (G)

z-Axis

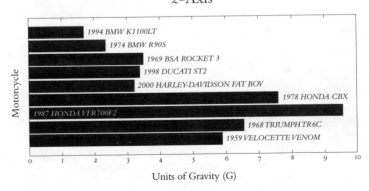

Units of Gravity (G)

OVERALL MOTORCYCLE COMPARISON
60mph Handlebar Vibration — Root Mean Square (RMS)

x-Axis

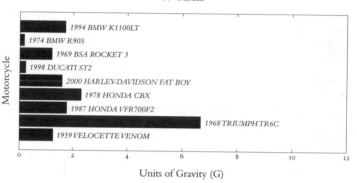

Units of Gravity (G)

y-Axis

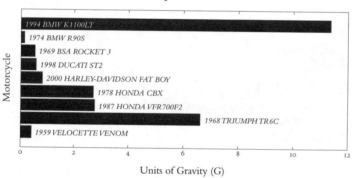

Units of Gravity (G)

z-Axis

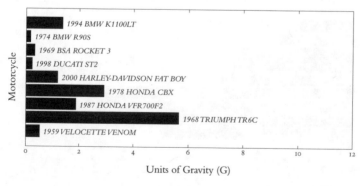

Units of Gravity (G)

OVERALL MOTORCYCLE COMPARISON

60mph Seat Vibration — Root Mean Square (RMS)

x-Axis

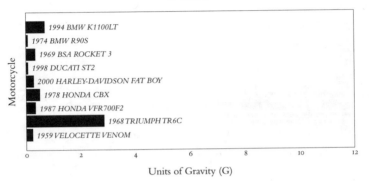

Units of Gravity (G)

y-Axis

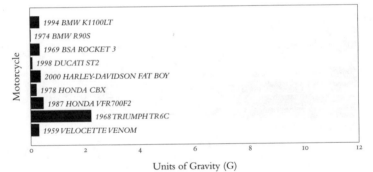

Units of Gravity (G)

z-Axis

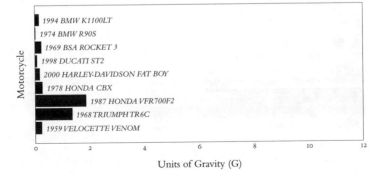

Units of Gravity (G)

OVERALL MOTORCYCLE COMPARISON
60mph Footpeg Vibration — Root Mean Square (RMS)

x-Axis

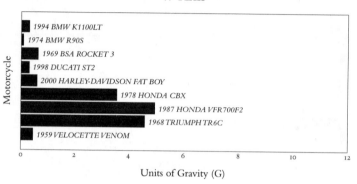

Motorcycle

1994 BMW K1100LT
1974 BMW R90S
1969 BSA ROCKET 3
1998 DUCATI ST2
2000 HARLEY-DAVIDSON FAT BOY
1978 HONDA CBX
1987 HONDA VFR700F2
1968 TRIUMPH TR6C
1959 VELOCETTE VENOM

Units of Gravity (G)

y-Axis

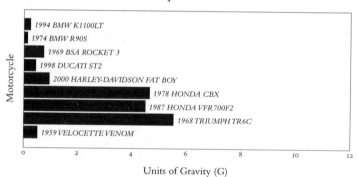

Motorcycle

1994 BMW K1100LT
1974 BMW R90S
1969 BSA ROCKET 3
1998 DUCATI ST2
2000 HARLEY-DAVIDSON FAT BOY
1978 HONDA CBX
1987 HONDA VFR700F2
1968 TRIUMPH TR6C
1959 VELOCETTE VENOM

Units of Gravity (G)

z-Axis

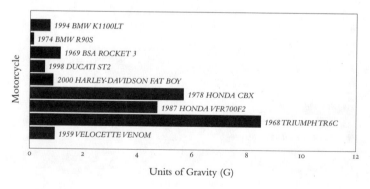

Motorcycle

1994 BMW K1100LT
1974 BMW R90S
1969 BSA ROCKET 3
1998 DUCATI ST2
2000 HARLEY-DAVIDSON FAT BOY
1978 HONDA CBX
1987 HONDA VFR700F2
1968 TRIUMPH TR6C
1959 VELOCETTE VENOM

Units of Gravity (G)

It's important, in evaluating our results, to understand how the vibration forces were gathered by the accelerometers. For example, the transducers measured vibration with three axes of reference— *x, y, z*—aligned thus:

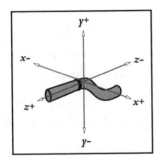

HANDLEBAR

x-axis: perpendicular to handlebar *(+ points backward)*
y-axis: perpendicular to handlebar *(+ points upward)*
z-axis: parallel to handlebar *(+ points left)*

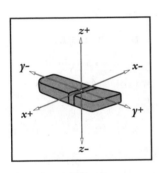

SEAT

x-axis: perpendicular to bike longitudinal axis *(+ points left)*
y-axis: parallel to bike longitudinal axis *(+ points backward)*
z-axis: perpendicular to bike longitudinal axis *(+ points upward)*

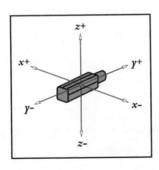

FOOTPEG

x-axis: parallel to bike longitudinal axis *(+ points forward)*
y-axis: perpendicular to bike longitudinal axis *(+ points right)*
z-axis: perpendicular to bike longitudinal axis *(+ points upward)*

The only variations to these orientations were made on motorcycles in which clutch-lever action interfered with the handlebar accelerometer; in those cases, the unit was rotated just enough to allow full clutch movement, since safety had to outweigh data-gathering. The extent to which this affected the data was not known, but the engineers did not consider the effects sufficiently significant either to run the test without handlebar data or to attempt multiple runs with different alignments to bracket the results. In practice, what this means is that the handlebar readings each reflect slightly different transducer orientations. This would be inevitable anyway, given that the handlebars themselves are each characterized by substantial differences in all the dimensions that define the rider's hand position: sweep, pullback, rise and drop-angle. The same problem beset the engineers in the instrumentation of the other data-gathering locations, which is why they had to design their test apparatus to be adaptable to each station.

It is clear even from a few moments' study of the displays that, as moto-lore and the experiment's hypothesis held, the vibration signatures and modes of the machines do indeed vary significantly. For example, even Triumph marque faithful have always admitted that the 650cc/750cc vertical twins could be among the worst teeth-rattlers of the postwar period, and the aggregated 60-mph G_{rms} test results show unequivocally the basis for the type's reputation. Because Triumph twins are also among the most beloved engines in the world, it's obvious that their popularity emerged not in spite of but because of their engines' characteristic vibration.

At the other extreme, the test results for the BMW R90S hint at the basis for the devotion of the Boxer faithful, who continue to this day to swear that the BMW opposed-twin engine is the sweetest powerplant ever devised. Only the 90-degree V-twin Ducati engine produced anything like as little vibration at the seat, handlebar and footpeg, but the BMW is clearly less affected by engine vibration than the other bikes. On the other hand, the BMW K1100LT, a mid-1990s luxury touring bike, shows that not even BMW's extensive vibration-control program (instituted after complaints about the K1100LT's predecessor, powered by an earlier version of this bike's engine) resulted in human-machine-interface vibration levels as low as those in older BMW R90S. This result, too, is consonant with much lore, in that BMW K-bike aficionados admit that the four-cylinder versions of the 'Flying Brick' manifest much of the 'buzziness' once associated only with so-called UJM ('Universal Japanese Motorcycle') transverse four-cylinder engines that dominated the big-bike market following Honda's launch of its epochal CB750 Four in 1969. The lore holds that inline fours buzz, no matter what is done to minimize the buzz, and our results support the lore.

The graphs here and in the Appendix are valuable in demonstrating the differing vibration signatures of the tested bikes, but as with all graphic displays of vibration, it is difficult to extrapolate how the displayed data 'feel.' Only experiencing the rides produced by the machines whose personalities are hinted at in these graphs can aggregate the stimuli to create a 'feel,' which is why no video game, amusement-park ride, simulator run or other replication of a motorcycle ride is ultimately anything like the ride itself. If we knew how a given motorcycle vibration mode affected human emotions, it might be possible to match vibration charts with personality types so that riders could pick out potentially pleasing engine/chassis combinations without having to experience them one by one. Something like this is done now by buyers as they look for performance data and descriptive specifications of various models on the marketplace to eliminate the machines that are obviously less attractive. But until our own collective and individual responses to moto-vibes are thoroughly charted, just charting the characteristics of the machines themselves won't help much.

All that is known by most riders is what they like and do not like, which they discover by experience. In the process, they often discover that a type that appeals to them for what amounts to cultural reasons may not appeal to them for psychobiological reasons. So the person who loves the way, for example, a Harley-Davidson Fat Boy looks and sounds might find, once in the saddle, that the ride itself is both uncomfortable and unrewarding. Or the person who thinks that he or she was born to ride a fast sport bike might find, once aboard that Suzuki GSX-R750, that the bike's high-power, four-cylinder engine generates such intensely uncomfortable heat and high-frequency, high-amplitude vibration that riding it is bearable only for a short time. And time, in all vibration issues, is critical, since vibration effects are cumulative. This is why the various standards-settings organizations worldwide commission researchers like Dr. Griffin to help establish "Vibration Dose Values" to limit worker exposure to occupational vibration. Motorcycle vibration can be so intense, as Griffin notes in his book, that the VDV can be exceeded in as little as 13 minutes of riding in certain circumstances.[43] How

[43] Griffin, *Handbook of Human Vibration,* p. 697.

can we know, then, what the effects are on us when we ride cross-country or compete in an endurance road-race? We can know only by experience, individual by individual.

Confronting such questions, some observers conclude that an element of masochism is essential to making an individual start to ride and continue riding. It seems obvious that vibration values like those shown in the graphs here lie far beyond our species' design envelope, just as it is obvious that the other exogenous stimulants we humans routinely make and use, from beer to crack cocaine, are not found naturally in our evolutionary heritage. Why, some people wonder, would any sane person seek the vibratory environment that our findings showed to be delivered by some of our tested bikes?

To say "different strokes for different folks" is a non-answer, though used frequently and with a shrug by many to whom the question is put. To someone who believes in cultural explanations for all behavior, the response suggests that the rider endures the ride's vibes for social reasons, just as a kid who tries cigarette smoking and hates it at first keeps lighting up to look cool or just to be part of the group. My experience has been that this view is inadequate. The kid who will keep smoking is, after all, more likely to succumb quickly to the biochemically addictive qualities of tobacco than the kid who really hates it and quits. Anti-smoking crusaders focus on finding ways to influence the kid who might be waffling about whether smoking is fun or not, but it is all moot if the chemistry kicks in. Similarly, an individual who thinks riding a Harley or a Triumph or a Ducati is really cool will find an excuse to stop riding if he or she can't stand the physical feedback generated by the huge vibration-machine between the legs. Contrariwise, if people find it addicting, they will seek any excuse to satisfy the craving.

Perhaps surprisingly, this situation takes us back to the power of vision to guide perception, and its role in shaping choices for motorcyclists who can pick among various types and models to buy and ride. As noted above, repeated efforts through the century of motorcycling to cloak the powerplant have been resisted consistently by many motorcyclists. This hostility has usually been interpreted as stubborn conservatism by those who think that progress in motorcycling is being impeded somehow by reluctance to enclose the engine, or to make other changes to the formulaic motorcycle style. This argument assumes that this is nothing more than a transitory cultural predilection for a 'look' in a motorcycle. Yet, if one acknowledges the power of the feel of a given engine type that has persisted—the H-D 45-degree V-twin, the BMW Boxer, the Triumph-style vertical twin, the large-displacement single, the transverse four—one can discern the outlines of another, albeit shadowy reason behind the supposed cultural conservatism. That reason is our need for a thing to look like what it is: an evolutionary preference for a lion to look like a lion, not like a whale, or for a bird not to look like a goat. These engines not only have cultural meanings, they embody differences that profoundly affect what they do to and for us, individual by individual.

How could this happen? I think that it occurs primarily via cultural evolution, as proposed by Dawkins and his followers. The marketplace works, in this case, as a Darwinian means of sorting out 'types' that connect with people more powerfully than other, competing machines. A century is not long enough to know for sure, but it seems that some engines have Orgasmatronic characteristics that are accidental byproducts of their creators' search for market success. The Harley-Davidson engine is an excellent example. Though once it was widely perceived to be a millstone for H-D and its dealers, it has come to be revered by millions with direct, personal experience of it. To be sure, cultural associations are immensely important in why and how that came to pass. But it would not have been possible had there not been something special about the configuration of mechanical parts that has so long defined 'Harley-ness.' The same is true to one degree or another for all archetypical engines, by whomever and whenever built.

How and why have such things emerged from the last century of automobility and motorcycling? The answers to those questions originate in what each individual experiences aboard different kinds of motorcycles, but do not end in 'the ride.' They take us, instead, from the realm of bodies in motion to the realm of bodies of motion, from the individual to the group, and from the group to the societal and cultural.

CHAPTER FOUR

MOTOTYPES, STEREOTYPES, AND EXHAUST PIPES

The question at the core of the consumer culture is "Which?" It is not simply a matter of value for money, or ensuring reliable performance of whatever sort the product promises. It is a question of identity, of 'positioning.' This is rarely more important than in vehicles, especially ones purchased primarily for recreation. When we choose this one over that one, we make a public statement about our values. This is why some advertising people think of cars as fashions or fashion accessories the owner drives, then changes not when they wear out, but when the owner's fashion changes. It is also why many who think seriously about motorcycle culture have come to believe that, for new riders, the primary guidance in selecting a specific bike is cultural associations. Once the urge to ride has been realized, people choose the specific motorcycle—thus their preferred public image—because they want to be like or look like someone they admire or wish to emulate.

Style always matters for those who can choose it, and motorcycle culture has always provided an array of styles from which to choose. Most who scrutinize the image-selection process attend to the visual details that define those styles. This is understandable, because getting the details right determines the success of the style to be 'worn' and the details are always in flux. But those details cannot illuminate their behavioral bases. Culture can make someone want to ride a certain kind of motorcycle and thus seek a certain kind of style but, as shown in the previous chapter, only the person's genetic inheritance can make the experience of the ride itself immediately into what is translated as pleasure, or fun.

Thus the process of finding fun and style is complicated, because a rider or would-be rider has to work through the cultural overlays that make one kind of machine or moto-mode more attractive than others. This process can take a long time, because the way to discover the right stimulus package is by experience, and the experience being sought changes with time and place. This phenomenon is not just an artifact of a neophyte's acquisition of sophistication about motorcycle styles. It is also an artifact of accumulated stimuli, some of which may have what amount to toxic effects on the nervous system or other components of the 'bodymind.' Vibration, for example, is known to be cumulative in its effects—hence the "Vibration Dose Value." If the same holds true for the effects of continuously applied or experienced high acceleration forces (as aeromedical research suggests it does), it is obvious that what is behind the change of modes for some intensely committed riders as they age is a kind of wearing out of the tolerances for, and the consequent savoring of, certain physical stimuli.

Among other effects, the individual search for the right moto-mode style-and-stimulus package has had two significant consequences. First, over the century of motorcycling, specific types of motorcycles have emerged to embody specific sets of capabilities, which themselves provide highly specific stimuli. These types are so highly refined that they become a virtual motorcycle subspecies, or what might be called a 'mototype.' Second, a flourishing market in used motorcycles from all eras, reaching back to the beginning of motorcycling itself, has also developed. The two phenomena are closely linked, because both are driven by the social manifestations of psychobiological preferences that riders have for certain packages.

A mototype resembles an archetype, at least in how we respond to it. An archetype is a pattern or original model, an 'ideal form,' or maybe just an idea itself, perhaps expressed as a style. It achieves archetypal status by shaping the other forms, products or processes used in the archetype's context, whatever that context might be. We need archetypes to make sense of the world. We guide our responses to things by comparing them to standard models, which we detect and categorize first by visual means. Our use of archetypes leads us to create stereotypes. Stereotyping in social terms is in deep disgrace these days among many people, because of its effects on the assumptions people often make about one another based on such things as religion, race or gender. Despite the existence of such effects, stereotyping is also a useful way to survive in a hostile world, which is why it is so widespread a behavior, and not just in people. Animals stereotype to survive; a rabbit is unlikely to conclude that the fox she meets in the field today is different in behavior from all those she and her species have learned to fear previously.

We humans can modify our stereotypes, but we still stereotype others, assigning them significances based on visual attributes that seem to connect the person to some previously established archetype. Fashion is entirely driven by the consequences of this, no less in automotive and motorcycle fashions than in clothing. Thus the development of motorcycle types, archetypal mototypes, and, finally, stereotypes over the century has not been an incidental or accidental process, but necessary to integrate the machines, their riders and what the riders signify for themselves and to others in society. Likewise, it has not been a process driven primarily by manufacturers trying to create more profit by making their product lines more complex and diverse. Instead of being mainly the result of manufacturer push, the mototype has resulted from consumer pull, as the riders themselves created the archetypes, usually by modifying some standard machine to embody certain styles or functional characteristics. The manufacturers responded and in the process accelerated the method by which a general-purpose bike became a mototype, at least when enough of a given type sold so well and so consistently that it established a new standard model for all others in a given category.

Though mototypes change with the times, some individual machines have achieved a kind of legendary status as embodiments of qualities widely believed to outlast transitory conditions. They include the Harley-Davidson Sportster, Norton Manx, BMW Boxer, Honda Super Cub, Vespa scooter, Honda CB750 Four, Ducati Desmo series, Indian Chief, Suzuki GSX-R, the Triumph Bonneville and a few others. Their automobile analogs include the Model T Ford, VW Beetle, Chevrolet Corvette, Porsche 911 and the Ford Mustang. Obviously, only the passage of much more time will demonstrate the social staying power of these vehicles but, so far, they remain potent symbols whose characteristics are profoundly important for millions around the world. Some come close to being vehicular icons.

An everyday mototype need not have such staying power; it need only be the model for the class or category for a given time period. The machines above achieved that in their respective production eras, and it was not immediately evident during those eras that they would become as symbolic as they did. They were merely immensely successful products, at least as perceived by their manufacturers and competitors. In several cases they were a little too successful, in that they made themselves tough acts to follow. Porsche, Harley-Davidson, Volkswagen and Ford all suffered somewhat from stereotyping by consumers due to the success of their products. A Harley 'meant' a certain kind of engine and chassis, as did a Porsche, which had to be powered by an air-cooled rear-engine—else how could it be a 'real' Porsche? Likewise the Beetle cemented the linkage of Volkswagen and the type so thoroughly that the manufacturer's attempts to escape the image were initially unsuccessful until generational turnover and time enabled the marque to redefine itself—only, later, to seek linkage with its brand heritage to capitalize on the Beetle yet again. However lucrative this seems now for Porsche, Harley-Davidson and Volkswagen, it was not evident that such an approach was useful or even desirable until recently.

However swift the technological developments that enabled manufacturers to accelerate from the Model T and the nearly contemporary first Harley-Davidson V-twin of 1907, however many model changes and mergers, acquisitions, bankruptcies and startups have filled the century with events, machines and busy-ness, the grandchildren of those who bought the first cars and motorcycles are themselves only now reaching late middle age. It shouldn't surprise us, given how human memory and culture work, that some beliefs and values crystallized in the first half or even the first third of the century persist and, with them, the machine types and archetypes that embody those values and beliefs. A lot has changed since 1910 but a lot more has not, especially inside the humans who buy and ride the bikes, thanks to those "Stone Age minds inside modern skulls." Examining several current major American street-based mototypes briefly shows how this works.

The cruiser mototype's objective, functionally, is to provide a stylish motorcycle platform for being seen, rather than for exploring the outer edges of performance (as with a sport bike) or exploring the outback (as with a dual-sport or dirt bike). Motorcycles configured for this role have also been called boulevard bikes, in reference to their emphasis on creating a two-wheeled frame of fashion for the rider to display himself or herself, as if on promenade. The mechanical specifics of the entire motorcycle can and do vary. So that, for example, though most people associate such bikes as the Harley-Davidson Fat Boy with the type, a cruiser can as easily be a Honda Valkyrie, a Suzuki Intruder or any number of other models from almost any manufacturer. Likewise, custom bikes, especially custom choppers, built by the owner or by a builder who specializes in such machines, are also cruisers, usually occupying the top rungs of the fashion world among riders who prize cruiser-fashion above all.

The engines for cruisers can also vary, though the large-displacement, air-cooled V-twin, as in a Harley, is considered mandatory by many aficionados. The exhaust pipes are expected to be entirely or largely unmuffled, so that the deep bass rumble of the big engine can be heard far and wide. The riding position, too, can vary, but most riders adopt the laid-back style popularized by the chopped Hogs and Triumphs of the 1960s, as portrayed most famously by Peter Fonda as Captain America in "Easy Rider." The handlebars are often tall, wide and put the rider in the 'ape-hanger' position, hands at or above shoulder level, leaning back, feet placed on forward-mounted footpegs or footboards. The saddle is sculpted to accommodate this position, often set as low as possible to the ground, with the passenger seat or pillion stepped up much higher on the rear fender, in keeping with the dictates of the chopper model. Because the cruiser rider is not looking for maximum speed around turns, the tires are configured for maximum footprint in gentle turns and highway riding. Chrome abounds, as do many other cosmetic touches and details as the rider's particular tastes determine, often including expensive and elaborate airbrushed scenes on the bodywork—fuel tank, fenders and side covers.

The experience of riding a cruiser is meant to engender a studied insouciance, cool-on-wheels. Cruising is all about Looking Good; the Going Fast part, to the extent that it is accommodated, is enabled by short bursts of acceleration, in keeping with the stoplight-to-stoplight genesis of drag racing whence, long ago, the stretched-out look of the cruiser bike derived as much as from just rumbling around town and, in the words of Steppenwolf's song "Born to be Wild" (the virtual anthem of boulevard cruisers): "lookin' for adventure, or whatever comes our way."

Stereotypes of the kinds of people who choose cruisers are the easiest to spot. This is neither accidental nor unintended. By the early 1990s, the 'Harley look' (which previous-era Harley-Davidson aficionados used to contend, somewhat ironically and sometimes heatedly, did not apply to all Harley riders) became almost a caricature: a middle-aged man, often overweight, wearing leather chaps, a black t-shirt with some kind of Harley logo-based artwork under a leather vest, itself adorned with many patches, pins and other paraphernalia, who might have a gray beard, a gray ponytail flapping in the breeze under his black bone-dome helmet, most visible skin colorfully tattooed, big black engineer's boots on the feet, a wallet hung by a chain looped around a big-buckled belt, looking at the world through the coolest of cool shades, controlling the bike through hands protected only by fingerless black-leather gloves. Such riders are sometimes sarcastically described by other motorcyclists as "rugged individualists proving it by dressing like every other Hog rider, riding only in groups, riding only Harleys."

Such was and remains the power of the visual-tactile-social assemblage of the Harley cruiser that it still seems to be growing in popularity, rather than shrinking. As will be discussed later, much more is behind this than just style, or even the way the 'potato-potato' Hog engine makes many feel. Note that at least one aspect of the seemingly outrageous riding positions of the cruiser world demands that the rider adopt and maintain a position that places considerable emphasis on strength. The ape-hanger handlebar, for example, with hands on grips at or above shoulder height, effectively makes the body into a drag-chute at speeds above 40 mph, as wind pressure shoves the rider's torso rearward (the same holds true with the 'flat' drag-style handlebars on choppers or cruisers, which require the rider to sit butt-aft, feet and hands forward). Unless one has experienced this, it is difficult to appreciate how much strength and stamina is required to go long distances; though the body adapts quickly to the position, as it does to almost any we can reasonably adopt, the weak cannot sustain the strain. The significance, in body-display terms, is clear: the rider who can manage the position is proclaiming his or her fitness, no matter what else he or she might think is being displayed. Thus the cruiser style has social significance in the prowess-power context of mate-searching and competitor confrontation. Whatever else that guy on the Hog is or is not, if he can ride long distances in that position, he's one tough hombre.

The dual-sport mototype's purpose is twofold: to let the rider go more easily where other kinds of motorcycles have difficulty going and to proclaim that the rider is an adventurous sort, in the old-fashioned sense. In previous eras the general-purpose nature of most motorcycles was taken for granted and riders routinely set off on long treks with motorcycles that were at least ostensibly street bikes, without much concern about having the right gear for every environment from pavement to crushed coral. But the increased complexity in all forms of automotive products that derived from the interaction of corporate push and consumer pull began delivering more and more dual-purpose motorcycles, even before World War II. Machines configured to be as useful in the unimproved or non-existent road milieu as on paved roads are always less than ideal in either zone, but work better in both areas than machines specifically tailored for either.

The machines made for such roles have usually featured visible and easily identifiable markers for their and their riders' identities. Exhaust pipes routed to stay clear of obstacles on the ground, for example, have been on dual-purpose bikes since the beginning. Crash protection around critical engine areas, braced handlebars, hand-protecting grip guards, wire-mesh headlamp screens, tires suited for on- and off-road use and styling that emphasizes ruggedness all signify that the rider is willing and able to find adventure by going where few dare to venture. (It's interesting to note that the same signals are intended to be sent by contemporary sport-utility vehicles, which far outnumber their two-wheeled counterparts.)

The dual-sport riders' style is now as fully developed as the cruiser riders'. Helmets specifically designed for the dual-sport role enable the rider to have a chin-bar or mandible, while also enabling him or her to remove a visor eye shield—common on the street—and replace it with goggles, much more useful on the dirt. Likewise, a flourishing aftermarket provides a wide range of water-resistant synthetic-material riding suits, along with special boots and gloves, to complete the look now generally accepted as *de rigueur* for the type.

Perhaps in response to the rising numbers of female riders, however, an artifact of dual-sport engineering has been introduced with visual consequences of great social importance to 'He-Man' types who need to display their manliness on any machine. Dual-sports, like motocross and enduro bikes, have taller seat heights than most street motorcycles, because negotiating rough terrain automatically demands suspension with longer wheel travel (at least with current suspension technology) than other bikes. Because female riders are typically shorter than males, this creates difficulties for some, resulting in gender-skewed ridership of the big dual-sports. To some extent, of course, the most ridiculously tall seat heights of the supposedly more serious dual-sports also deselect many men: even tall men find it difficult to touch the ground with both feet on big dual-sports, as with some motocross bikes and enduros. What is fascinating about this situation from the social standpoint is that it has remained unchanged since the advent of long-travel suspensions. One explanation is that the tall bikes' and long-travel suspensions' benefits in dynamic response—the ability to ride quickly and successfully where one otherwise could not or would not go—outweigh the unfortunate consequences they embody for shorter riders of both genders. However convincing that argument, the possibility cannot be ruled out that the social role of the machines' physical size is the real factor that keeps it in place. Men need certain ways to display physical attributes, often masked convincingly by entirely plausible engineering rationales.

Something like this phenomenon occurs, for example, among bicyclists who acknowledge the aerodynamic and ergonomic excellence of recumbent bicycles while eschewing them in favor of the more common diamond-framed bike. The standard bicycle format displays the rider in ways the recumbent cannot and does not—ways that evidently have profound social significance. Until and unless something changes to make recumbents as potentially important in 'display' terms, it seems unlikely that they will achieve the acceptance that the now century-old standard diamond-frame bicycle has established.

In motorcycles, the equivalent to the road-racing bicycle is the sport-bike mototype, which places its rider in much the same position the bicycle racer must assume, because of aerodynamics. The bicycle racer also must be placed to provide maximum thrust and recovery through the pedal cycle, which is not necessary for the sport-motorcycle rider, but it is surely not coincidence that the athletic prowess the bicycle rider displays finds its cognate in the ability of the sport-bike rider to sustain a riding position almost as punishing for the unfit, the overweight or those with inferior reflexes. Just as the performance road bicycle is modeled after the racing bike, so the sport-bike motorcycle is modeled after the road-race motorcycle. Elaborate wind-cheating fairings on sport bikes imply great speed and acceleration, and the bikes, for the most part, deliver the goods. One can buy a street-legal motorcycle able to accelerate brutally to almost 200 mph and sustain almost equally astonishing speeds around corners. Sport-bike riders prize their bikes' raw performance; their riding positions and riding gear often emphasize their affection for and implied mastery of sheer speed. Though once seen rarely in the United States, full racing-style riding leathers are now as common a sight on American sport-bike riders as black leather jackets. This style shift alone signals the depth of the cultural changes that motorcycles reflect and embody, since such 'mission-specific' clothing was disdained by many, maybe most, motorcyclists only 25 years ago in the United States. It should be noted in this context that many sport-bike riders continue to wear nothing more than an expensive helmet, a t-shirt, jeans or shorts, and sneakers, however, and it would be foolish not to conclude that this 'uniform' has as much significance and importance for those go-fast riders as full leathers do for other sport-bike riders.

Some attribute the now-common trait of dressing the part to aggressive commercial activity by manufacturers. This conclusion derives from the same viewpoint that underlies the belief that the increasing complexity of all vehicle product lines, both automobiles and motorcycles, is due primarily to increasingly persuasive advertising and marketing by the manufacturers. In my experience, the view is most fervently held by people who have a negative assessment of corporate activity and capitalism in general. In their eyes, buyers are gullible rubes who succumb to savvy come-ons, conditioned by a lifetime of lies about buying happiness through hardware.

It is easy to become sufficiently jaded by our commercial culture to believe so, but what must be kept constantly in mind is that—as the manufacturers always try to remind their most vociferous critics—they might, with their wares and advertising, 'propose,' but the buyers really do 'dispose.' When people do not want a consumer product, for whatever reason, it is dead on arrival at the stores. Moreover, the advertising people I know who have worked most successfully in the business all believe that their work primarily influences choice among competing products.

Consider, in this context, the development of the touring-bike mototype. 'Touring' itself on or in motor vehicles has a long history, but has been characterized by substantial changes in its exact dimensions and nuances over the century, country by country and age by age. Though it has been obvious from the beginning that manufacturers 'pushed' people to use their machines for touring, the real stimulus has always been curiosity about what might be over the next ridge, which is yet another form of sensation-seeking, as will be shown more fully later.

At the beginning of the 20th century, touring among automobilists referred to the 'voyages' made by the wealthy few who could afford automobiles, almost all of which were chauffeur-driven. These cars were more like boats than the vehicles now so common; many were as large as modern trucks, though not fast (except, perhaps, by contemporary standards), and exposed their occupants to weather. The 'tourist' dressed in motor-clothing, prepared for the voyage as if going on a sail around a bay, and frequently overnighted with equally well-off friends.

Though motorcycles had been used to explore the world since their advent, widespread motorcycle touring developed quickly after more reliable machines appeared in the first decade of the 20th century, and the primary components that characterize touring bikes today have been in use since before World War II. Large, upright windshields and saddlebags or panniers are the easiest components to spot, whether on a new Honda or a 1935 Indian Chief. Since the objective is not to go fast but to go long, the riding position is 'relaxed,' with handlebars that usually place the hands well below chest level, pulled back to minimize the stress of stretching to grip the bar. The rider's spine is usually upright, or inclined slightly forward or rearward depending on his or her build, and feet can be placed on footboards forward of where they are usually found on standard street or sport bikes. Likewise, 'highway pegs' placed even farther forward enable the rider to sprawl with legs outward like a cruiser rider, but with the crucial difference that the touring bike's windshield and fairing keep the wind from shoving the rider backwards. Touring-bike saddles also are configured to allow long hours on the road and thus provide much more buttock and thigh support than do bikes designed for environments that require riders to move around a lot. Current touring-bike technology even provides for ventilated and heated seats, electrically-adjustable screen height and (for many other classes of bike, as well) heated handgrips.

Some current 'turn-key' touring bikes (those that can be ridden from the showroom to Alaska, stopping at home only to stuff the saddlebags with clothing and other necessities) are dynamically superb machines capable of being ridden aggressively and quickly in every kind of environment, but the popular stereotype inevitably locates the machine and rider on Interstates or other less-challenging roads. The subtype of sport-touring bikes (typically combining the powerplants and suspensions of sport bikes with less exaggerated riding positions, big fuel tanks, and all-weather fairings of touring bikes) has become significant for riders who want something more sporting.[44]

Each of the mototypes can be and is analyzed extensively in every issue of the enthusiast publications to locate bikes in the rider-interest spectrum. In this context, what is most relevant about them is how they have emerged from the buyer-manufacturer dialog over the century. That dialog has resulted in ever more narrowly-defined types of machine, as many observers of the motorcycle scene have noted. What is often overlooked is that the signals sent visually by the mototypes' stereotyped styles embody significantly different kinds of sensation-seeking. A person who really finds it fun to ride through miles of dusty trails, often standing on

---

[44] The precise lines of market demarcation between touring bikes and sport-touring bikes are often difficult to find in machines obviously capable of both roles, but with tongue firmly in cheek, we at *Cycle Guide* used to put it this way: "On a touring bike, you look at the butterflies as you ride along a two-lane road in a verdant valley. On a sport-touring bike, you look *through* the butterflies, which are usually splattered all over your windscreen and visor." It is of course possible to ride a sport-touring bike at a leisurely pace, but for many—maybe most—riders, "sport" actually means "speed," and thus the machine is configured with more rear-set footpegs, lower handlebar, and greater cornering ground clearance than the 'straight' touring bike.

the footpegs to ensure better balance in uncertain surface conditions like sand, mud or gravel, is indeed experiencing different stimuli from those of someone who prefers rumbling through a town on a cruiser, or someone who seeks out the twisties to use as a dance floor for a sport-bike jitterbug. To the extent that sensation-seeking itself differs, these people are signaling important things about themselves that transcend 'mere' style.

The different kinds of sensation-seeking are thus the essence of the stereotypes we have developed in automotive culture, not just in motorcycles but throughout the vehicle spectrum. If all sensation seekers were the same, or all sensations sought had the same behavioral causes and effects, this would not matter much. Neither is the case; sensations do differ, as do their social consequences when embodied in machines meant to deliver them. The mototypes' purpose is to reflect these differences both in physically functional and socially useful ways related to group and individual associations. None is more important than mate-searching, since both biological and cultural evolution rely on reproductive fitness.

In the mate-searching process, detecting differences between potential mates is essential. In a culture in which so many costumes can create so many fake personas, those which are harder to create and sustain deceptively are increasingly valuable as indicators of real personal characteristics. Any that depend on sensation-seeking therefore illuminate capabilities related to fitness. A fondness for making or listening to music of any kind is a useful social signal, as is a fondness for making and listening to motor-music, by means of the wind instrument that is an internal combustion engine. No one disputes the value of learning, for example, that a potential mate's personal musical tastes are dramatically different from one's own, for better or worse; similarly, the aural preferences in motor-music are important in indicating a range of behaviors, values and personal abilities that may have profound mate-selection influences.

Since research into sensation-seeking began in earnest during the 1960s, a vast research base has been assembled by psychologists to show how the types of sensations sought can be significant in socially organizing terms. Attuned to the need for careful evaluation of race, gender, class and other demographically differencing characteristics, researchers have produced a literature of results and analyses that yields fascinating insights and interpretations, with implications for understanding such behaviors as motorcycling in general and stereotyped mototype-based emulation in particular.

It is useful, in considering sensation-seeking, to pay particularly close attention to the lessons that the most senior researchers have drawn from their experiments. For example, Marvin Zuckerman, now emeritus professor of psychology at the University of Delaware, arguably the guru of the field, notes in his 1994 work, *Behavioral Expressions and Biosocial Bases of Sensation Seeking* that "Sensation seeking is essentially a greater disposition to approach novel and intense stimuli, people or situations, whereas low sensation seeking is the tendency to avoid such stimuli. The advantages of high sensation seeking in other animals, and perhaps in our own hominid ancestors, are increased access to new potential food sources and mates, but the advantages are somewhat offset by the risks." [45] He adds, a few sentences later, that "A successful hunter must take some risks and even enjoy predation. Because of the risks, a moderate but not too high level of the trait was probably optimal for survival, reproduction, and insuring the survival of one's offspring."[46] In this context—survival—he continues: "Human types are not so biologically differentiated, but a society may accommodate high sensation seekers in one role, such as warriors and explorers, and low sensation seekers in another, like diplomats, priests, and record keepers. The balance between the adventurous and the cautious members of society may determine the fate of everyone in the society."[47] The consequences in modern life are made clear by Zuckerman when he writes: "There is a strong possibility that the fundamental trait of sensation seeking has not changed since the Pleistocene period when it may have had an adaptive value at moderate levels. Assortative mating may have maintained variability in the trait. Of course, the phenomenal expressions have changed from activities like hunting to reckless driving."[48]

Or, perhaps, to riding motorcycles, when driving in increasingly reliable and safe automobiles is an alternative. (When one has no choice and must use a motorcycle of some kind because one lacks access to automobiles or other forms of transportation, the issue of social significance of motorcycling is substantially changed, of course.) Because, as Zuckerman

---

[45] Marvin Zuckerman, *Behavioral Expressions and Biosocial Bases of Sensation Seeking* (Cambridge Univ. Press: Cambridge, 1994), p. 287.

[46] Ibid.

[47] Ibid., pp. 287-288.

[48] Ibid., p. 289.

notes, *"58% of the sensation-seeking trait is heritable* [original emphasis],"[49] it seems clear that motorcycle riders are signaling something important about themselves to potential mates, as to everyone in society. Thus it is also clear why stereotypes in moto-imagery are useful socially, since shadings in the sensation-seeking traits one pursues are important, like the differences in plumage among birds, or any sexually-linked trait among animal populations.

Trying to understand how a person's taste for novelty on two wheels translates socially into signals about character has to take into consideration the Orgasmatronic aspects of the sensations actually sought on two wheels. In this quest, the ride becomes the destination, in effect, just as acquiring the drugs an addict ingests becomes the objective of living. The social and cultural aspects illuminated here may seem to be secondary artifacts of highly individualized self-stimulation for purely internal pleasures; I suspect that few motorcyclists would agree that they ride primarily for what amounts to social purposes, though many will readily refer to the substantial social benefits they enjoy in riding. Moreover, the interactions between the internal biochemical rewards of riding, which occur pre-cognitively, and the social consequences of such riding might not always be linked in a causal relationship. But Zuckerman's conclusions about the social role of sensation seeking, vis-à-vis its universality and persistence as well as its origins in species survival, point to the real reasons we even seek sensations, in whatever form.

Motorcycles should be understood in this context as expressing the behavior, not causing it. Those who seek the

---

[49] Ibid., p. 291.

sensations motorcycles deliver are nearly genetically identical, so far as is known, to our ancestors in our Environments of Evolutionary Adaptedness. The reproductive significance of that fact is clear in the mate-searching consequences of motorcycling behavior. Likewise, so is the societal significance, as hinted at by Zuckerman's comments.

In the less socially complicated America in which I grew up, conventional wisdom was distilled in sayings that expressed a kind of 'social common sense' passed down over the ages. Among men, the belief was that there were only so many types: fighters, lovers, thinkers and priests. This was, of course, stereotyping at its most basic, and though our culture has developed along lines that make all social stereotyping anathema, everything in the human experience shows the persistence and power of stereotyping, from its biological roots to its continued existence. Any scientist, studying such a persistent phenomenon, must conclude that it persists because it is useful. Thus the old saw about how men's fundamental characters shake down probably captures something important; though we know that all men can at some point probably be induced to fight, all men love (or try to love or seek love) and so forth, the behavioral traits hinted at by such conventional wisdoms sometimes resonate with what science shows us about ourselves. In sensation-seeking terms, the importance of the phenomenon lies in how men, especially, decide how to collect in groups, and why.

In this context, the role of differentiated motorcycle mototypes and the stereotypes they create provides the means by which such groups can align themselves. The mototypes summarize preferred sensation-sets, appearing as engineered, functional differences between the motorcycles, which attract people with similar tastes both for such sensations and for the environments that enable them. Because we humans need symbols to summarize values and beliefs, the particular marques or models of motorcycles that have become archetypical are vital symbols of much more than just the array of values usually associated with them.

Harley-Davidson, for example, is thought to embody something uniquely 'American' as a consequence of the marque's history. But it seems clear to me that the physical stimuli produced by a Harley-Davidson motorcycle are as important in creating its mystique as the history of the company that makes them. The company's history and the values it supposedly embodies are obviously important, but in the sensation-seeking context it is essential to focus attention on the Harley's unique ride characteristics, which persisted through many H-D models for so long that, even though other manufacturers have attempted to replicate them, they are still perceived in reference to the 'original.' It's obvious that, had Harley-Davidson not continued to produce machines with such characteristics, the social and cultural interpretations of the marque would be radically different today; but H-D did, and thus, 'Harley-ness' is as real to millions of people as if it were a purely quantifiable quality.

Harley-ness makes it clear, were there any doubt, that the manufacturer's identity *is* important in our experience of the product. The history of vehicle manufacturing so far has focused on clear manufacturer identity, so the processes by which we sort the machines and assign their social and societal significance is linked irremediably to the maker's name and nationality. Stereotyping is of course operating in this process, and for good reason; among much else it provides, socially, it enables us to assemble in clubs organized around a particular motorcycle marque or model. The attraction of the stereotype's stimulus-set lies hidden for most people well behind the machine's logotype, because the storytelling done to cement the allegiances of the club members usually focuses on the symbol, not what it symbolizes on the sensation-seeking scale.

This club-formation, by means of shared stimuli and the symbols for it, is also rooted in our evolutionary inheritance. Since the Neolithic revolution created farming and with it urbanization and everything we mean by civilization, we have lived to one degree or another in environments for which our evolution did not previously prepare us as a species. Though our cultural evolution has enabled us to prosper in such environments, clearly, many of our tensions individually and societally derive from the mismatch between our biological and cultural evolutionary heritages. Despite ideologically-driven scholarship, philosophies, politics, polemics and other forms of imaginative expressions of what ought to be rather than what is, in terms of the human character, what we have discovered about ourselves in the last 10,000 or so years is that we are not infinitely adaptable socially. Given the chance, we revert to certain forms of social interaction whenever and wherever we can. Among those forms is the virtual band or clan or tribe: the club. The "right crowd with no crowd-ing," as they said of the Brooklands race track in England in the '30s.

Crowding is not so much a description of a physical state of proximity as a social state, a pressure felt especially keenly when the 'wrong' person is too close for comfort. We sort ourselves whenever we can, and the problems of how and why have occupied students of sociology and anthropology for the last century, at least. The problems of proximity are especially acute among males in many primate societies, and humans are no different. Designed to compete for everything from females to food, males can ally themselves and even make friends, but our predisposition to competition creates certain cultural consequences that have appeared throughout our history. One reason why motorcycle clubs are so useful is that they contain and channel male competitiveness in ways other cultural constructs do not.

Male competitiveness exists not just in the much-studied, much-feared 'outlaw' motorcycle clubs such as the Hell's Angels and their ilk. Any gathering of men, young or old, has the potential for conflict over status. Jammed into close proximity in a single container, men have to subdue their natural competitiveness. It is the genius of our species that we have evolved social mechanisms by which we can do so, more often than not. Thus busloads of basketball players, soldiers or corporate executives have developed intrinsic systems by which they can arrange themselves without too much friction. Most of modern life, in fact, requires learning how to contain, channel and contextualize the powerful urge to compete among us males.

Motorcycles present a male with an ideal vehicle both for experience and expression, and thus might be particularly dangerous socially. They can create emotional states of high system arousal, understood often as the fight-or-flight state of our 'bodymind.' Set thus on a kind of emotional 'half-cocked trigger,' a male motorcyclist might easily be considered the equivalent of a trigger-happy gunfighter walking into a Dodge City saloon in search of trouble. The extent to which this might be true is as yet unknown, so far as I have been able to tell, since it depends on a level of analysis of the behavioral effects of the human-machine interface over time that appears not to have been undertaken, at least not seriously. Anecdotally, of course, we see Hollywood images of biker-gang members arriving at peaceful campgrounds ready to rumble, rape and rampage. In my experience, after riding a large-displacement, V-twin-engined motorcycle without fairing or windshield for more than a few hours, one is interested mainly in just getting off the motorcycle, not looking for combat.

Whatever might happen when the bikes are parked, the salient feature of the motorcycle gang or club is that it lets males sort themselves out on the road without having to be too close to each other. Moreover, each rider retains power in ways he does not afoot or in sharing space with others in a single vehicle, since he can, at any time, simply peel off and go solo. Likewise, since each rider can choose his own mount and modify it to his own tastes, his group identity is never wholly dependent on externally applied criteria he cannot control. This issue of control over oneself is at the core of the social utility of the club, whether an outlaw gang or a small group of off-road riders.[50] Being in the driver's seat is possible in an automobile only for one male at a time, which imposes

[50] Though it is claimed that outlaw-club membership requires obedience to riding rules, as to all club authority. Clearly, this limits the scope of free action by an outlaw-club member, if not other riders.

hierarchical and behavioral constraints that every other male in the vehicle feels to some extent. Aboard a motorcycle, each man is the captain of his own ship, the 'pilot in command.'

As with much in motorcycling culture, behind club behavior is indeed, as the cultural-constructivists claim, the motorcycle's usefulness as an archetype. It simultaneously symbolizes a set of cultural associations and the sensations that lie deep under the associations. The stereotypes we create to summarize those associations in social form help us deal with the stresses of surviving in a civilization that has little in common with the world our ancestors walked out of, so long ago. Among them were many hunters, as Zuckerman pointed out, and among us today are many whose biological inheritance includes the predisposition to seek stimuli far beyond the range most people seek—on motorcycles, in cars or anywhere else. Dr. Zuckerman suggests that some find these stimuli in "reckless driving." While perhaps true, the culture we have created with motorcycles has one important category of experiences that itself is far more important to those who inhabit its regions and those who study it than the "reckless drivers." The category is racing, and the hunter-racers who explore its outer limits do much more for themselves and for society than merely entertain.

CHAPTER FIVE

FAST IS NEVER
FAST ENOUGH

Because of how they expose themselves to danger, motor-cycle racers are often considered the ultimate thrill-seeking speed junkies, perhaps even more than their automobile-racing counterparts.[51] There may be something to this view,

---

[51] An online project called the Motorsport Memorial (*http://www.motorsportme-morial.org/*) has the ambitious goal of recording every racing fatality, to honor the memory of those who died in competitive motorsport, whether on land, sea or in the air. To demonstrate the relative lethality of motorcycle and car or truck racing, as of 28 February, 2008, the number of motorcycle racers listed was 1545 (solo

at least insofar as it helps us understand what initially draws anyone to race motorcycles as opposed to just riding them. But there's a problem with understanding motorcycle racing that way: To be at home on a racetrack at speeds and accelerations most people cannot imagine, surrounded by others doing everything they can to pass each other, motorcycle racers must become inured to the physicality of the experience, to concentrate on racecraft. In short order, the sensations fade into the background of competition itself.

I found this out in my first motorcycle road race, in March, 1967. I'd decided to go racing after watching only two motorcycle road races the previous fall. It was, I soon discovered, a highly stimulating, satisfying, engrossing and thoroughly exhausting experience that I could never truly explain to anyone, unless he or she was also a racer. I found that within a few laps of my first practice sessions at Cotati Raceway, in Northern California, I was comfortable with lean angles and speeds that would have seemed insane on the roads outside the track. Whatever thrills I got from adrenaline spikes came *after* some event on the track—a crash in front of me, a broken component on my bike, a near-crash on my part from a mistake or a malfunction. The rest of the time I was so completely enmeshed in the activity that I was oblivious

rider, sidecar pilots and sidecar passengers), while the number of car and truck racers who died in competition was listed as 3429 (drivers, co-drivers, riding mechanics, and on-board navigators). Thus, although there are many more car and truck racers in the world than motorcycle racers, motorcycle racing claimed almost half the number of lives as car and truck racing. An even more dramatic comparison is of the most lethal racing circuits, by type, for cars/trucks and motorcycles; Indianapolis Motor Speedway has had the most fatalities among car/truck competitors, with 55; while the Isle of Man Mountain Course, upon which motorcyclists compete in the annual Tourist Trophy and Manx Grand Prix races, has claimed 228 lives.

to any sensation at all, attending only to those sights, sounds, odors and other stimuli that had significance related to the state of my racing machine, the track or the other racers. In this, I soon discovered, I was very much in the middle of the racer mentality and experience; nobody I ever knew who raced longer than a single season ever mentioned being thrilled by anything, save victory or a particularly good save when the bike seemed about to depart the track or dismantle itself dramatically.

This was not the result of a need to appear 'cool' in the social sense. Contrary to the images many people have of what racing consists of and of who does it, racers must be cool-headed and steady-handed to survive. In all forms of racing, the core experience—indeed, the central demand for survival—is total concentration. In my experience and that of those whose opinions I value, this complete concentration, unlike anything else in daily life, is what ultimately makes racing so powerfully addictive an activity.

The relationship between the environmental extremes that characterize speed-sport and the extreme concentration needed to sustain the speed seems clearly linked to our evolutionary heritage. The link might be to hunting, or possibly to combat, though in the latter, fear plays a much more powerful role than in racing. Motorcycle racers who suddenly develop serious fear about what they are doing quickly hang up their leathers. Less debilitating fear can play a role in racing, obviously, as when, in attacking a corner as it should be attacked to maintain or improve a position, actions must be taken that induce a certain amount of fear, until the new fear levels are in place and the 'bodymind' is unfazed the next time the actions are taken. This is why racers strive to extend themselves in practice sessions and to keep themselves up to speed between races and in the off season.

An old racer's saying is: "Pain is nature's way of telling you to pay more attention." This wry summary itself illuminates one way the racer's world differs from the non-racer's. An injury, for most racers, is not a reason to quit, only a reason to do something differently and better, assuming that a mistake induced the injury in the first place. In this, motorcycle racing is hardly unique, given the personal-damage toll taken in football and other contact sports. But the immediate, sometimes severe and often fatal injuries that may ensue from a mistake in motorcycle racing makes moto-sport much less forgiving. Racers understand and accept the costs because the benefits, in experiential terms, are priceless to them, in ways that are hard for others to understand. It is not just a question of risk, it is a question of which risks to take, and why.

For example, I raced at Bathurst, Australia, in 1988 with Paul Dean, editor of *Cycle World*, aboard the 1987 Suzuki GSX-R 750 that I had campaigned under the *Team Cycle World* banner at the Isle of Man TT the year before.[52] Because we had such a good time in the Island, we decided to ship the bike and the TT team manager, Terry Shepherd, to the annual races at Bathurst, where we would race it in the Arai 500 endurance road-race. The race would draw Australia's top talent, since the world-famous Mount Panorama circuit was used for racing only twice a year, for the James Hardie 1000 car race and for the annual motorcycle races. The Mount

---

[52] I wrote about the Bathurst event in the October, 1988 *Cycle World* ("Thunder on the Magic Mountain," pp. 53-68), and about racing in the 1987 Isle of Man TT in the September, 1987 issue ("The Long and Winding Road," pp. 40-47).

Panorama circuit was celebrating its 50th anniversary, having been built just before World War II to train Aussie riders for the Isle of Man TT races, then as now the world's most grueling, dangerous and prestigious road-race events.

After Paul Dean's first stint in the saddle, the team was lying well up in the standings. During my session, I soon came upon a rider on a much larger and faster Formula One bike, who would slow down substantially in the tight turns at the top of the mountain, then unleash his formidable engine's power down the mile-long Conrod Straight. Realizing that I'd have to get him behind me to keep our place, I planned a pass where he slowed the most—the tight downhill left-hander known as Forrest's Elbow. All went well as we dove into the braking area for the turn; I pulled out from behind him, leaned over further and rolled on the throttle, taking a much tighter line through the turn than he did until, just past the apex, the Suzuki's fairing grounded against a slightly upthrust section of concrete I hadn't seen, instantly kicking the rear wheel out and throwing me to the ground. The bike and I slid across the track and slammed into the trackside concrete barrier, not removed for the motorcycle race, set up to protect the grandstands from race cars.

Though the Suzuki bounced off the wall and slammed back into me as I was still sliding toward it, I was only bruised. The corner workers quickly got the broken bike off the track while I leaned on a fence near the grandstands, trying to figure out whether we could continue if I could get the bike back to the pits.

At that point an Aussie came down from the grandstands. Facing me across the fence, smiling broadly, he said: "Bloody hell, mate, that was one nasty prang. Want a cigarette?" He pulled out his pack and offered them to me. Without thinking, I replied: "No thanks—smoking's bad for your health." At that, the grandstand burst into roars of laughter and applause, as if the whole thing had been scripted. It did seem funny in the circumstances, but it revealed, in a more serious way, the differences between the world on each side of that fence. Most racers I have known well are obsessive about physical fitness and many are extremely health conscious. Yet all put themselves at great physical risk every time they climb aboard a racing motorcycle. How to square these contradictions?

The answer lies in the nature of what we actually got out of racing. In the sensation-seeking sense, we obviously found something immensely stimulating about life on the edge at speed, and yet could not and did not ever think seriously about what it might be since few of us could recall, after any given race, more than one or two sensations. What we remembered most were details of our racecraft: how we passed or blocked a pass, how we dealt with a broken brake pedal, a split exhaust pipe, a tire wearing out too fast. Even so, all of us would say that we lived life to its fullest on the track, and we were never more alive than when we pitted ourselves against our competitors, most of whom were good friends and almost all of whom we trusted literally with our lives. Moreover, we could not wait to get back out there to do it again.

In this, our experiences echoed those of hunters. Hunting requires total commitment of the 'bodymind' among those who do it to survive. Every movement has to be carefully made when closing on the prey; every sound, every sight, every odor can be significant and has to be closely observed and analyzed. Hunting is thus a series of challenges or problems to be solved. Considering the way our brains evolved to solve just such survival problems, one by one, it is not surprising that some people enjoy using them in the 'bodymind' sense to their fullest capacity in a blood sport like motorcycle racing. All sports demand full integration of mind and body for the contestant to be successful, but those that place the person in immediate jeopardy obviously recapture at least some key parts of the most intense conditions from our evolutionary experiences—escape from predation, combat and hunting.

In social and societal terms, the personal payback enjoyed by racers has significant benefits for everyone else. All sports provide a socially non-destructive outlet for the need to compete and to be seen to be competing. This is important to emphasize in the context of automotive and motorcycle competition because a large part of that competition is unofficial and unsanctioned. Nobody knows how many street races occur daily in chance encounters on the road, but my experience is that, were it possible to tally the number, it would astonish most people. I have driven test cars and ridden test motorcycles all over the world. Everywhere I have done so, I have been challenged by someone to an impromptu and of course illegal race.

However this street racing may endanger those who do it and those who also happen to be on the road while the race is underway, it must be understood as part of the inevitable repertoire of human behavior, not something unique to using automobiles and motorcycles. Moreover, all street-racing events are not the same. Some, like my chance encounters on test drives, are opportunistic and whimsical. Some, however, are as serious as anything that happens at Indianapolis or Daytona. By all accounts, every major city has a thriving illegal street-racing culture of some kind. The purpose of this racing, as in sanctioned competition, is manifold. First, it enables competitive display by riders—mostly male, mostly young—to enhance their reputations and thus their status. Second, it provides a way to make money, sometimes a considerable amount of money, by the racers themselves. Third, just as the sanctioned racing does, this illegal racing contains and directs the potentially highly destructive built-in male competitive forces.

Safety experts rightly argue that street racing itself is potentially highly dangerous, destructive and deadly, especially when it occurs not on deserted back alleys or rural roads but in congested traffic when two would-be-racer heroes encounter and challenge one another. The problem of finding the means by which they can take their confrontation from the freeway, say, to the racetrack opens up the questions of how and why some choose to do that and others resist doing so, despite the blandishments of their peers.

In Hollywood representations of racing, the storyline demands that the fast kid be impecunious but brave and tremendously talented so that his 'breaking-into-the-majors' tale can be told. For some this occurs, albeit often without the Hollywood elements. For others, the disincentives to take it to the track are as great or greater than the incentives. Going racing in sanctioned competition demands adopting a viewpoint alien to many Alpha Male types, because it demands that they submit to being institutionally inducted into a different world, one in which their actions must be fitted into rules they probably don't much like, most centrally because somebody else composed them. Real Alphas of the most intensely competitive and combative sort like to make their own rules and force everyone else to abide by them. Thus on the street a top-gun type merely needs to build a machine and drive or ride it with such skill that others challenge him. There are no podium finishes in this kind of racing: you either win or lose.

By contrast, in sanctioned competition, social and cultural constraints are omnipresent. Governing rules dictate everything from what the racer can race, when, where and how, to what he or she must wear. Though it was not always so, motorsport in the United States now is a highly organized and bureaucratized enterprise. It demands insurance, lawyers, civic interaction, responsible behavior and environmental consciousness that's anathema to the personality types common among street racers.

Whatever the racing environment, to be an activity with adaptive function in the evolutionary sense it must enable its practitioners to achieve reproductive advantages over their competitors. Racing illegally or legally can do so in several ways, some obviously economic and some, less obviously, social. At a minimum, success as a racer means mastery of self and machine, both important signals for mate-searching in a highly technological culture. Just as a first-class hunter who fashions his own weapons and other tools and uses them to bring home the meat can achieve high status, so too can a racer who builds his or her own machines and drives or rides them to victory, or even to high status without outright victory (as happens often in sanctioned racing). The particular social environment in which the racer operates can of course direct choices about what to race, where and when. Motorcycle racing, even more than automobile racing, was and still is seen by many middle-class Americans as a self-indulgent, wasteful and foolishly dangerous sport. This attitude can negatively influence someone looking for approved means of achieving status. Moreover, at a visceral level, most people know that putting oneself in danger—not for others but for one's own purposes—is not heroic in any meaningful sense. Many young men and boys idolize racers, but only because the racers represent classical male values of bravery in the face of death, along with control close to what everyone who watches racing knows is the edge of disaster.

A friend summarized the view many have of motorcycle racers when he told me, knowing that I was a veteran pro racer: "Motorcycle racing is for guys with nothing to lose." This is nonsense, but it illuminates the belief among middle-class men who choose socially safe paths through life that anyone who does not choose those paths cannot, either because he is too dumb or too foolish. Motorcycle racing, in this formulation, is for the dumb *and* foolish.

There is a schoolyard-faceoff quality to the intensity with which some men display disdain and dislike for racing and racers that should attract our attention while considering the social significance of motorcycle racing. Whenever such powerful emotions are aroused by something, it is a signal that the something is important in some way. I am inclined to think it derives from competition for mates.

Marvin Zuckerman emphasizes the sexual role played by sensation-seeking differences, both between mates and among competitors for mates. Males generally score higher on sensation-seeking scales that include sensations common to motorcycling and especially racing of all kinds. Research data show the importance of high sensation seeking. For example, Zuckerman notes: "D. Buss et al. (1990) did a study of preferences for mate selection in 37 cultures. The first three highest-ranking traits for both men and women in the entire cross-cultural sample were (1) kind and understanding; (2) intelligent; (3) exciting personality. It is not clear what an 'exciting personality' means to subjects but I suspect it is something like an extraverted high sensation seeker." [53]

If Dr. Zuckerman is correct, the dislike of the low-sensation seeker (who looks for stability and predictability and avoids challenges) for his high-sensation-seeking competitor is obviously based in a certain psychobiological and demographic reality. Continuing his commentary above, Zuckerman writes: "Because these are all highly desirable traits in a potential mate and there are [sic] a limited supply of persons high on these traits, then the highs are attracted to each other and the lows have to make do with each other. Much as the lows would prefer a mate with an exciting personality, providing he or she is also kind and understanding, it is probably just as well that they end up with someone closer to their own low levels of sensation seeking since there is evidence that a lack of congruence on sensation seeking can be a source of marital dissatisfaction." [54]

---

[53] Zuckerman, *Behavioral Expressions and Biosocial Bases of Sensation Seeking*, p. 194.

[54] Ibid.

Research in sensation-seeking underscores repeatedly that high sensation-seekers do not seek risk *per se*; they seek it to create challenging environments, to enable them to use all their mind and body faculties. This perfectly defines the track-based motorcycle racer, because sanctioned competition is safer than everyday street riding. This is not evident to most casual onlookers, but the details that define organized, sanctioned racing make it clear. It is worthwhile in this context—risk selection and management—to itemize a few of those.

First, the racer himself or herself must undergo physical tests to apply for a racing license, even at the novice level. Second, the machine on which he or she will race is inspected for compliance with class rules and with safety criteria such as tire condition and 'safety wiring.' Third, the neophyte racer must undergo scrutiny in his or her first races to ensure that he or she can engage safely in competition with peers at speed. This scrutiny also often includes mandatory training or proof of riding competence. Fourth, the racer must use approved safety clothing, head to foot, all mandatory for admission to any racetrack, even for practice. Fifth, at any racetrack, the traffic is all going the same direction, comprised of equally committed (if not equally skilled or talented) riders, all having agreed to rules of conduct set forth in the sanctioning body's rulebook. Sixth, the racetrack's own insurance requires the circuit to have fire and rescue personnel on duty, even in practice sessions; during races, every corner is staffed by people—often volunteers—trained in safety techniques necessary to save lives. Likewise, during races, at least one and sometimes several medical officers are on duty, often with ready access to a fully outfitted medical suite for emergencies, including helicopter medical evacuation to a major medical facility when locally available. Seventh, the track itself is maintained as no public highway could be, swept clean continuously and examined carefully after every accident or incident to ensure that safe racing can and should continue. Finally, racing's social structure often ensures that rank novices and highly advanced professionals are not on track at the same time, to minimize speed and skill differentials for safety purposes.

The contrasts with the situation on public roads could not be starker. This is why some street racers think of themselves as the 'real' racers: they accept risks that those who compete on tracks do not and will not. As noted above, I believe they take those risks for several reasons, all social. To begin with, there are few closed-circuit racetracks in the United States, especially road-race tracks, though many more dirt tracks and motocross tracks exist. This means that someone—a teenager, typically—who develops, through street riding and culturally associative values, an intense interest in road racing faces a set of serious problems in trying to go racing if he or she lives in the wrong part of the country. Certainly, the last few decades have seen a huge and important process by which manufacturer-supported programs make it possible to walk into a motorcycle dealership and find the hardware and the organizational links to go racing. But distances to the tracks can still be a problem for those without the means. So street racing, with the same production-class sport bikes that one would race on a track, is a real alternative. In addition, that would-be road racer can achieve great in-group status with derring-do in unsanctioned competition, where there is also, frequently, real money to be made.

For those who select the organized-racing path to motorcycle racing, profitable careers in racing are possible. Motorcycle racing is now big business worldwide and the social mechanisms by which talented newcomers are spotted and given their chances in the spotlight are now sophisticated. The ubiquity of motorcycle racing of all kinds on cable and satellite television has helped cement the activity into the public consciousness as never before. No one can say where this will lead institutionally, but the coverage ensures that the manufacturers will most likely continue to compete with factory-backed teams worldwide. This commercial competition will have social-societal significance beyond the moto-world itself, in the form of the machines developed from the technologies refined continuously on racetracks.

People who like fast cars and motorcycles are fond of saying: "Fast is never fast enough." This is usually taken as a mild form of boasting when a bunch of riders or drivers are bench racing in a buddy's garage or having lunch after a morning ride. But it captures the psychobiological reality reflected in sensation-seeking generally and speed-sports particularly. Sensation-seeking has strong and identifiable neurochemical bases. Research into the brain chemistry of high and low sensation-seekers shows how their neurochemical activity differs when presented with novel stimuli. One important difference between the high and low sensation-seekers in this context is in the rate at which any novel stimulus becomes boring. At the sensory-cell level, this is reflected in differential rates of stimulus habituation and adaptation, in turn influencing the rate at which mood-influencing neurochemicals are inhibited or disinhibited at the synaptic gaps between neurons. The upshot is that high sensation-seekers are more likely to seek an increase in the stimuli that create novelty than low sensation-seekers. When those stimuli involve the visual and somatosensory artifacts of speed or acceleration, as with motorcycles, fast really is never fast enough. The habituation process quickly sets new and higher speed requirements for creating the environment most stimulating to the high sensation seeker, absent other environmental changes.

In short, racers, among others who relish the challenge of higher speeds and accelerations, need ever-higher plateaus of moto-motion to have fun. This is *not*, therefore, socially-constructed behavior, but pre-cognitive response to accommodation processes in the brain and body. The same evolutionary equipment that makes us such good problem-solvers, hunters and all-around motion-seekers keeps us continuously looking for the next higher high. This phenomenon explains, among much else, why and how so many new riders so quickly 'outgrow' their starter bikes, whatever they might be. It also explains how societal standards for speed and acceleration change. Though we experience motion individually, we experience the limits of the motion in a social setting over which we have no control, beginning, as noted earlier, even before birth. It might be impossible to prove that a fetus developing in a womb whose host is subject to consistently high accelerations emerges at birth more accommodated to those forces than other newborns, but research suggests there is reason to believe so. Likewise, if one grows up riding in cars and on motorcycle passenger seats experiencing higher speeds

than one's parents did, the processes by which one habitu-
ates to those speeds is mediated evidently not by conscious
thought but by the array of mechanisms our evolution has
built into each of us to respond quickly and appropriately to
the external world.

Racers, whether on street or track, face the same general limits, psychobiologically, as the rest of humanity. So
it is likely that the technology of motorcycles (or any other
technology, for that matter) will eventually produce machines
that nobody can actually use because they will create forces
beyond our 'design envelope.' Military aviation has already
encountered this problem, leading to the realization that the
days of piloted aircraft are over, at least for some missions. We
can build machines capable of creating and surviving forces
and environments that humans cannot.

Meanwhile, tires, suspensions and other factors continue to limit the speeds riders can achieve even with the most
powerful engines on race tracks, due to the inherent limita-
tions of the motorcycle design itself. Because of this, riders
can continue to matter in motorcycle racing—on or off the
track—in ways they already do not in automobile racing, due
to the relative masses of rider and machine, and the ways in
which motorcycles steer. Just as with horse racing, which has
never gone out of style for spectators or onlookers alike, this
'human-essentialness' will keep motorcycle racing relevant for
those who seek to do it, as well as for those who seek thrills by
watching it. We will always find new ways to ensure that fast
is never fast enough.

CHAPTER SIX

PERFORMANCE ART

Concentration and full use of the mind and body, which defines the essence of motorcycle racing, also defines something else central to the human experience: art. All art, of whatever kind, is made. Someone has to shape it, whether the shaping is done with a musical instrument, a paintbrush, a chisel, a computer keyboard or a motorcycle engine. As many have pointed out, the distinctions we draw between what we do for art and what we do for commerce, or so-called practical reasons, are as artificial as the distinctions between the arts and the sciences. What integrates them is their human-ness, which we need no persuasive argument to understand. Even so, in the context of what fun consists of in motorcycling, it is essential to keep an open mind, to be able to see and hear and feel how ingredients that might seem to be just so much hardware or noise are actually art to many, many motorcyclists.

The ride itself is art, visually, as well as aurally and kinesthetically. Though physiologists use 'kinesthetics' to mean something highly specific about the interaction of muscle, nerve and mind, I use it here in the sense in which it has entered popular culture: the dancing sense. Derived from the Greek words *kin'ma*, meaning motion, and *aisth'sis*, meaning sensation or perception, kinesthesia can mean "of, or relating to, a sense of bodily motion." The sense is the key, of course, in the 'bodymind' context, because it is the means by which emotions—and thus fun—come from such motion, as demonstrated in the previous chapters. What is less often evident to non-riders is how the visual experience of riding itself is performance art to the rider, if not to onlookers.

It is not merely the interaction of kinesthesia with the exhaust pipe's motor-music or the other sound-generating components of the machine, from the tires to the particular aerodynamic features of the bike, that create a unique rider-machine airflow package and thus a unique sound at any speed that generates the art of the ride. Those are important components but less so than the visual stimuli, thanks to the visual-dominance effect in human life. Sound and feeling are crucial to us in every way, but vision remains dominant among our primary senses. Hence the dominance of appearance in our lives, especially for those things with which we choose to decorate or enliven our world.

The motorcycle itself is usually assumed to be the motorcyclist's primary decorative-art object and so it is. But the *ride* creates a continuously changing set of images for the rider that provide aesthetic reward. The sensation-seeker's thirst for novelty (the probable source of *Wanderlust*, among much else) greedily drinks in this kind of visual reward. Nothing, as the ancient philosophers noted, is ever really the same over time, so the road, the roadside scenery, the destination and the traffic itself are highly stimulating elements—at least potentially—for the art generated by any motorcycle ride. Most motorcyclists who ride for any length of time comment on some aspect of this, noting how just riding a bike as opposed to driving a car or being a passenger on a bus changes their perceptions so that they enjoy what they see much more and more intensely than otherwise. Moto-lore is filled with tales of how this influences people as well as what it is about motorcycles that creates this effect.

The preference for shiny, highly reflective surfaces on all our machines is a clue to how the art component of a ride functions. Our eyes evolved to detect things in the natural world related to survival. Our peripheral vision and central (or 'foveal') vision have overlapping but distinct purposes in this regard, both having evolved significantly in the arboreal environment. To survive, our ancestors lived by knowing when to move fast or slowly, what to lunge at and grab, what to avoid and what to embrace.

From our evolution in this world of trees came our tastes for everything visual. We see parts of the electromagnetic spectrum invisible to other animals and delight uniformly across all cultures in decorating ourselves and our world with whatever we can, absent pressures not to do so. Why, then, might we have a predilection for juxtaposing matte and shiny surfaces in certain ways? Though different cultures at different times seem to have had different preferences from our modern proclivities, sufficient evidence has accumulated to convince me that the actual scope of these differences is not as important as the similarities we all share through space and time.

Light is the key. We like the way light reflects off or refracts through some materials better than others. Is this, too, an artifact of our arboreal past? Anyone who has spent much time in tree settings, above the ground or on it, with all the trees gloriously in leaf under a bright sun and particularly in the presence of wind, knows how rewarding the sensations can be, most of all visually. What characterizes such environments is movement. The trees are living things, never truly still. The slightest wind animates the leaves and smaller branches, which twitch and reflect light to catch our eyes, and for sound evolutionary reasons, since such motion might indicate the presence of a predator, a competitor, an ally, a mate, offspring or the beginning of a change in the weather—all important to our survival.

The motorcycle in motion thus can be conceived of, once again, as a limb of that rare African moto-tree, capable of its own movement, creating its own wind and its ever-changing world. The motion itself is rewarding visually and can become art because we are in a state of high arousal. Likewise, because we adorn the machine we are riding in certain ways, even when the surrounding terrain palls, the light dancing off the motorcycle's components can be a stimulant of considerable reward, not least since it changes continually. There is a strangely fascinating effect just in how a highly-polished fuel tank reflects the world as one rides. Most of the long-haul touring riders I know report that they never get as bored crossing the prairies or plains on a motorcycle as they do in cars or other closed vehicles. This is due largely to the continuous vigilance needed to keep the bike doing what one wants it to do, even when the bike has a modern cruise-control throttle and comfortable seating behind a full fairing. However, almost as important, I think, is the continuously fascinating art show that unfolds as one rides, in a connection to the rider that is much more direct than one experiences in a closed vehicle.

From this perspective, the importance of the mototypes includes their relatively different visual environment. It is difficult for a non-rider to grasp how different the world looks from the different riding positions that characterize the touring bike, the dual-sport, the sport-bike and the cruiser. There are many obvious similarities among bikes that position their riders within a few inches or degrees of each other, and any given motorcycle can be modified to suit any rider. But the archetypal cockpits and riding positions, and the bodywork that goes with them (or, in the case of 'naked' bikes and cruisers, doesn't go with them), change the environment-theater for the rider dramatically.

For the terminally practical-minded, this emphasis on the visual stimuli that amount to art in the motorcycling context might seem overwrought. It is not. Research continues to show how the origins of most of the technology that took us from one stage of life to another, through the last million or so years, emerged from purely decorative or aesthetic purposes. A pioneer in the study of such techno-origins was Cyril Stanley Smith (1903-1992), a famed metallurgist who turned his attentions to the ways in which technology, history and art intersected. In 1970, he wrote an essay called "On Art, Invention, and Technology" that summarized key aspects of his pioneering research in using metallurgy to understand history and thus human behavior. A practical scientist himself, he understood well the disinclination of practical people to believe that anything other than economic or other necessity was "the mother of invention."

"Necessity," he writes, "is *not* the mother of invention—only of improvement. A man desperately in search of a weapon or food is in no mood for discovery; he can only exploit what is already known to exist. Discovery requires aesthetically motivated curiosity, not logic, for new things can acquire validity only by interaction in an environment that has yet to be." [55] In so boldly contravening conventional wisdom, Smith knew whereof he spoke: he investigated the past not only through the documentary evidence of the historian but also through the 'microstructures' of archaeological artifacts and art objects, which, he said, "instantly reveal to a knowing eye the technical history of making the object."[56] This amounts to what we would today call forensic archaeology: "[T]hrough such records, I have communicated," Smith writes, "with dozens of craftsmen, including a Luristan smith of 800 B.C., a bronze founder of Shang China, an ancient

[55] Cyril Stanley Smith, "On Art, Invention and Technology," in *A Search for Structure: Selected Essays on Science, Art and History* (Cambridge, Mass.: 1970, reprint 1981), p. 325.

[56] Ibid., p. 328.

Greek goldsmith, and a thirteenth-century Japanese sword-smith, and I have understood them better than I understand some of my English-speaking colleagues today!"[57]

In the context of understanding the centrality of aesthetics to the whole human experience of any technology, modern or ancient, motorcycle or megalith, Smith's iteration of the techniques created for aesthetic purposes should be cited in full:

> Practical metallurgy is seen to have begun with the making of necklace beads and ornaments in hammered native copper long before 'useful' knives and weapons were made. The improvement of metals by alloying and heat treatment and most methods of shaping them started in jewelry and sculpture. Casting in complicated molds began in making statuettes. Welding was first used to join parts of bronze sculpture together; none but the smallest bronze statues of Greece or the ceremonial vessels of Shang China would exist without it, and neither would most of today's structures or machines. Ceramics began with the fire-hardening of fertility figures molded of clay; glass came from attempts to prettily glaze beads of quartz and steatite. Most minerals and many organic and inorganic compounds were discovered for use as pigments; indeed, the first record that man knew of iron and manganese ores is in cave paintings where they make the glorious reds,

---

[57] Ibid.

browns, and blacks, while the medieval painter controllably used pH-sensitive color changes long before the chemist saw their significance. In other fields, archaeologists have shown that the transplanting and cultivation of flowers for enjoyment long preceded useful agriculture, while playing with pets probably gave the knowledge that was needed for animal husbandry. To go back even earlier, it is hardly possible that human beings could have decided logically that they needed to develop language to communicate with each other before they had experienced pleasurable interactive communal activities like singing and dancing. Aesthetic curiosity has been central to both genetic and cultural evolution.[58]

It is easy to gloss over the phrase "aesthetic curiosity" without thinking in depth about what it might mean. But it is not only vital to understanding what Dr. Smith intended, it is also essential in the context of understanding what people who create with their motorcycles experience as art. The key word is *experience*, since the artist literally makes something new, as noted above, each time he or she creates it with a ride or a process. Historians of technology categorize a lot of what I conclude is artistic/aesthetic activity as 'making and fixing,' which is what someone watching a welder or a bead maker at work would presumably see. The welder who fabricates structures for himself or herself is easily understood as an artist, while the one who welds to repair for profit is per-

---

[58] Ibid., pp. 328-329.

ceived as a worker or craftsman. These distinctions center on the economic purpose of the work, but they do not recognize that the psychobiological payback for the welder may be identical in each situation. Nevertheless, for the motorcyclist who works on his or her bike or who modifies it to suit personal taste, the actual 'work' itself involves utter concentration, coordination and movements (albeit sometimes tiny) that are themselves aesthetic for the worker.

Smith himself explicitly recognized this: "Personally," he writes, "I believe that the life of a craftsman, indeed of any man making something to be enjoyed or used, is a fine example of what it is to be human: mind, eye, muscle, and hand interacting with the properties of matter to produce shapes reflecting the purposes and cultural values of his society, and sometimes extending them." [59]

The motorcycle can thus be seen as a uniquely aesthetic object. Because of its size and configuration, it encourages (or at least, does not discourage) the sort of fiddling and tinkering that automobiles no longer do, and thereby invites involvement. Motorcycle dealers have always rued this attractiveness of the machines they sell and service, for whenever a clueless but adventurous customer is afflicted with, as the British used to say, "an attack of spanners [wrenches]," the resulting basket-full of bits must be reassembled by someone who knows what the customer did not. But in an automotive world decreasingly suited to amateur mechanical fiddling, due to the interlocking effects of manufacturers protecting themselves against liability lawsuits by customer-proofing their products in the user-serviceability sense, by government establishing

[59] Ibid., p. 326.

consumer-protection rules that have the same effect, and from their increasing reliance on highly complex electronics systems in sealed boxes, the open-ness of motorcycles to spanner-attack makes them increasingly important.

The core experience in the garage or shop is tool use, ostensibly for problem-solving. But most hobbyist-mechanics will admit that a problem to solve is an excuse to buy, make and use tools. It is the *use* that makes the sometimes frustrating, often complicated process of 'making and fixing' so rewarding in such a subtly aesthetic way. Kinesthesia is crucial because repair, restoration and every other operation involved with machines is literally 'hands-on.'[60]

Given the way our 'bodymind' operates, we shouldn't be too surprised by the artistic side of spinning wrenches, but we are culturally conditioned to perceive what happens in our own workshops as something other than art. To understand how all our machines of automobility have come to be so central to our culture, though, we must note that the making-and-fixing experience may be as close to the kind of creative expression routinely assigned to studio artists as millions of people will ever come. Likewise, just going for a ride of any kind is aesthetically rewarding for those who themselves might believe they have no artistic capacity whatsoever.

For the more explicitly artistic, the motorcycle has obviously been both challenging and highly satisfying to decorate. For individuation, motorcyclists have always sought to personalize their machines. The results are not only visual and aural but also kinesthetic, as customizers tailor the

---

[60] Sociologist Douglas Harper deftly and thoroughly explores this world in his book, *Working Knowledge: Skill and Community in a Small Shop* (Univ. of Calif. Press: Berkeley and Los Angeles, 1992).

machine to suit preferred handling qualities. Just as clothing fashion is much more than how it looks—think of the crucial quality the garment trade calls the 'hand' or feel of fabric—moto-fashion (art by another name, ostensibly for a different purpose) includes sharply differing feel for the rider, to generate different aesthetic-emotional states.

This is nowhere more clear than in tuning the exhaust system. Though to some ears all motorcycles sound alike, most people can tell that they are not. To the motorcyclist, the rumble of a big cruiser's V-twin is as different, aesthetically and culturally, from the frantic wail of a four-cylinder sport-bike as a bass drum's beat is from a trumpet's call. Aesthetically, the obvious consequence is that people like some motor-music and not others.

All music depends ultimately on rhythm, so it is no surprise that the internal-combustion engine's rhythms can and do create sympathetic responses in some people. What is surprising is how many find the sounds of engines to be music. As with so much in the motorcycling world, the roots of this behavior must be experienced first-hand for real comprehension. The unmuffled Harley-Davidson that passes on the street might sound like mere noise to some, but to the person riding the sound is sweet. There are obviously cultural overlays to the choice of which sounds one chooses to be immersed in or surrounded by, but I am convinced that the affinities on such evident display with loud exhaust pipes derive primarily from riders' pre-cognitive responses.

The interaction between exhaust-pipe music and all the other aspects of the ride were made clear to me long ago when a tuner told me that one of his customers had a problem with his BMW's vibration. In explaining how he dealt with the problem, the tuner said that in riding the customer's bike he noted that the stock exhaust pipe was still in place. The engine note was thus so quiet—the bike being a BMW K100RS—that the rider noticed the tingle generated by the four-cylinder engine (a stressed member of the frame) more than he might otherwise. The tuner replaced the exhaust pipe with a slightly louder one and the rider was convinced the tuner had worked some kind of magic on the engine-frame interface, since he said no longer felt any vibration at all.

What must be kept in mind about a bike's exhaust note is that it, too, is mediated by discrete rider actions. He creates what is to him an aesthetically pleasing composition with every movement of the throttle twist-grip. Everyone has encountered the situation of being stuck at a traffic light behind or near a motorcyclist who cannot seem to stop revving the engine. This was more common in the bad old days because the high-performance tweaks so commonly used by so many riders resulted in engines that would die if not revved while stopped. These days it is more clearly a cultural behavior. Even so, it is important to remember that the rider is not only influencing his arousal state but also, possibly, savoring the sound of his wind instrument.

It is useful to think about the ubiquity of the human urge to drum in this context. Our musical heritage, which of course includes drums, is itself rooted in evolutionary biology. Linguist-musicologist Jean Molino makes this point in his essay, "Toward an Evolutionary Theory of Music and Language" in the book, *The Origins of Music*. Citing Igor Stravinsky's famous line—"I consider music, by its nature, to be incapable of *expressing* anything"—as the problem of what music signifies, Molino writes: "I believe that to have a less artificial and less inexact idea of musical signification, one must abandon 'great' music and instead turn to contemporary and primitive forms of dance music, from ritual to disco. The issue is not about representational semantics but about what I call 'rhythmo-affective semantics,' which involves the body, its movements and the fundamental emotions that are associated with them. This point seems to be essential: our conception of music, based on 'great' European classical music, distances ourselves irremediably from the anthropological foundations of human music in general."[61]

Molino's point is fundamentally simple and highly relevant to the question of what moto-music might signify. Though the actual instruments that make the music—the engine and exhaust pipes—are quite sophisticated and the sounds thereby emitted likewise complex, the human response is likely to be primitive, just as our response to music to which we can dance is primitive: we want to get up and dance, not sit and watch others do it. Moto-music similarly encourages participation, at least for the rider who, recall, is controlling it continuously as surely as if he or she were fingering a keyboard or a flute.

The aggregated aesthetic responses of the human to the mechanical on and with motorcycles are undeniably powerful stimuli in their own right. It's no exaggeration to say that the motorcycle *is* the art, or that it makes possible the art that so many find so entrancing, rewarding, and continuously

---

[61] Jean Molino, "Toward an Evolutionary Theory of Music and Language," in *The Origins of Music*, Eds. Nils L. Wallin et al. (MIT Press: Cambridge, Mass., 2001), p. 170.

stimulating. The motorcycle as art, in that sense, shows us the universal parts of our human-ness, since the call of the wild exhaust pipe seems to know no cultural or social boundaries. With motorcycles, as with so much else, people may not know why, but they do know *what* they like—and it is art, by any other name.

CHAPTER SEVEN

YESTERDAY'S RIDE TOMORROW—AND BEYOND

Motorcycles have changed significantly since the dawn of the 20th century, but fundamentally they remain little more than bicycles with engines in place of pedals. What this might mean about motorcycles' roles in society as society changes in the future is an open question. I believe that, like the bicycle, the motorcycle format has embedded itself into our lives so firmly that it embodies something like the mathematical expression 'necessary and sufficient,' albeit for purposes more psychobiological than transportational. Some motorcyclists, however, see such stability as stagnation. These riders crave the development of daring technologies to make the motorcycle safer, easier to ride under bad road or weather conditions and somehow—as they see the situation—less socially divisive. They want a motorcycle that a 17-year-old could not crash in a fit of absentmindedness and annoy old ladies in Oldsmobiles, as I did in 1965. [62]

Such vehicles have been invented periodically in one form or another, but motorcyclists around the world have continued to stay away from them in droves. The question is, yet again: Why? Why hasn't the mototype template been substantially altered by technology?

Some believe that today's relative design stasis results from innovation deliberately restrained by commercial interests. They think that the history of innovation in all forms of motorcycling has convinced the manufacturers or would-be manufacturers that there is no point in seeking breakthroughs, since they won't sell. This view is based on a sour assessment on the part of motorcyclists themselves, whose biases are the ultimate inhibitor of progress: satisfied with what is, too many motorcyclists are not interested in what might or 'should' be.

---

[62] The Piaggio MP3 three-wheeled scooter, in its 250cc, 400cc, and 500cc forms, is reputed to be just such a 'motorcycle' – though of course, because it has three wheels and the engine in the 'wrong' place, for many motorcyclists wedded to the current archetypes, it must remain an oddity. Time will tell if this view long prevails once the added grip and stability the Piaggio platform confers is fully understood.

What lies behind this assessment is of course related entirely to the concept of what a motorcycle is 'for.' In places where people depend on motorcycles—usually small bikes, mopeds, and scooters—as primary transportation, the question of what powered two-wheelers are 'for' is obvious. However, in the United States and other more industrially developed nations, most motorcycles are used for pleasure. That makes them what amounts to stimulus-delivery devices, potentially useful for transportation, but actually used primarily for fun of the kinds explored in this book. Were that situation to change, were the motorcycle to become as important a transportation tool in the First World as it is in the Third, its mototype molds would, I think, quickly be changed, and the frustrated techno-progressives would equally quickly find a wide-open market. Until then, however, especially in the United States, the contours of the motorcycling terrain are determined by three interlocking markets: new bikes, used bikes, and classic bikes.

It would be easy to think that the three categories of machines are defined primarily by purchase cost, but that typically economic view misses the true difference between them, in the stimulus-delivery sense. Though today's motorcycles still follow the same layout as the first mass-market machines, in terms of the experience delivered by the bikes in each market category, the differences for the rider-operator are significant. Machines from these three categories—which of course have constantly shifting boundaries—demand entirely different skills and interactions from their rider-owners. Thus, motorcyclists who grow bored with one form can always find another; this satisfies the thirst for novelty, while delivering the essence of two-wheeled motion.

The category we now call classic bikes demonstrates the power of yesterday's bikes today. While some collectors have always sought yesterday's machines for fun or profit, widespread interest in classic bikes did not occur until the 1960s. As with all social or cultural developments, there are differing opinions about what caused—and is still causing—the boom in old, 'classic' and 'vintage' bikes. Some believe that it is a mixture of nostalgia for a fondly remembered past that never was, fueled by widespread increases in disposable income. Others say it is just the standard human interest in antiques and collectibles transferred from the clock shop to the bike shop.

Both probably capture important elements of the reasons for interest in old bikes. But something is missing in those explanations: they do not emphasize the experiences provided by the older machines, focusing instead on the machines as symbols. Underestimating the radical differences in the experience provided by previous-eras' motorcycles (and cars, boats, airplanes and all other 'auto-mobiles') is a serious mistake, for the old bikes were in many cases uniquely quirky in every way. For example, until the United States Federal Motor Vehicle Safety Standard Act mandated that all motorcycles sold new in America for Model Year 1975 and afterward be equipped with standard controls for the primary systems—throttle, clutch, brakes, lights, horn—many manufacturers followed their own beliefs in designing how the rider controlled the bike. Hand-shifting once was commonplace, but nobody could agree, seemingly, on where the shifter should be located, what the shift pattern should be or how the clutch-shifter interaction should work. Similarly, since the beginning of motorcycling, throttle control has been assigned to various devices, including left-hand twist-grips or levers on the handlebars. Likewise, the long-lived practice of making motorcycles with foot-shifted transmissions that required the rider to use the right foot to shift and the left to work the rear-brake pedal was ended only by the FMVSS edict.

Motorcycles from the pre-FVMSS era thereby provide a rich array of experiences and stimuli that any rider today can explore. A good case in point is the renewed interest in two-stroke street bikes. New two-strokes, such as the Yamaha that I was riding when I encountered the lady in the Oldsmobile, have been outlawed effectively by exhaust-emission and noise regulations in the United States. Yet millions have been produced, because they were cheap to build and easy for neophytes to understand and work on, whether as motor-scooter, moped or motorcycle engines. Many historically important motorcycles have been two-strokes, many of them Japanese (Suzuki, Kawasaki, and Yamaha, for example, established themselves as immensely important manufacturers almost exclusively with two-stroke motorcycles). Such Japanese bikes as the Yamaha RD and RZ-series twins, the Kawasaki Triples (the H1 and H2, 500cc and 750cc, respectively), the Suzuki 250cc X6, 750cc Water Buffalo and Gamma are often restored and collected. The iconic BSA 'Bantam' was a copy of the German DKW RT 125. French, Spanish and Italian scooters, particularly the Vespa, were and still are enormously culturally important, and have created their own aficionados, who seek out and savor the rides those machines provide.

For a rider today, real novelty in stimulus-package can be had with almost any older bike. Because of the cycles of engine and chassis development since the advent of motorcycling in volume-produced vehicles (effectively, since around 1910), an inventory of widely differing experiences exists in the form of bikes that have survived, have been restored and can be ridden. More and more such machines emerge daily from long storage, where many lay for decades in dust-gathering neglect. Still more emerge from parts bins, assembled as 'Bitsas.'

The consequences of this continuing worldwide interest in old and classic bikes include important commercial and social changes to the moto-world. Not only are more old bikes coming out of storage to be restored and used, but the moto-lore that goes with the bikes has influenced designers and manufacturers to create a continuing series of so-called Retro machines. Some believe the trend began with the late-'80s revival of Harley-Davidson, which, through the 1990s, sold many machines on the benefits of the less-explicitly 'techno' look and feel of the big V-twins. In this analysis, Harley's success suggested to the other manufacturers that the way to go forward in sales was to evoke the past. In fact, the mototypes developed for differing market segments offer riding experiences as different as their styling. Really successful Retro machines replicate as much of the feel of the 'original' experiences as their manufacturers can engineer into them, using contemporary technology to satisfy modern safety and environmental requirements. Thus the search for sales of new bikes has indeed taken the manufacturers back to the future, as it were, while they continue to explore what can be done with leading-edge technologies for other market segments. The implications for the future of motorcycling of this continuing interest in older machines are unclear, just as the extent to which the classic-bike market will continue to be robust is unclear.

Does this robustness, and the continuing importance of the mototypes explored earlier mean that that motorcycling is at a technological dead end? Though it might seem that the best answer for this question would be found in defining the limits of the technologies that make motorcycles possible, I think the answer lies in understanding motorcycling as a part of automobility in the largest sense. Automobility itself is usually considered by those who concentrate on such matters as a mature system comprised of many sub-systems, much as railroading was mature at almost exactly the moment automobility burst on the scene. The famous S-shaped curve of invention, innovation, exponential growth and finally, asymptotic leveling-off, applied so often by historians of technology to the analysis of any discrete technology, can be and has been applied to automobility. But, however seductive the notion of capturing human behavior with such schemas may be, we have only been 'auto-mobile' as a species for little more than a century and unevenly at that. Nothing makes the immaturity of automobility more clear than the situation of motorcycle and automobile use in China.

In China, the history of mass motorization is even briefer than in the West, and has involved fascinating differences from the Western experience due to the unique features of Chinese society and culture. Despite the recent liberalization of the Chinese economy, for example, Chinese politics remains a top-down affair in most situations involving national policies. Thus the questions relating to how automobility would be introduced, encouraged and actually developed throughout the nation were and still are directed by members of the ruling communist elite. It was decided in the early postwar period—when the so-called New China was established following Chiang-Kai Shek's defeat and expulsion from the mainland by Mao Zedong's forces— that bicycles would be replaced not by cars but by motorcycles, and only gradually, in Five-Year Plans. The chaos of the Cultural Revolution disrupted those plans as much as everything else in Chinese life, but by the 1980s motorcycles were being built through-out China. However, by the late 1990s, motorcycles stopped being the solution to mass automobility for urban Chinese and became the problem that cars are in the West. Even ear-lier, in 1984, controls on motorcycles use were instituted in Beijing. In January 2002, the city of Nanning in southeastern China halted new motorcycle sales and registrations, citing congestion, pollution and crime related to motorcycle use.

Among much that is intriguing about the Chinese moto-story as it is unfolding are reports that motorcycle use and ownership became recreational and status-linked (at least for those who have benefited enough from economic liberaliza-tion). Clearly the Politburo did not count on the fun factor's power to change culture, even Chinese culture. As the 21st century unfolds, we are seeing what this means, too, in how the Chinese are buying and building cars in huge numbers, as well as motorcycles. Do they 'need' them? Of course: the way to measure a need is to watch how it sells, and automobility in China, as this is written, is selling very well indeed.

As the Chinese experiences remind us, automobility cannot be understood without putting it in the context of what historians sometimes call "big-H History." That kind of history isn't the history of a nation, a state, a company or an intellectual trend; it's the whole world's history, so far as it can be known. Motorcycling, however central to those who make it the center of their commercial or recreational lives, has been only a facet of that big-H History, embedded in the intersections of what modern historians usually characterize as chaos, contingency and context. This view of how history works emphasizes that any particular outcome of human interactions in love, war or commerce is unique to the situation: no overarching theories are likely to describe what happened at any time or place, let alone why.

This viewpoint clearly attracts many historians and other intellectuals. But it omits the power of our evolutionary inheritance, which, as shown previously, includes a profound preference for fun whenever possible. The significance of the fun factor in the context of what motorcycles of tomorrow will be like does not mean 'more of the same,' for two important reasons. First, the larger socio-cultural realities frame what is possible for any technology, and nobody knows what those will be for tomorrow, in the United States, in China, or anyplace else. Second, the same search for novelty that drives the used-bike and classic-bike markets as powerfully as any other factors will ultimately result in wholly new or even 'revisited' mototypes. Three-wheeled motorcycles, for example, have never been as successful in the United States as in Europe, for reasons usually ascribed to economics, which enabled American 'utility' motorcyclists to transition quickly to cars early in the 20th century, while Europeans more typically moved first to sidecars and only much later to cars. In the United States, the 'trike' format, which places a solo wheel up front, coupled with a side-by-side, car-like rear end, has been much more popular than the traditional solo-'chair' combination. Three-wheeled designs of other kinds have never entirely disappeared, even in the aftermath of the regulatory transformation of all road-going machines, as inventors and investors have sought to convince people to give up their cars for the delights of trikes and cyclecars of all kinds. So far, these attempts have been mostly in vain. But new three-wheeled machines, from serious manufacturers suggest that the century-long lock on riders' imaginations that the tandem two-wheeler has had might be loosening.

It is always tempting to use perceptions of the past to guide predictions of the future, but if the past century of motorcycling has shown us anything, it is that, whenever they are given a chance, some sensation-seekers will put their bodies in motion on motorcycles any way they can, while others will do it only because they have no reasonable alternative. In other words, though economics does limit what is possible for people, regardless of what kind of powerplants they might have in the future—electric, fuel-cell, internal-combustion—a substantial portion of humanity will always seek to merge fun and transportation on motorcycles, and *motorcycle* itself might well become a term expanded to include entirely novel configurations. I know at least one lifetime motorcyclist who will welcome the day that happens—and I am surely not alone.

CHAPTER EIGHT

Evolution and the Automotive Transformation

Our use of machines that make automobility possible clearly affects us individually and collectively. If it is safe to say we are more or less hard-wired to enjoy automobility, it is also safe to say that we seem to have done a rather poor job of integrating automobility into our societies without paying a huge price for it.

Nobody alive today created the systems at the heart of how automobility currently functions. From the nature of our roads to the means by which our governments seek to regulate our use of the machines made for the roads, the systems architecture was conceived and built by our forebears. People living today have tinkered with it but have not changed it fundamentally.

As noted in the Introduction, Americans have inherited a nation-state built on the idea and the ideal of self-government, according to notions of such governance held by men who were mostly progeny of the Enlightenment. Our nation's founders generally held that rational discourse and what we today call 'science' could lead to a better life by helping an educated people find and use truths and disregard falsehoods about pretty much anything. A key use of such truths would be to embrace those that applied to self-government.

Alas, history is not a tale of rational discourse and truth-finding, let alone truth-using. Indeed, among some contemporary intellectuals, the idea of truth itself is in disrepute; many allege that truth is another cultural construct. Many of today's influential thinkers consider the truths of the United States' founders to have been merely convenient ways for them to understand their world. These ideas about the relativity of truth are ancient, but are found in their most currently relevant form in the beliefs of Karl Marx. Marx sought and thought he'd found a way to understand how and why humans work, literally and figuratively, in societies and cultures. He believed that we are all born into cultures that shape us, willy-nilly, apart from a few universal appetites, drives and fears. Thus, to Marx and those whom he influenced, the idea that people are born as more or less blank slates upon which almost any beliefs or behaviors can be written was and still is literally a liberating concept.

Marxism's tenets have been experimented with on various scales in various places around the world since the mid-19ᵗʰ century. The casualty lists created by those who shackled Marx's thought to their political agendas have run to the hundreds of millions. Despite the attempts by Marx's followers and apologists to claim as many or more millions as victims of their own most-hated '-isms,' it's difficult not to conclude that the attempt to use the belief that human nature is essentially a cultural construct has been history's most catastrophic exercise. Human nature, as the sciences continue to reveal, is indeed somewhat flexible, but not nearly as elastic as Marx's diehard followers believe.

The matter of what constitutes human nature is essential to the question of how effective our social and cultural constructs have been in dealing with automobility. Anyone who delves seriously into those constructs might be surprised by the assumptions about human nature on wheels made by their creators. For a 1995 study, I researched the social and legal causes and effects of one aspect of the mechanisms developed to cope with automobility—driver's licensing—and found myself sympathizing with the late 19ᵗʰ and early 20ᵗʰ century lawyers in various jurisdictions around the country as they tried to cope with cars and their drivers. Just how profoundly the machines changed everything is captured somewhat by quotes from then-Secretary of Commerce Herbert Hoover's 1924 speech in Washington, D.C., opening the first national convention seeking to synchronize the nation's widely-differing laws relating to motor vehicles of all kinds:

> The automobile is no longer a luxury—it is a complete necessity.... It is here to stay, and to stay in constantly increasing numbers. If it has brought about the present traffic conditions so quickly that we have been unable to cope with it, if our roads and streets were laid out for other purposes and are inadequate to the situation, then it is fitting and proper that the public officials, the transportation interests, the business interests, the motorists, and those engaged in the business of alleviating suffering should gather together to assist in straightening out the tangle...we must find constructive measures to meet the crisis of tens of thousands of deaths annually, with hundreds of thousands of serious personal injuries...There is but cold comfort in the statement that it has crept upon us almost unawares and that our traffic lanes are inadequate. True it is that the dreams of the inventors of the automobile have been realized in a fashion that would take the pen of Jules Verne to portray. True, the advance of the industry is almost incredible. True it is that there are almost 12,000,000 active cars probably transporting more people daily than all our railways. True it is that but few people can visualize the staggering sum of two billions of dollars spent each year for passenger cars alone. True it is that

all this has come about within the short space of 25 years and even more largely in 10 years.

But all these truths do not alter the fact that with all this admirable development...we are facing a crisis in our city streets and rural highway traffic that must be met at once, and must be met in such a manner as to leave in no uncertainty the permanent result of such corrective measures as we can suggest.[63]

How much has the situation changed since 1924? The roads are better, the vehicles are better and the drivers...well, what about the drivers? Apparently, we—today's drivers and riders—are still human beings who continue to act in ways that make automobility dangerous. Despite all the advances, the death toll on our roads continues to hover around 40,000 killed annually. The obvious question—yet again—is: "Why?"

I believe the answers lie in how human nature is influenced by and responds to our machines and 'systems' of automobility. People have long known that machines 'did things' to those who used them. By 1950, when Walt Disney's cartoon "Motor Mania" was released, the ways in which people were changed by driving were catalogued by the character Goofy. He was mild-mannered and courteous as Mr. Walker but when he became Mr. Wheeler he was aggressive and dangerous to himself and others. 'Everybody' knew this...but nobody had a panacea for the bad that automobility brought with the good.

[63] Herbert Hoover, "Opening Address," in *First National Conference on Street and Highway Safety* (U.S. Dept. of Commerce: Washington D.C., 1924) pp. 7-8.

The initial legal response to the challenges of adopting automobiles was registration and licensing, first to know who did what to whom (without an identifying tag on a vehicle, how could anyone know which vehicle did what at which location and time?), then to control, via driver's licensing, who had access to automobility as an 'operator' of the machine. Additionally, regulation of road behavior by enforcement of traffic laws was supposed to rein-in the worst tendencies of those who had been duly licensed to drive or ride. The system can be said to have worked, in the sense that utter chaos has not since ruled American roads. But all the legal apparatus brought to bear on managing automobility was based on 19th-century assumptions about human nature, the primary assumption being what used to be called the 'reasonable man.' This imaginary person constituted the common denominator of behavioral modeling for the lawyers who erected the socio-legal architecture that was supposed to control automobility. A reasonable man would do *this* and not do *that*, the thinking went. Road-going automotive devices were understood in such thinking as no different from a buggy or a horse-and-rider combination.

Was that kind of thinking justified? Certainly, from the standpoint of those who were on duty at the time. For just as they assumed much about how cars and their drivers could be regulated properly, they assumed that automobility was merely another transportation mode—an assumption still in place today. It takes a conscious effort to defeat a form of 'instinct blindness' to see it otherwise, but what does it look like if we do that?

As Hoover's speech makes clear, automobility spread more like a disease than a mere transportation system. This is because it 'infected' individuals, whose individual actions, aggregated, changed them and the world—and continue to do so. As this is written, China and India are experiencing astounding growth in personal transportation choices, as people in those countries buy and use cars, trucks, and motorcycles in unprecedented numbers. Serious manufacturers talk about further expanding the use of cars in India and China by building astonishingly cheap cars, making automobility affordable to more and more millions. Because of the near chaos reigning on roads throughout India and mainland Asia in major metropolitan areas, it is a safe bet that fatalities will climb as fast as automobile use.

It is because of automobility's historically unprecedented effects on individuals and societies that I proposed, in my 1995 study of driver's licensing, that the advent of powered, personal transportation was actually as socially and culturally transformational as upheavals such as the Protestant Reformation, whose effects continue to ripple through our lives today and will far into the future. The 'Automotive Transformation' can be understood as a much more profound influence on humanity than merely the substitution of horse-drawn wagons with motor vehicles. Because of its toll specifically in human life, it has been a literal change in the physical environment of the world, as important as the much-feared global warming (or, previously, cooling) forecast by environmentalists. Indeed, they specifically indict the automobile in their analyses, and in so doing, edge up to recognizing the potential power of the Automotive Transformation as a force for other kinds of change.

That power lies in how it might be operating as an evolutionary force, as surely as a worldwide disease epidemic. It is no secret that the demographic groups most vulnerable to death or maiming from automobile use are the young and the old, but primarily the young. Automobile crashes are the number one killers of young people in America, and have been for a long time. Year after year throughout the postwar period, car-related deaths have been changing the way genes are distributed throughout the American population. If we grant that Dawkins' idea of memetic, or cultural evolution is a real possibility, would it not likewise be wise to consider the possibility that automobility itself is acting upon our population as an evolutionary force?

Long before the Scopes Monkey Trial in 1925, Charles Darwin's ideas about natural selection and speciation were hijacked by people with all kinds of agendas, often related to 'purifying' or 'improving' humanity through what amounted to eugenics. Biological evolution itself is so widely misunderstood that the word *evolution* has come to signify much more—and much less—than it does in biological science. Nevertheless, if we accept the hypothesis that automobility has been acting as a lethal as well as a benign environmental pressure, in the process becoming a new Environment of Evolutionary Adaptedness, selecting the young who can overcome its lethality and thus reproduce, we find ourselves confronted with the need to rethink what is actually happening on our highways, and why. In so doing, especially in the context of motorcycles, some startling hypotheses about motorcycling are entirely reasonable.

For example, because road-riding motorcyclists routinely must encounter and survive the most dangerous conditions in automobility, any who do so and reproduce are passing on potentially heritable traits that can better fit at least some of their progeny to an automotive environment. Medical staff in emergency rooms around the nation often joke that a dead-on-arrival motorcyclist is actually a 'donor cyclist,' and wags are wont to term riders who kill themselves in stupid stunts as Darwin Award winners. There might well be something important behind such observations, because by the ruthless logic of real-life dangers, those young people who are drawn to motorcycling by its cultural display but who can't master its physical demands are indeed de-selecting themselves from the reproductive process (at least if they haven't reproduced before death).

As noted earlier, I believe we are too close to the beginning of the Automotive Transformation fully to comprehend its breadth and depth, so in the event that biological evolution is under way because of automobility, nobody can know for certain what, if any, its effects are. Even so, the successful motorcyclist's model is instructive, because it suggests that, rather than being marginal to automobility, motorcycling might well be central to it, in terms of potentially desirable traits. The motorcyclist who exposes himself or herself frequently to dense traffic and who flourishes in that environment is one who has a very high situational awareness, a quick perception of potentially lethal developments, and an array of skills to deal successfully with them when the worst case does occur. It is not exaggerating to say that the motorcyclist is, in this sense, like a hunter in our past, when the species' survival depended on hunting and gathering to survive. The hunter must notice everything, project possible outcomes of every action or reaction very quickly, and remain on high system arousal at all times. Hunters have always been potential prey as well as predators, of course, but any who reproduced their genetically heritable traits made possible the continuation of the species in the long prehistoric period in which anatomically modern humans were hunter-gatherers.

However, there is also an entirely different and equally reasonable way to interpret motorcycling in the current automotive context. Speculating about a bio-social selection process in an automotive environment now dominated by cars and trucks which have been continuously refined to provide as much passive safety and isolation from the outside environment as possible, it is also reasonable to wonder if the motorcyclist in an EEA defined by safer and safer cars is less the product of post-Industrial evolutionary-environment adaptations than the product of decreasingly relevant genetic traits. More and more technological solutions to the problems posed by automobility appear to be minimizing the role of the driver, with onboard and data-linked computers making possible so-called driverless cars much sooner than seemed likely even a decade ago. It is thus possible to foresee a near future in which motorcycles as vehicles will be legislated into extinction because they fit less and less well into computer-controlled traffic mix.[64]

---

[64] The requirement for a human operator to stabilize the motorcycle makes computer-control of the machine unlikely any time soon, and without such hands-off control, a motorcycle cannot be integrated into a truly 'intelligent' vehicle net-

Because of the uncertainties about whether any sort of evolution is happening due to automobility, and if so, what traits, behavioral and otherwise, it might be selecting for, it would be easy to dismiss the notion entirely. Easy, but in my view, wrong. The physical world into which we are born, and in which we must survive, profoundly influences what we do and why in the automotive environment, as it does everywhere else.

Yet as wise men and women remind us, to be human is more than to be a biological machine, and a human body is always in motion, if not externally, then internally, the mind and spirit free even when the body is not.

work. If such on-board autonomous non-human control becomes possible, the situation would change radically—but it is an open question whether a motorcyclist would give up personal control to a computer, even more so than the question of how many car drivers will do so.

CHAPTER NINE

RIDING INTO
THE INEFFABLE

If indeed the many stimuli that comprise a motorcycle ride are the foundation of the affection so many have for riding, and also are the foundation for the cultural consequences of the experience of riding, can they likewise be the neurochemical basis for the spiritual experiences so many have in motion on two wheels? Like emotions, spiritual experiences are well nigh impossible to quantify, though, like emotions, they can be cataloged and described. Given enough time, enough research, and enough commitment, someone, someday will be able to put calipers of some kind on the spirit, and from that will flow scientific understanding.

Until then, we are left with the observation of the phenomenon that, to state it as simply as possible, a physical stimulus can lead, on a motorcycle, to a spiritual response. This would not be news to philosophers, ancient and modern, who have struggled endlessly over all the questions relating to mind and body, *psyche* and spirit, and seemingly have managed to entangle themselves in thickets of argument and counter-argument without useful results—that is, without providing knowledge or wisdom which can be used to improve lives. These days, anyone interested in navigating the thickets need not buy massive tomes; the World Wide Web provides many keyword-searchable sites, where simple phrases such as 'mind-body dualism' will reward the curious with succinct but thoughtful summaries of the beliefs and conclusions of the greatest thinkers in history—or at least those whose thoughts have been recorded and transmitted to us by the gatekeepers of cataloging in all eras and locales.

The latter point is very important, for it reminds us that we each live in times and places with particular sorting mechanisms which operate visibly and invisibly to shape the conceptual worlds in which we function. Social scientists focus their attention on these mechanisms in trying to clarify what historians usually call the *mentalité* of a group of people, or the *Zeitgeist* (literally, "time-spirit") of an era. Ever since Charles Darwin's *On the Origin of Species* changed the way people thought about the most fundamental questions of humanity ("Who am I? What am I? Why am I here? Where did I come from?"), one enduring feature of Western *Zeitgeist* has been the schism between those who believe that mankind is divinely created (or "inspired") and those who believe that the strictly material and unguided processes of biological evolution have resulted in all life, including human beings.

As this is written, in the first decade of the 21st century, the schism has opened wider, and the issues dividing people seem clearly salient to the questions of behavior that lie at the heart of this book. I am persuaded, obviously, that the artifacts of our evolution—specifically, our ancestors' arboreal adaptations, many of which seem to have been preserved throughout our species' history—are the fundamental reasons why some of us are effectively addicted to motorcycling while others are not, and *Bodies in Motion* has attempted briefly to identify the major reasons I've found. However, it is essential to recognize that, for the purposes of the 'bodymind' bases of our behavior on wheels or in any other environment, it does not matter whether human nature is the result of divine inspiration or 'blind' evolution. What matters is that there actually exists a definable and quantifiable realm of human behaviors that, aggregated, constitute human nature, and that, though it is somewhat elastic, in proven contrast to the claims of the Marxists and other diehard cultural constructivists, human-ness has biologically defined qualities that manifest themselves whenever and wherever possible.

Just as cartoonist Gary Larson's cow is designed to eat and like grass, we are designed to like or dislike certain activities based more on our genetic inheritance than on our culture. The social consequences of being thus designed are innumerable, and maybe most important among them is a widespread propensity for attempting to persuade others that their understanding of how and why we are so designed is wrong, but that is an argument which, though clearly involved with the ideas and evidence in this book, is not central to it.

In the context of this study's animating question, though—the "why do some ride?" question and its significant subordinate questions—the key point is that it is simply undeniable that many motorcyclists do find far more than mere enjoyment from their riding, if not always, then at least often enough to differentiate their decision to ride their bikes for certain purposes, and drive their cars for others. So it is with Fr. John Staudenmaier, S.J. who so vividly reminded us in Chapter Two, when he says that motorcycling "helps me to like being small in a large domain. It is one of my favorite ways to make myself present to God." The "large domain" is the universe outside ourselves, and when this Jesuit wants to make himself "present to God," he is speaking for the millions who are not religious, but who feel something powerful, something transcendent, something that connects everyone and everything…and that something, though available to anyone anywhere and any time, is very commonly detected by motorcyclists, often quite unexpectedly on short rides and long, and if not revered as the Christian God, then understood in the depths of the bodymind in ways for which there are neither adequate words nor pictures.

This experience is a common gift of motorcycling, I believe, because our evolution leads us to seek certain physical experiences in which are embedded, like gold veins in rock, spiritual experiences. Does this mean that the experiences awaken some part of the brain, triggering what Richard Dawkins calls "The God Delusion," the triggering being a genetically transmitted predisposition? Maybe, but if so, it has yet to be proven. What is undeniable is that the quantifiable components of a motorcycling experience combine in some people in some way to foster non-quantifiable–'spiritual'–experiences.

If my own experience is any guide, to undergo an unlooked-for and unexpected spiritual soaring while riding can lead one to find similar episodes in other ways, in other places and times. I never felt the fleeting moments of spiritual uplift when riding were religious, and thus never translated them as revelatory. Others of course might do so or not. What is significant is not that different translations and understandings of the spiritual events exist, but that the events themselves irrefutably do exist.

It helps, I think, to understand the motorcycle's role in such spiritual events in the context of big-H History, in order to glimpse, perhaps, some reasons why such events are so startling and precious to those who experience them while motorcycling. In the largest sense, Western culture since the Industrial Revolution of the late 18th and 19th centuries has been profoundly influenced by changes in life due to technological and scientific developments. Largely agrarian before the Industrial Revolution, the populations of the West have become overwhelmingly urban and suburban. This transformation has been exhaustively chronicled and examined by scholars in every affected nation, almost since the transformation began. Few have attempted to understand it in terms of our evolutionary heritage, however, at least until the last three or so decades, the period in which 'evolutionary' became an academically respectable modifier for 'biology.'[65]

When we attempt to survey the differences in daily life and lifetimes for agrarian and post-Industrial Revolution Westerners, using the conceptual lenses of evolutionary biology, what leaps out as we focus them is how increasingly insulated from the natural world people have become. As we have sought to use technology and science to help us live longer and more comfortably, through the relentless and efficient markets typical of consumer-capitalist societies, we have of course lost our daily-life connections with the natural world. Consequently, many attempt to use their income and leisure time to return to nature, traveling far and wide in search of what have come to be called authentic experiences. Millions use automobiles of one type or another to get to the locations where such experiences will, they hope, be available. And many find them, in the majesty of the Grand Canyon, the exhilaration of mountain climbing, the challenges of sailing small ships into great seas, or in lengthy hikes into deliberately preserved wilderness. They are explicitly attempting to reconnect with our past. Just like those who leave good office jobs and take up the hard, endless work of the farmer, the rancher, the commercial fisherman.

Atop a rocky scarp, looking down at the dawn breaking over the clouds far below, a mountain climber cannot help

---

[65] A rare but important exception is Gregory Clark, whose book, *A Farewell to Alms: A Brief Economic History of the World* (Princeton Univ. Press: Princeton, N.J., 2007) broke new ground by proposing that biological evolution might have worked to enable the post-Industrial Revolution West to break the "Malthusian trap" that had kept mankind in economic bondage since the Neolithic revolution in agriculture.

but feel his spirit soar. Just as a sailor far out on the blue water, with all sails set and the beautiful ship leaned hard over, a bone in her teeth, must experience something transcendent when the clouds clear, the sun is setting in red-gold glory, and dolphins dance alongside. The common thread is always the same: We who were born into the wide world need to find it sometimes to find ourselves, and we do it best when our spirits lead the way.

For millions of motorcyclists, putting our bodies in motion on two wheels is the way to liberate our spirits. We need not travel to the ends of the earth, climb mountains, sail seas, abandon one way of life to start another. All we need do is climb aboard our motorcycles and ride, putting ourselves in mortal danger just as our ancient ancestors did simply by living in their arboreal Eden, our destinations always different but always the same: the ride itself and wherever in the real, dangerous, delicious, awe-inspiring, eternally new world it takes us.

Why do we seek this ride? Far better to ask, many of us believe, an entirely different question, one asked continually through the long history of our species by seekers of all sorts, eternally baffling to those who do not share the seekers' compelling need to go, to do, and to discover: not *Why?* but *Why not?*

SELECT BIBLIOGRAPHY

Books

Adams, James L. *Flying Buttresses, Entropy, and O-Rings: The World of an Engineer.* Cambridge: Harvard University Press, 1991.

Brooke, Lindsay and Gaylin, David. *Triumph Motorcycles in America.* Osceola, WI: MBI, 1993.

Brooks, Sammy Kent. *The Motorcycle in American Culture: From Conception to 1935.* Unpublished Ph.D. Dissertation. Washington, D.C.: George Washington University, 1975.

Clark, Gregory. *A Farewell to Alms: A Brief Economic History of the World.* Princeton, N.J.: Princeton Univ. Press, 2007.

Clarke, Massimo. *100 Years of Motorcycles: A Century of History and Development.* New York: Portland House, 1986.

Corn, Joseph J. *The Winged Gospel: America's Romance with Aviation, 1900-1950.* New York: Oxford University Press, 1983.

Dregni, Michael and Dregni, Eric. *Scooters!* Osceola, WI: MBI, 1995.

Dodge, Pryor. *The Bicycle.* New York: Flammarion, 1996.

Fukuyama, Francis. *The End of History and the Last Man.* New York: Avon, 1992.

Gaulin, Steven J. C. and McBurney, Donald H. *Psychology: An Evolutionary Approach.* Upper Saddle River, N.J.: Prentice-Hall, 2001.

Girdler, Allan. *The Harley-Davidson and Indian Wars*. Osceola, WI: MBI, 1997.

Graves, Robert. *Lawrence to His Biographers, Robert Graves and Liddell Hart*. New York: Doubleday, 1963.

Griffin, Michael J. *Handbook of Human Vibration*. San Diego: Academic Press, 1990.

Harper, Douglas. *Working Knowledge: Skill and Community in a Small Shop*. Berkeley: Univ. of California Press, 1992.

Honda Motor Company. *World Motorcycle Facts & Figures, 1998*. Japan: HMC, 1999.

Hughes, Thomas P. *American Genesis: A Century of Invention and Technological Enthusiasm, 1870-1970*. New York: Penguin, 1990.

Hughes, Howard C. *Sensory Exotica: A World Beyond Human Experience*. Cambridge: MIT Press, 1999.

International Road Federation. *World Road Statistics, 1998, 2002*. Geneva: IRF, 1999, 2002.

Joseph, Rhawn. *Neuropsychiatry, Neuropsychology, and Clinical Neuroscience: Emotion, Cognition, Language, Memory, Brain Damage, and Abnormal Behavior* (Second Edition). Baltimore: Williams & Wilkins, 1996.

Maines, Rachel P. *The Technology of Orgasm: Hysteria, the Vibrator, and Women's Sexual Satisfaction*. Baltimore: Johns Hopkins Press, 1999.

Mandel, Leon. *Driven: The American Four-Wheeled Love Affair*. New York: Stein and Day, 1977.

McGowan, Chris. *Diatoms to Dinosaurs: The Size and Scale of Living Things*. Washington, D.C.: Island Press, 1994.

Partridge, Michael. *Motorcycle Pioneers: the Men, the Machines, the Events, 1860-1930*. New York: Arco, 1977.

Pert, Candace B. *Molecules of Emotion: Why You Feel the Way You Feel*. New York: Scribner, 1997.

Pierson, Melissa Holbrook. *The Perfect Vehicle: What It Is About Motorcycles*. New York: Norton, 1997.

Post, Robert C. *High Performance: The Culture and Technology of Drag Racing 1950-2000*. Baltimore: Johns Hopkins, 1994, 2001.

Powell, J. David and Brennan, Richard P. *The Automobile: Technology and Society*. Englewood Cliffs, N.J.: Prentice Hall, 1986.

Pursell, Carroll. *The Machine in America: A Social History of Technology.* Baltimore: Johns Hopkins, 1995.

Riley, Robert Q. *Alternative Cars in the 21ˢᵗ Century: A New Personal Transportation Paradigm.* Warrendale, PA: SAE, 1994.

Scharf, Virginia. *Taking the Wheel: Women and the Coming of the Motor Age.* New York: Free Press, 1991.

Sheets-Johnstone, Maxine. *The Roots of Thinking.* Philadelphia: Temple University Press, 1990.

Smith, Merritt Roe and Marx, Leo. *Does Technology Drive History? The Dilemma of Technological Determinism.* Cambridge: MIT Press, 1998.

Staudenmaier, John M., S.J. *Technology's Storytellers: Reweaving the Human Fabric.* MIT Press: 1989.

Sucher, Harry V. *Inside American Motorcycling and the American Motorcycle Association, 1900-1990.* Laguna Niguel, CA: Infosport, 1995.

Suzuki, Takashi. *The Romance of Engines.* Warrendale, PA: SAE, 1997.

Swallow, Tom. *Flywheel: Memories of the Open Road from Stalag IVB Germany 1944/45.* Exeter: Webb & Bower, 1987.

Temple Press (Staff eds.). *Motor Cycling Manual: A Complete Guide to Motor Cycling* Third Edition (Revised and Enlarged). London: Temple, 1914.

Wallin, Nils; Merker, Björn, and Brown, Steven, eds. *The Origins of Music.* Cambridge: MIT Press, 2001.

Weiss, Mark L. and Mann, Alan E. *Human Biology and Behavior: An Anthropological Perspective.* Glenview, IL.: Scott, Foresman, 1990.

Wilson, Edward O. *On Human Nature.* Cambridge: Harvard Univ. Press, 1978.

Wilson, Frank R. *The Hand: How Its Use Shapes the Brain, Language, and Human Culture.* New York: Vintage, 1998.

Wilson, Hugo. *The Encyclopedia of the Motorcycle.* New York: Dorling Kindersley, 1995.

Wilson, Paul. *Chrome Dreams: Automobile Styling Since 1893.* Radnor, PA: Chilton, 1976.

Zuckerman, Marvin. *Behavioral Expressions and Biosocial Bases of Sensation Seeking.* Cambridge: Cambridge University Press, 1994.

_____. *Sensation Seeking: Beyond the Optimal Level of Arousal.* Hillsdale, N.J.: Lawrence Erlbaum Assoc., 1979.

Journal Articles and Chapters

Aerts, Peter, et. al. "Spatio-Temporal Gait Characteristics of the Hind-Limb Cycles During Voluntary Bipedal and Quadrupedal Walking in Bonobos (*Pan paniscus*)" in *American Journal of Physical Anthropology*, 111:503-517 (2000).

Foley, Robert A. and Elton, Sarah. "Time and Energy: The Ecological Context for the Evolution of Bipedalism" in *Primate Locomotion: Recent Advances* (419-433), Strasser, Elizabeth et al., eds. New York: Plenum, 1998.

Hunt, Kevin D. "Ecological Morphology of *Australopithecus Afarensis*" in *Primate Locomotion: Recent Advances* (397-415).

Hur, Yoon-Mi and Bouchard, Thomas J., Jr. "The Genetic Correlation Between Impulsivity and Sensation Seeking Traits" in *Behavior Genetics*, Vol. 27, No. 5, 1997, 455-462.

Jonah, Brian A. "Sensation Seeking and Risky Driving: A Review and Synthesis of the Literature" in *Accident Analysis and Prevention* Vol. 29, No. 5: pp. 651-665, 1997.

Kerr, J. H. "The experience of arousal: a new basis for studying arousal effects in sport" in *Journal of Sports Science*, 1985 3(3): 169-179.

Kjellberg, A. "Psychological Aspects of Occupational Vibration" in *Scandinavian Journal of Work Environment Health* (1990; 16: 39-43).

Lewkowicz, David J. "The Development of Intersensory Temporal Perception: An Epigenetic Systems/Limitations View" in *Psychological Bulletin* 126 (2), 281-308, 2000.

Lundberg, Thomas C. M. "Vibratory Stimulation for the Alleviation of Chronic Pain" in *Acta Psychologica Scandinavica Supplementum 523*. Stockholm: Karolinska Institutet, 1983.

McCrossin, Monte L., et al. "Fossil Evidence for the Origins of Terrestriality Among Old World Higher Primates" in *Primate Locomotion: Recent Advances* (353-389).

Piazza, Pier Vincenzo et al. "Corticosterone in the range of stress-induced levels possesses reinforcing properties: Implications for sensation-seeking behaviors" in *Proceedings of the National Academy of Science USA* Vol. 90, (Dec. 1993), pp. 11738-11742.

Povinelli, Daniel J,, and Cant, John G. H. "Arboreal Clambering and the Evolution of Self-Conception" in *The Quarterly Review of Biology*, Vol. 70, No. 4 (Dec., 1995), pp. 393-421.

Ruff, Christopher. "Evolution of the Hominid Hip" in *Primate Locomotion: Recent Advances* (449-469).

Smith, Cyril Stanley. "On Art, Invention and Technology" in *A Search for Structure: Selected Essays on Science, Art, and History* (Cambridge, Mass.: MIT Press, 1970, reprint 1981), 325 ff.

Tuttle, Russell H. et al. "Heel, Squat, Stand, Stride: Function and Evolution of Hominoid Feet" in *Primate Locomotion: Recent Advances* (435-448).

Wasserman, Donald E. "Human Occupational and Industrial Vibration" in *The Journal of Environmental Sciences* Vol. 31 (2), March/April 1988, 58-62

Zuckerman, Marvin. "The Psychophysiology of Sensation Seeking" in *Journal of Personality* 58:1 (March, 1990)

_____. "Sensation Seeking, Mania, and Monoamines" in *Neuropsychobiology* 13: 121-128 (1985).

Periodical Articles

Thompson, Steven L. "Racers on the Runway," in *Car and Driver*, April, 1992, pp. 153-162.

_____. "The Long and Winding Road," in *Cycle World*, September, 1987, pp. 40-47.

_____. "Thunder on the Magic Mountain," in *Cycle World,* October, 1988, pp. 53-68.

Online Resources

Cosmides, Leda and Tooby, John. *Evolutionary Psychology: A Primer.* Online: *www.psych.ucsb.edu/research/cep/primer.html* (URL verified 28 February 2008). Center for Evolutionary Psychology, University of California, Santa Barbara, Jan, 13, 1997.

Eldridge, Louis D., and Northrup, Susan E. "Chapter 4: Effects of Acceleration" in *USAF Flight Surgeon's Guide.* *http://wwsam.brooks.af.mil/af/files.fsguide/HTML/Chapter_04.html* (URL verified 8 August 2002; as of 28 February 2008, no longer active).

Foale, Tony. "Camber Thrust." 1985-1997. Online:
http://tonyfoale.com (URL verified 28 February 2008).

International Haplotype Consortium. "A Haplotype Map of the Human
Genome," in *Nature,* Vol. 437, pp. 1299-1320 (27 October 2005), Online:
http://www.nature.com/nature/journal/v437/n7063/full/nature04226.html
(URL verified 28 February 2008).

Kliewer, Gary. "The Mozart Effect" in *New Scientist* 6 November 1999. Online:
http://www.newscientist.com/article/mg16422115.100-the-mozart-effect.html
(URL verified 28 February 2008).

Motorsport Memorial. *http://www.motorsportmemorial.org/*
(URL verified 28 February 2008).

Simmons, Ryan (National Aeronautics and Space Administration).
"Calculating Grms (Root-Mean-Square Acceleration),
1997. Online: *http://femci.gsfc.nasa.gov/random/randomgrms.html*
(URL verified 28 February 2008).

Vance, Bill. "Terraplane," in *CanadianDriver.* Online:
http://www.canadiandriver.com/articles/bv/terraplane.htm.
(URL verified 28 February 2008)

Voshell, Martin. "High Acceleration and the Human Body."
28 November 2004. Online: *csel.eng.ohio-state.edu/voshell/gforce.pdf*
(URL verified 28 February 2008).

Weinberger, N. M. "Lessons of the Music Womb" in *Musica:*
Univ. of California, Irvine: Winter, 1999. Online:
http://www.musica.uci.edu/mrn/V6I1W99.html
(URL verified 28 February 2008).

Wikipedia. "Fast Fourier transform." Online:
http://en.wikipedia.org/wiki/Fast_Fourier_transform.
(URL verified 28 February 2008).

Sound Recordings

Cosby, Bill. "The $75 Car," in *Bill Cosby/Why Is There Air?* Warner Bros.:
New York, 1965, re-released 1998 as audio CD (WB 1606). Originally
recorded live on 28 November 1964 at the Flamingo Hotel, Las Vegas.

ACKNOWLEDGEMENTS

Without the dedicated assistance of others, this book would never have been written, much less published. My wife, Laning Pepper Thompson, had more influence in getting *Bodies in Motion* into print than anyone else. Not only did she give me excellent editorial advice, as a seasoned newspaper writer/book editor, but she worked tirelessly to keep me alive after my near-fatal collision in 2004. Aiding her in the latter effort were the many people who prayed for and directly aided me while I was near death and recovering. The list of those people who sustained me by giving so much, so selflessly and for so long is far too lengthy for this space, but I hope they will understand that I am eternally grateful to every one of them.

My friend and fellow motorcyclist, Howard E. Boyer, Jr., originally commissioned this book in 1997 while at the University of California Press. Understanding, as he did, so much about psychobiology, Howard enthusiastically embraced the idea of changing the book from a social history to an exploration of the 'why' questions. He died, unfortunately, before it saw print, but his influence is in it, as it is in so many other books by many now-famous scientists whose work has changed our understanding of our world.

Another friend and motorcyclist, James L. Adams, now professor emeritus of engineering and design at Stanford University, not only offered advice but directly assisted by enabling me to commission graduate students in his department to do the vibration tests for the book. Under Jim's direction, Matt Ohline, then head of the Stanford Smart Product Design Lab, arranged for engineering graduate students John Norwood, Omer Atesman, and Geoff Dolan to do the tests, and thereby to accumulate credit towards their graduate degrees (they might also have benefited in other ways: John Norwood, for example, bought a Velocette after our tests!).

Crucial to those vibration tests was another engineer-motorcyclist friend, Paul Adams. A retired airline pilot and former naval aviator, Paul has gained world renown for his unmatched restorations of Nortons, especially Manxes. Paul provided most of the motorcycles in the tests from his extensive personal collection and also let us use his home/garage/shop as the base for the tests. He also enlisted other friends to provide 'iconic' test bikes: Tom Findleton, who built Paul's superb motorcycle shop-cum-museum, allowed us to use his Harley-Davidson Fat Boy, Adrian Page kindly lent his BSA Rocket 3 to us, and John Niesely graciously provided the BMW R90S. My stepson, Andrew Williams, brought his

Ducati ST2, and, like Paul, did some of the test riding, being as superb a motorcyclist as he is a mountain bicycle racer and engineer.

Other friends aided significantly with the science and historical contexts. Thomas Wehr, M.D., formerly deputy chief of psychobiology at the National Institute of Mental Health, helped guide me through the biochemistry of the brain whenever I found the evidence contradictory or confusing. His wife, Elizabeth Wehr, J.D., made incisive and useful comments. Robert C. Post, Ph.D., former president of the Society for the History of Technology, and editor of the Society's journal, *Technology and Culture,* helped me with historical context, a task made easier for him because he grew up with and in Southern California hot-rodding. Bob's book, *The Culture and Technology of Drag Racing in America*, is the definitive work on the subject, written with a unique blending of the scholar's and enthusiast's viewpoints.

My old friend James E. Williams, who served with me at *Car and Driver* and provided the graphic components of my redesign of *Cycle Guide* and *AutoWeek*, gave me indispensable advice and guidance at critical points. Similarly sage advice came from my friend Harlan W. Hadley, an architect-racer esteemed highly for his judging at national-level automotive and motorcycle concours d'elegance. Noted racer-journalist John L. Stein, another old friend and colleague, also provided help in many ways, as did veteran motorcyclist and old friend Steve Tillett. My mentor in human-factors research, C. Tyson Rose, Ph.D., used his extensive background in HF and experimental biology to aid me in clarifying my research into the complex problem of motorcycle vibration—made easier for him because of his decades of experience as a rider himself, and because he'd been a very successful motorcycle dealer. Every author needs a good editor, and I was fortunate that, in addition to my wife, my friend John Joss brought his more than five decades of experience as a pilot, motorcyclist, racer, journalist, author and editor to the task of copy-editing a later version of the book, though, of course, any errors in the work are my responsibility alone.

Finally, this book would not be in your hands were it not for the unstinting support of Andy Goldfine. When Andy found out that the University of California Press had decided that it did not want to publish the version of the book Howard Boyer had authorized, Andy volunteered to help and ultimately decided the best way was by publishing a revised and updated version. In his Foreword, Andy ably explains for himself why he chose to do so. I am grateful to Andy, as to all those who helped to bring *Bodies in Motion* to life in print.

—Steven L Thompson, February 2008

INDEX

APPENDIX

STANFORD UNIVERSITY VIBRATION STUDY

On Wednesday, 21 March 2001, a Stanford University team instrumented and tested nine different motorcycles for vibration as perceived by riders. Headed by James L. Adams, Ph.D., Senior Associate Dean for Special Projects of the Smart Product Design Laboratory, the team had previously worked with the author to design the test. It was conceived as an experiment, there being no publicly available database of such tests for motorcycles at the time. The experiment's hypothesis, as proposed by the author, was that, in keeping with motorcycle lore, motorcycle engine-chassis combinations produce significantly different vibration at the 'human-machine interface' points of the seat, the footpegs, and the handlebar grips. Experience tells even the neophyte that this hypothesis is valid, but quantifiable data showing the nature of the vibration at those points was not publicly available. The tests would provide the first such data known to the author or to the members of the team.

Under the aegis of Prof. Adams, Lecturer Matt Ohline of the SPDL arranged for Stanford engineering graduate students Omer Atesman, Geoff Dolan, and John Norwood to design the experiment, design and fabricate the test equipment, to undertake the test with the apparatus, and to translate the raw data into visual form, for the purposes of comparing the motorcycles in the study. The engineers designed the test equipment so that the data-gathering would be done using a notebook computer, connected to custom-made brackets for the left handlebar grip, the left footpeg, and the forward section of the seat.

The testing system used the following components and methodologies:

— Computer: Toshiba Satellite 1735

— Accelerometers: Crossbow CXL 10HF3 (3 axis)
- -10G to +10G range
- $300\mu G_{rms}$ resolution
- 0.3 Hz to 10 kHz bandwidth

— Analog-to-Digital (A-to-D) Hardware:
ComputerBoards DAS 16/16
- 16 bit resolution
- 16 channels
- 100 kHz maximum sample rate

— A-to-D input scale: -10V to +10V

— A-to-D sample rate: 2500 Hz

— Number of samples for 'idle' and
'60 mph' datasets: 2500 (1 second)

— Number of samples for 'acceleration'
data sets: 25,000 (10 seconds)

— Software: MatLab (™The MathWorks)

The test location was a private residence in the Sierra
Nevada foothills, near the town of Placerville, California. The
tests began at 10:30 a.m. and testing continued for approxi-
mately six hours. Because the tests were to be conducted to
determine the vibration 'signatures' of the nine motorcycles,
a 'road-test' method of testing was adopted. As noted in
Chapter Three, this method inevitably includes variables not
controlled for in the testing, such as air temperature, pressure, and humidity, as well as the condition of the surfaces on
which the bikes were ridden. The stationary-idle tests were
conducted on the cement parking area adjacent to the garage

of the private residence, and the mobile tests were conducted on the nearby two-lane road, paved with asphalt.

The motorcycles tested were:

1994 BMW K1100LT

IMAGE COURTESY OF BMW MOTORCYCLES.

- 1092cc liquid-cooled DOHC longitudinal in-line four, 100 bhp @ 7500 rpm
- Weight (dry, unladen): 606 lbs.
- Seat height (unladen): 31.9 in.
- Wheelbase (static): 61 in.

1974 BMW R90S

- 898cc air-cooled OHV longitudinal opposed twin, 67 bhp @ 7000 rpm
- Weight (dry, unladen): 452 lbs.
- Seat height (unladen): 32.2 in.
- Wheelbase (static, unladen): 57.7 in.

1969 BSA ROCKET 3

- 740cc air-cooled OHV transverse
    in-line triple, 58 bhp @ 7250 rpm
- Weight (dry, unladen): 503 lbs.
- Seat height (unladen): 32.25 in.
- Wheelbase (static, unladen): 58 in.

1998 DUCATI ST2

- 944cc liquid-cooled SOHC transverse
    90-degree V-twin, 83 bhp @ 8500 rpm
- Weight (dry, unladen): 467 lbs.
- Seat height (unladen): 32 in.
- Wheelbase (static, unladen): 56.3 in.

2000 HARLEY-DAVIDSON FAT BOY

- 1449cc, air-cooled OHV transverse
    45-degree V-twin, 63 bhp @ 5200 rpm
- Weight (dry, unladen): 665 lbs.
- Seat height (unladen): 25.5 in.
- Wheelbase (static, unladen): 64.5 in.

1978 HONDA CBX

- 1047cc liquid-cooled DOHC transverse
  in-line six, 85.5 bhp @ 9000 rpm
- Weight (dry, unladen): 555 lbs.
- Seat height (unladen): 32.9 in.
- Wheelbase (static): 58.9 in.

1987 HONDA VFR700F2

- 700cc liquid-cooled DOHC transverse V-four,
  76 bhp @ 11,000 rpm
- Weight (dry, unladen): 436 lbs.
- Seat height (unladen): 31.9 in.
- Wheelbase (static): 58.3 in.

1968 TRIUMPH TR6C

- 649cc air-cooled OHV transverse vertical twin,
    45 bhp @ 6500 rpm
- Weight (dry, unladen): 384 lbs.
- Seat height (unladen): 32.2 in.
- Wheelbase (static, unladen): 55.5 in.

1959 VELOCETTE VENOM

- 499cc air-cooled OHV transverse vertical single,
     36 bhp @ 6200 rpm
- Weight (dry, unladen): 380 lbs.
- Seat height (unladen): 30.5 in.
- Wheelbase (static, unladen): 53.75 in.

The transducers were mounted so that they recorded data at the seat, handlebar, and footpeg, thus:

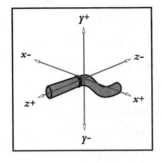

HANDLEBAR

x-axis: perpendicular to handlebar *(+ points backward)*
y-axis: perpendicular to handlebar *(+ points upward)*
z-axis: parallel to handlebar *(+ points left)*

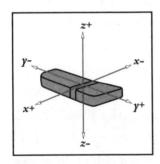

SEAT

x-axis: perpendicular to bike longitudinal axis *(+ points left)*
y-axis: parallel to bike longitudinal axis *(+ points backward)*
z-axis: perpendicular to bike longitudinal axis *(+ points upward)*

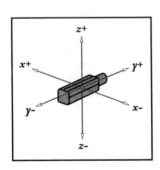

FOOTPEG

x-axis: parallel to bike longitudinal axis *(+ points forward)*
y-axis: perpendicular to bike longitudinal axis *(+ points right)*
z-axis: perpendicular to bike longitudinal axis *(+ points upward)*

The data displayed in graphic form are best understood by comparing each motorcycle's vibration recorded in the same test modes (idle, 60 mph, hard acceleration) at the same location (handlebar, footpeg, seat) and same axis. In so doing, it is essential to remember that these tests were undertaken *only* to compare the data collected for these machines on a certain day, with certain riders, in a certain location, at slightly different times. In short, these charts should not be expected to be descriptive of every similar make and model tested, or to be predictive as to how those similar models will 'feel.' Though the charts might well be reasonably accurate in those terms, only extensive further testing could disclose that, and such testing was beyond the scope of this book.

What the data do show, as noted in Chapter Three, is that, in consonance with motorcycle lore, there is indeed a substantial and significant difference in the vibration 'signatures' of these motorcycles, and thus, we can be sure, in others. How any given rider might respond to the vibration is the key question that follows the quantitative proof of wide differences in stimuli fed to the rider shown in this experiment, and it is a subject rich with possibilities for exploration by future researchers.

STANFORD UNIVERSITY
VIBRATION STUDY
Idle Vibration

OVERALL MOTORCYCLE COMPARISON

Idle Handlebar Vibration — Root Mean Square (RMS)

x-Axis

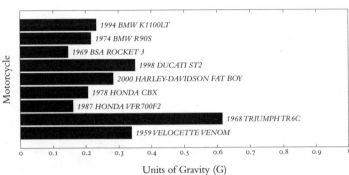

Units of Gravity (G)

y-Axis

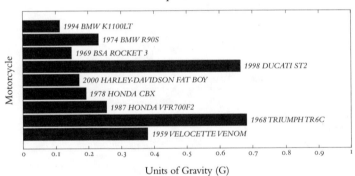

Units of Gravity (G)

z-Axis

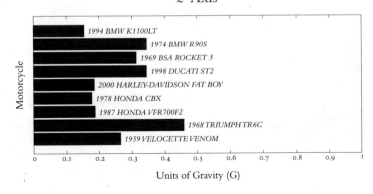

Units of Gravity (G)

OVERALL MOTORCYCLE COMPARISON
Idle Seat Vibration — Root Mean Square (RMS)

x-Axis

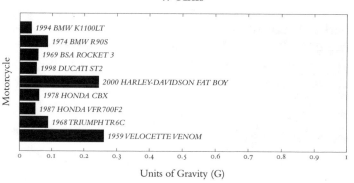

Units of Gravity (G)

y-Axis

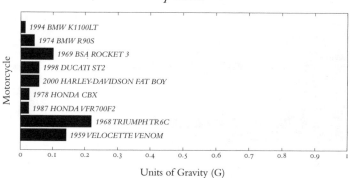

Units of Gravity (G)

z-Axis

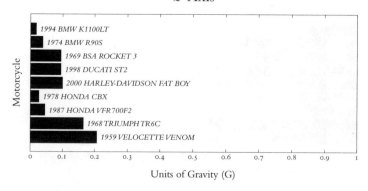

Units of Gravity (G)

OVERALL MOTORCYCLE COMPARISON

Idle Footpeg Vibration — Root Mean Square (RMS)

x-Axis

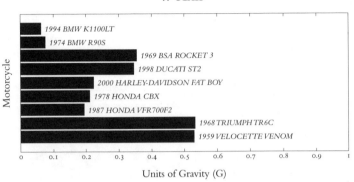

Units of Gravity (G)

y-Axis

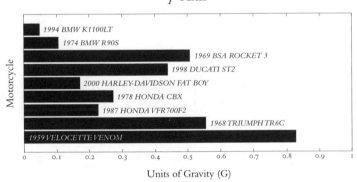

Units of Gravity (G)

z-Axis

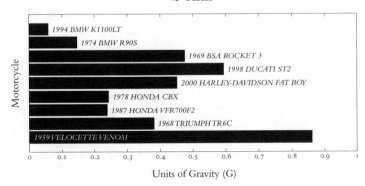

Units of Gravity (G)

1994 BMW K1100LT

Idle Handlebar Vibration — Transducer Data

x-Axis

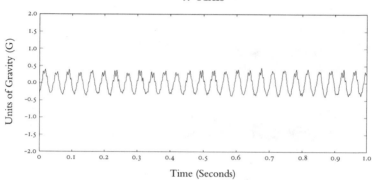

Time (Seconds)

y-Axis

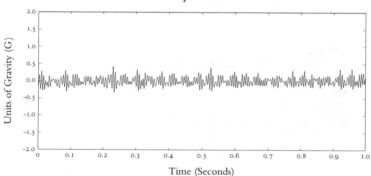

Time (Seconds)

z-Axis

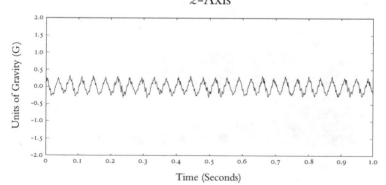

Time (Seconds)

1994 BMW K1100LT

Idle Handlebar Vibration — Fast Fourier Transform (FFT)

x-Axis

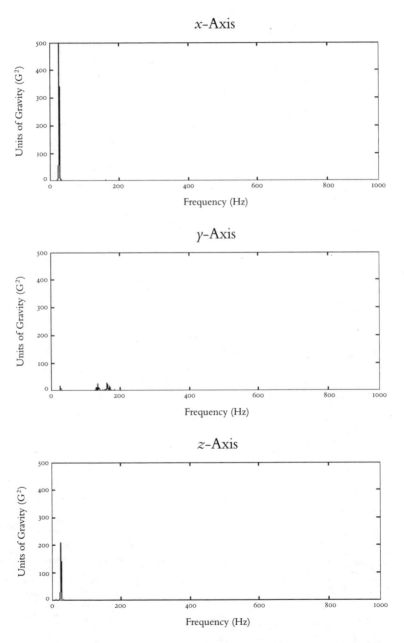

y-Axis

z-Axis

1994 BMW K1100LT

Idle Seat Vibration — Transducer Data

x-Axis

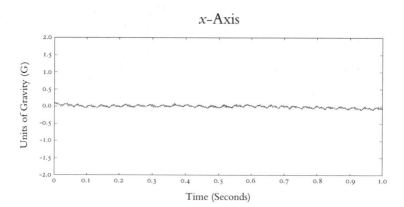

Time (Seconds)

y-Axis

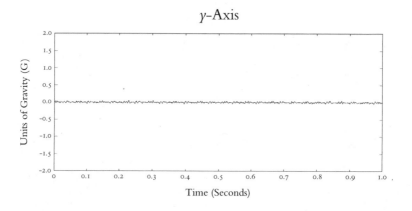

Time (Seconds)

z-Axis

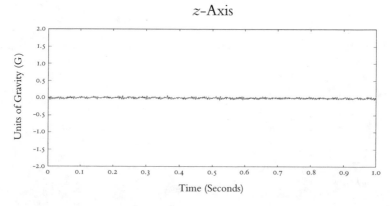

Time (Seconds)

1994 BMW K1100LT

Idle Seat Vibration — Fast Fourier Transform (FFT)

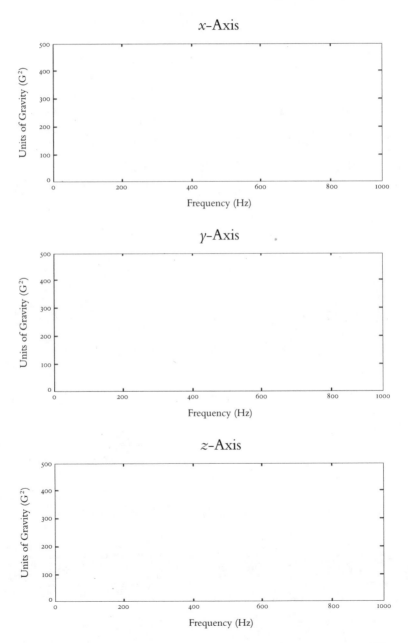

1994 BMW K1100LT

Idle Footpeg Vibration — Transducer Data

x-Axis

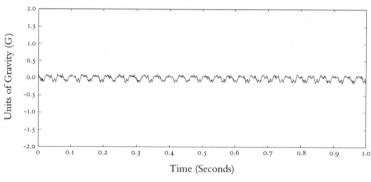

Time (Seconds)

y-Axis

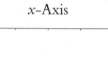

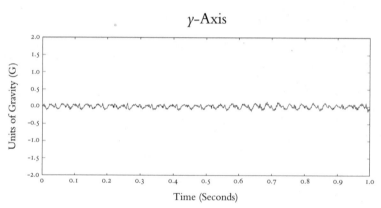

Time (Seconds)

z-Axis

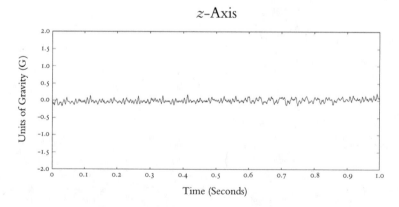

Time (Seconds)

1994 BMW K1100LT

Idle Footpeg Vibration — Fast Fourier Transform (FFT)

x-Axis

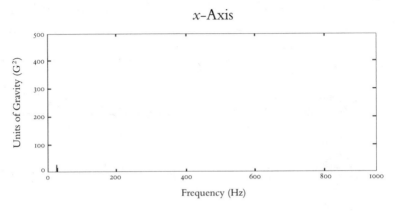

y-Axis

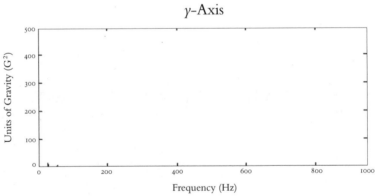

z-Axis

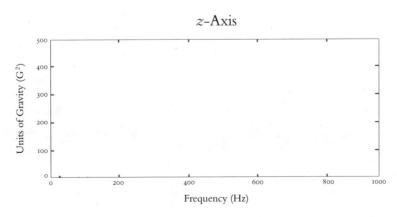

1974 BMW R90S

Idle Handlebar Vibration — Transducer Data

x-Axis

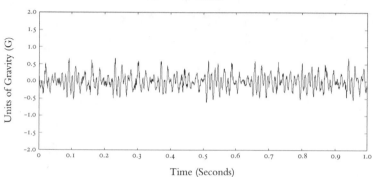

Time (Seconds)

y-Axis

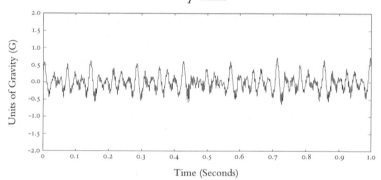

Time (Seconds)

z-Axis

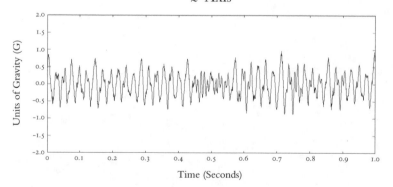

Time (Seconds)

1974 BMW R90S

Idle Handlebar Vibration — Fast Fourier Transform (FFT)

x-Axis

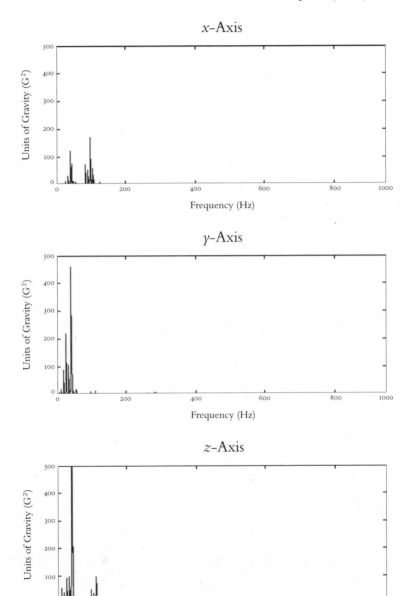

y-Axis

z-Axis

1974 BMW R90S

Idle Seat Vibration — Transducer Data

x-Axis

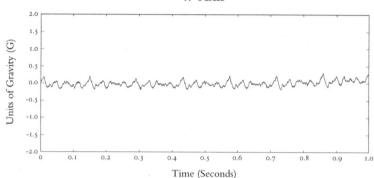

Time (Seconds)

y-Axis

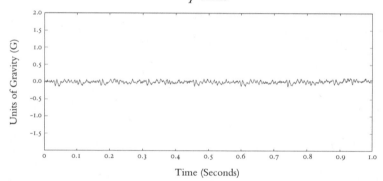

Time (Seconds)

z-Axis

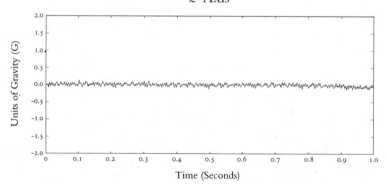

Time (Seconds)

1974 BMW R90S

Idle Seat Vibration — Fast Fourier Transform (FFT)

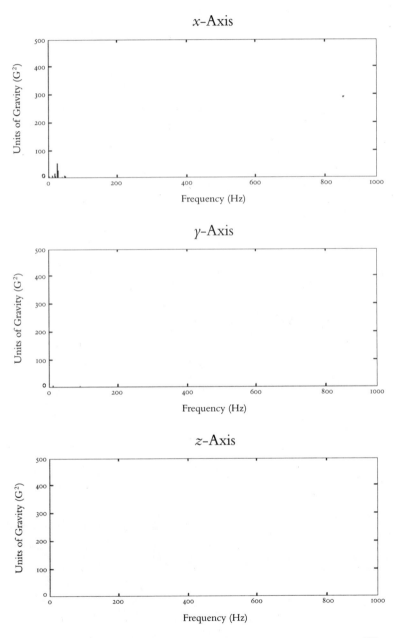

x-Axis

y-Axis

z-Axis

1974 BMW R90S

Idle Footpeg Vibration — Transducer Data

x-Axis

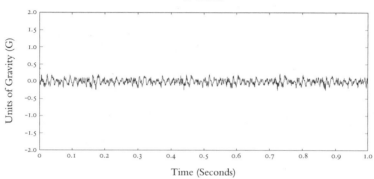

y-Axis

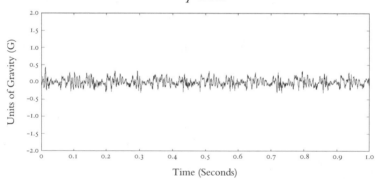

z-Axis

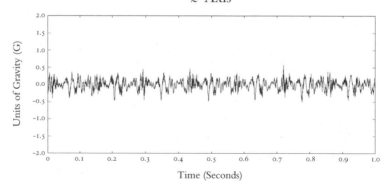

1974 BMW R90S

Idle Footpeg Vibration — Fast Fourier Transform (FFT)

x-Axis

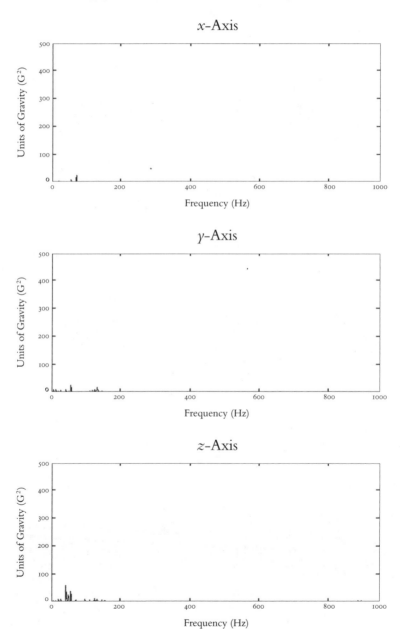

y-Axis

z-Axis

1969 BSA ROCKET 3

Idle Handlebar Vibration — Transducer Data

x-Axis

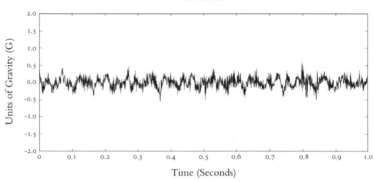

y-Axis

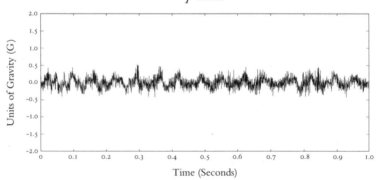

z-Axis

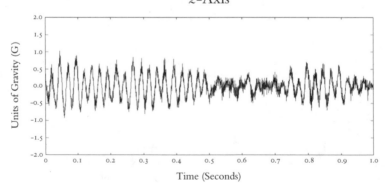

1969 BSA ROCKET 3

Idle Handlebar Vibration — Fast Fourier Transform (FFT)

x-Axis

y-Axis

z-Axis

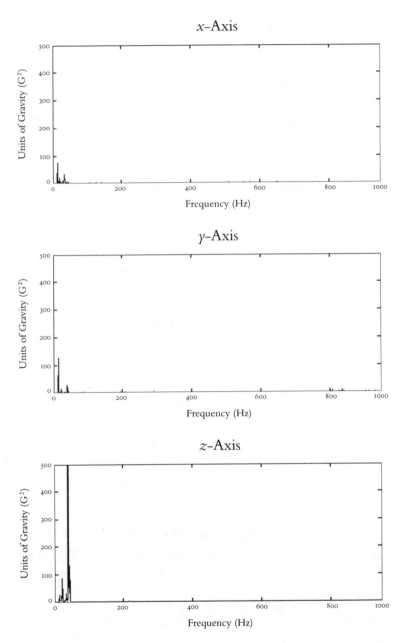

1969 BSA ROCKET 3

Idle Seat Vibration — Transducer Data

x-Axis

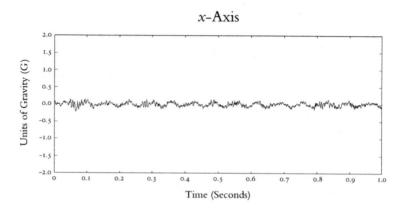

y-Axis

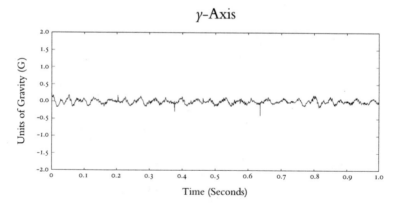

z-Axis

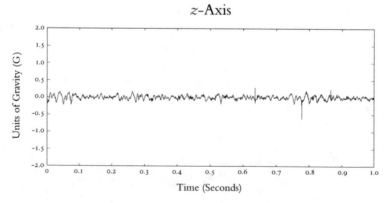

1969 BSA ROCKET 3

Idle Seat Vibration — Fast Fourier Transform (FFT)

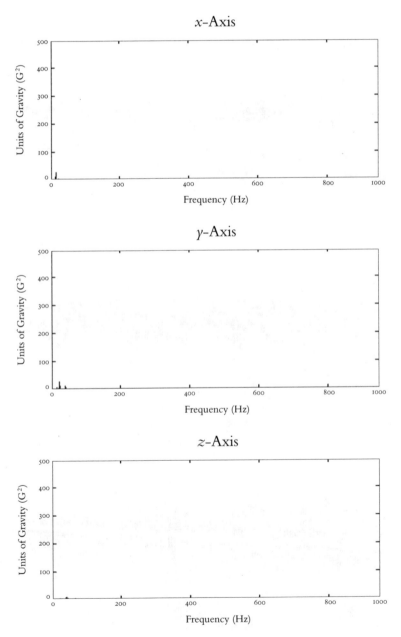

x-Axis

y-Axis

z-Axis

1969 BSA ROCKET 3

Idle Footpeg Vibration — Transducer Data

x-Axis

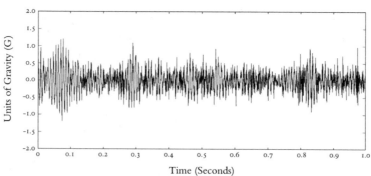

y-Axis

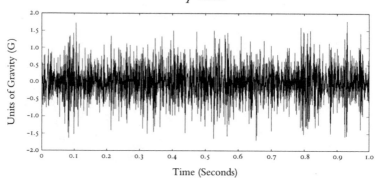

z-Axis

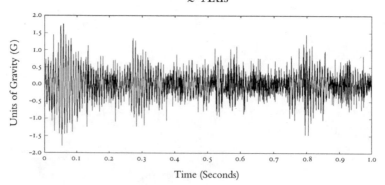

1969 BSA ROCKET 3

Idle Footpeg Vibration — Fast Fourier Transform (FFT)

x-Axis

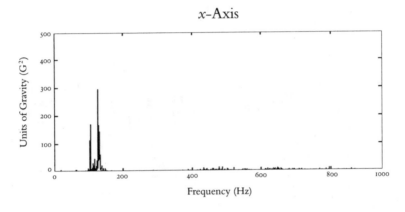

y-Axis

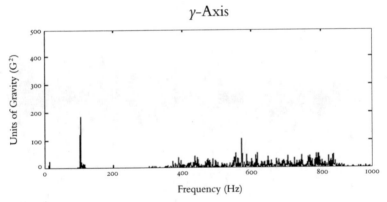

z-Axis

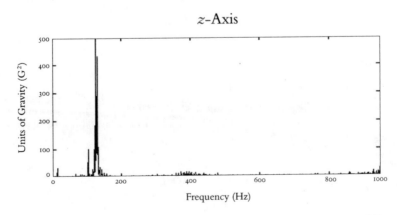

1998 DUCATI ST2

Idle Handlebar Vibration — Transducer Data

x-Axis

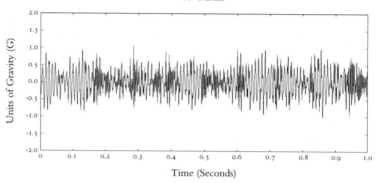

Time (Seconds)

γ-Axis

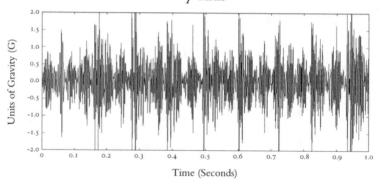

Time (Seconds)

z-Axis

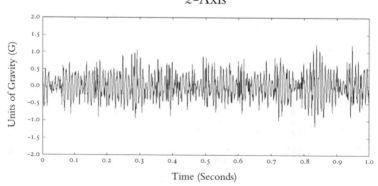

Time (Seconds)

1998 DUCATI ST2

Idle Handlebar Vibration — Fast Fourier Transform (FFT)

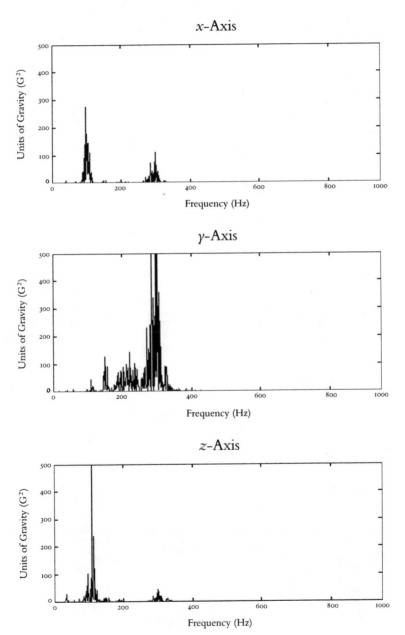

1998 DUCATI ST2

Idle Seat Vibration — Transducer Data

x-Axis

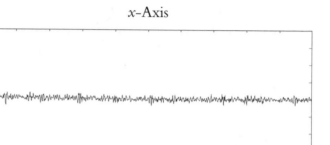

y-Axis

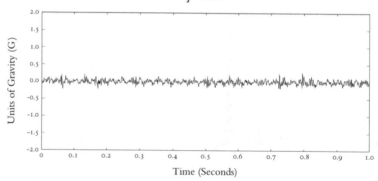

z-Axis

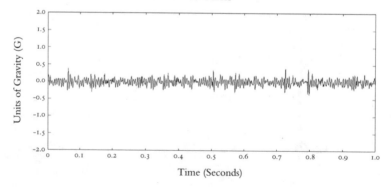

1998 DUCATI ST2

Idle Seat Vibration — Fast Fourier Transform (FFT)

x-Axis

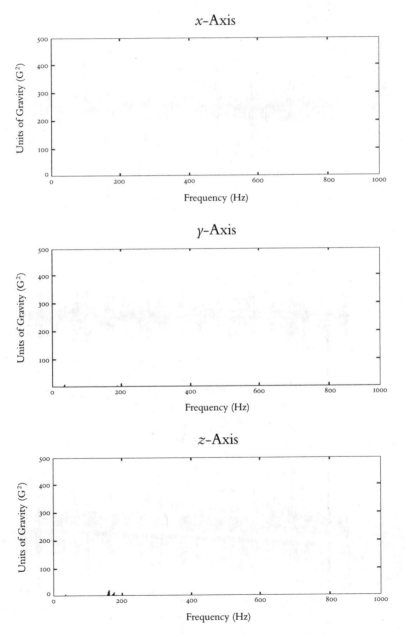

y-Axis

z-Axis

1998 DUCATI ST2

Idle Footpeg Vibration — Transducer Data

x-Axis

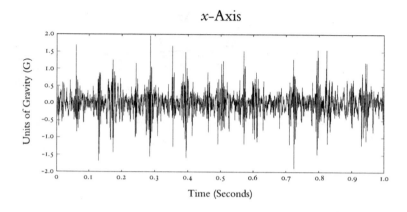

γ-Axis

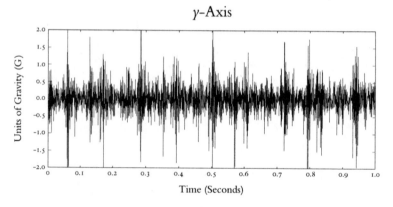

z-Axis

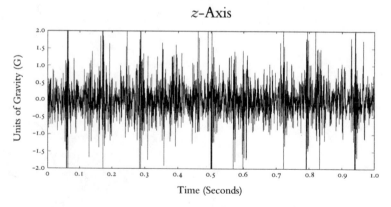

1998 DUCATI ST2

Idle Footpeg Vibration — Fast Fourier Transform (FFT)

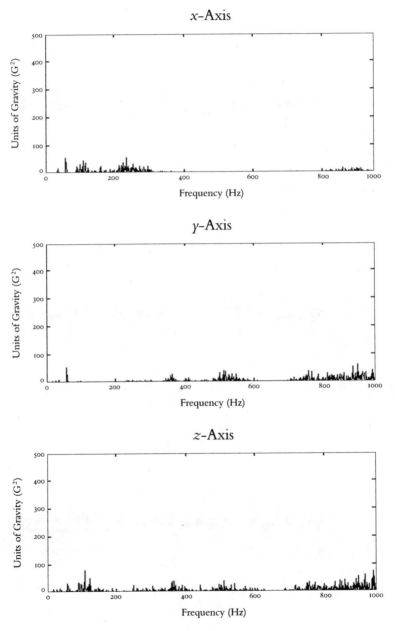

2000 HARLEY-DAVIDSON FAT BOY

Idle Handlebar Vibration — Transducer Data

x-Axis

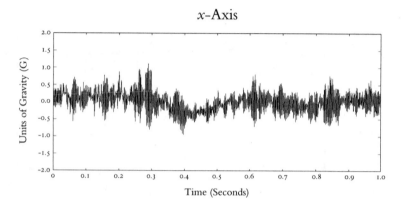

Time (Seconds)

y-Axis

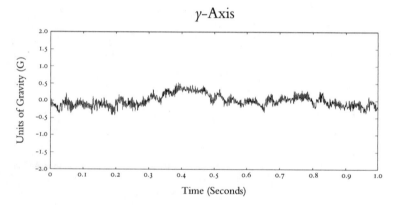

Time (Seconds)

z-Axis

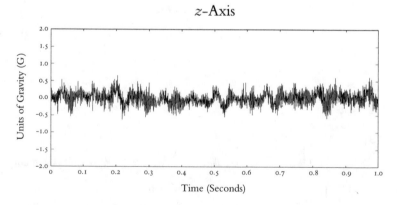

Time (Seconds)

2000 HARLEY-DAVIDSON FAT BOY

Idle Handlebar Vibration — Fast Fourier Transform (FFT)

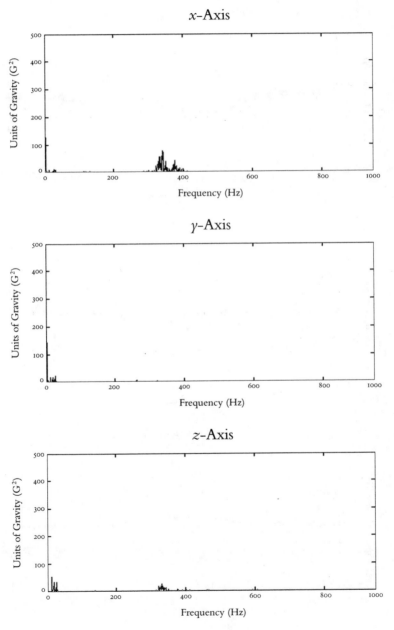

x-Axis

y-Axis

z-Axis

2000 HARLEY-DAVIDSON FAT BOY

Idle Seat Vibration — Transducer Data

x-Axis

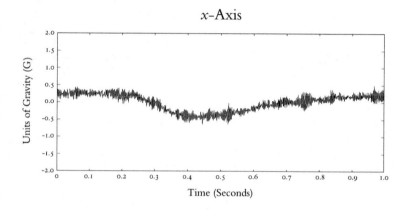

γ-Axis

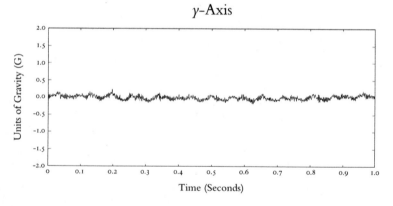

z-Axis

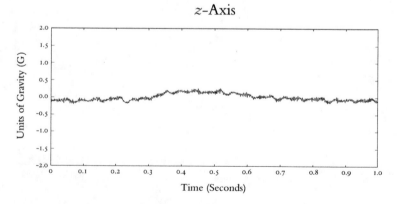

2000 HARLEY-DAVIDSON FAT BOY

Idle Seat Vibration — Fast Fourier Transform (FFT)

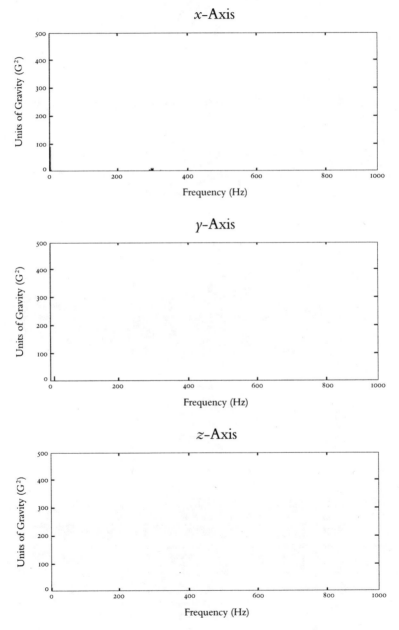

2000 HARLEY-DAVIDSON FAT BOY
Idle Footpeg Vibration — Transducer Data

x-Axis

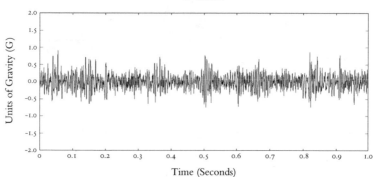

Time (Seconds)

y-Axis

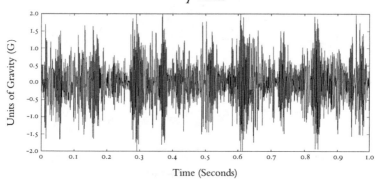

Time (Seconds)

z-Axis

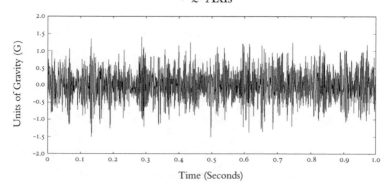

Time (Seconds)

2000 HARLEY-DAVIDSON FAT BOY

Idle Footpeg Vibration — Fast Fourier Transform (FFT)

x-Axis

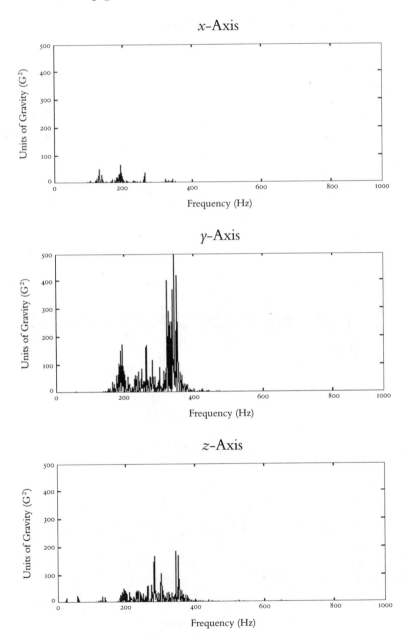

y-Axis

z-Axis

1978 HONDA CBX
Idle Handlebar Vibration — Transducer Data

x-Axis

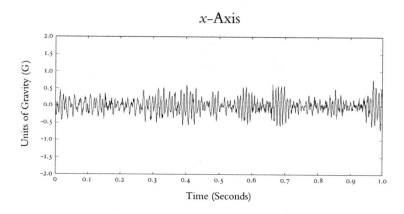

y-Axis

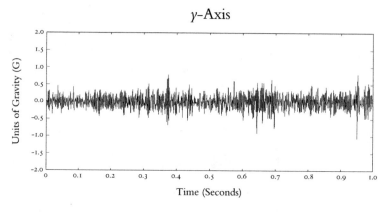

z-Axis

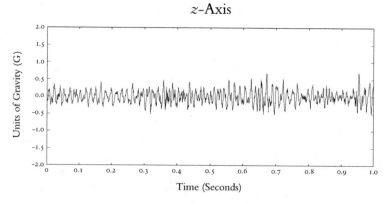

1978 HONDA CBX

Idle Handlebar Vibration — Fast Fourier Transform (FFT)

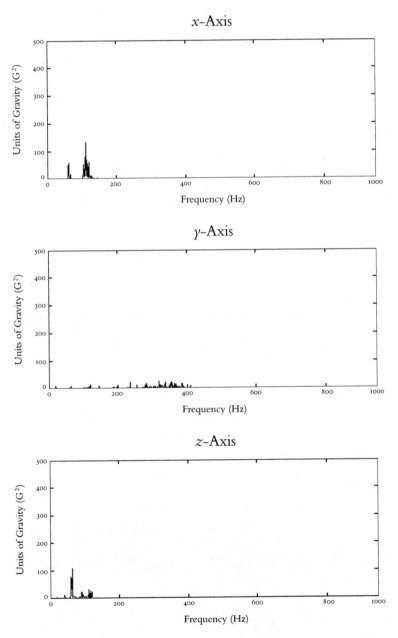

x-Axis

y-Axis

z-Axis

1978 HONDA CBX

Idle Seat Vibration — Transducer Data

x-Axis

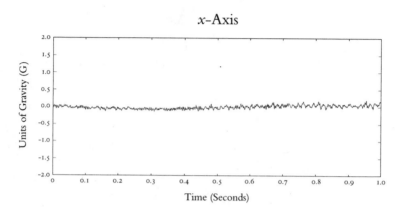

Time (Seconds)

y-Axis

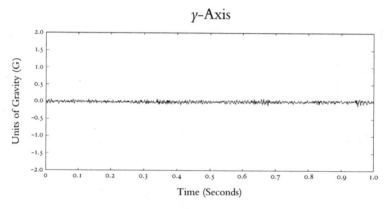

Time (Seconds)

z-Axis

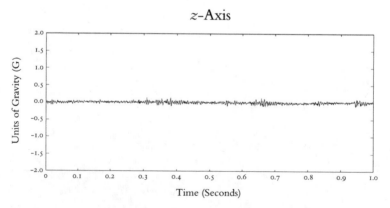

Time (Seconds)

1978 HONDA CBX

Idle Seat Vibration — Fast Fourier Transform (FFT)

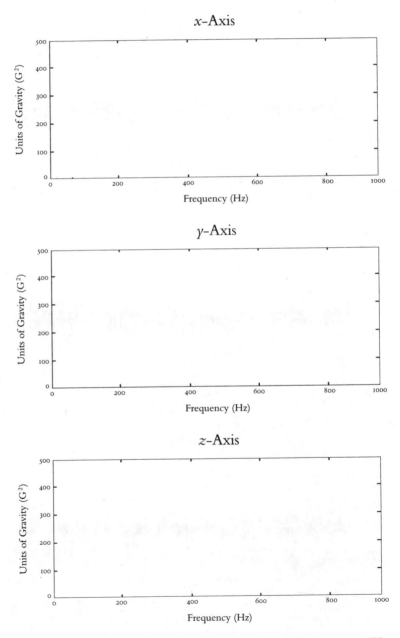

1978 HONDA CBX

Idle Footpeg Vibration — Transducer Data

x-Axis

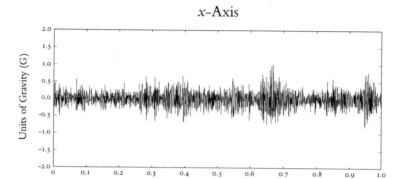

y-Axis

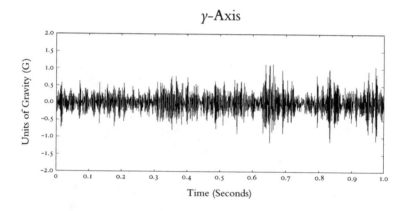

z-Axis

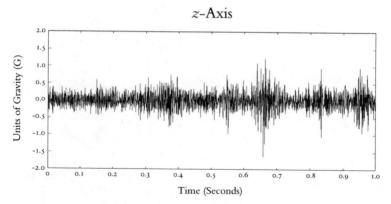

1978 HONDA CBX

Idle Footpeg Vibration — Fast Fourier Transform (FFT)

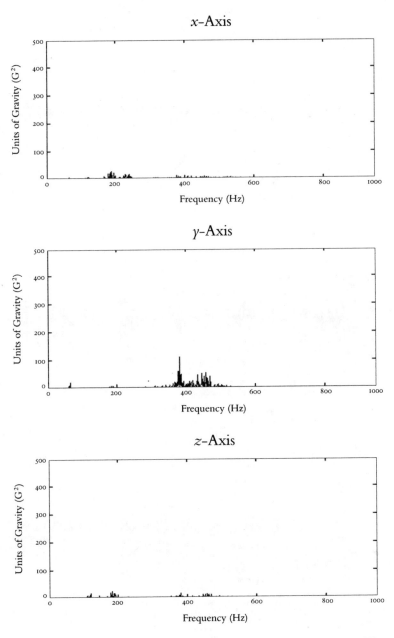

1987 HONDA VFR700F2
Idle Handlebar Vibration — Transducer Data

x-Axis

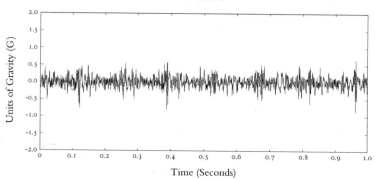

γ-Axis

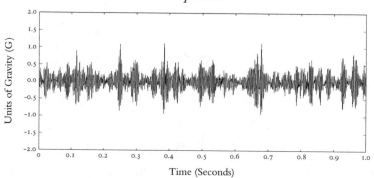

z-Axis

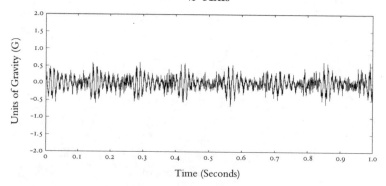

1987 HONDA VFR700F2

Idle Handlebar Vibration — Fast Fourier Transform (FFT)

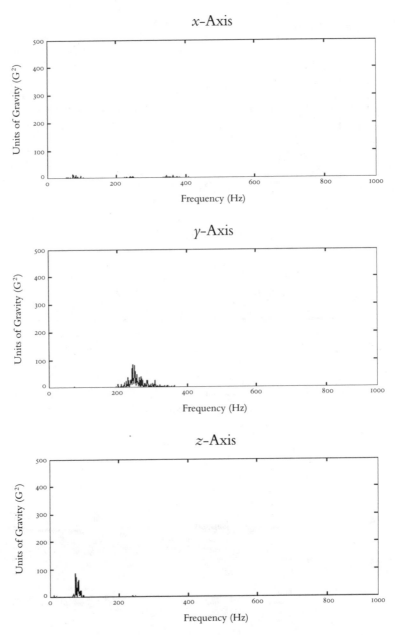

x-Axis

y-Axis

z-Axis

1987 HONDA VFR700F2

Idle Seat Vibration — Transducer Data

x-Axis

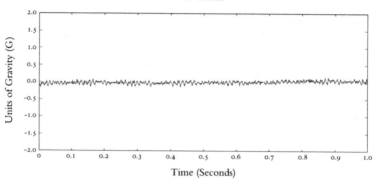

y-Axis

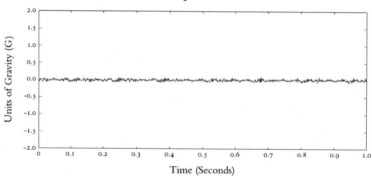

z-Axis

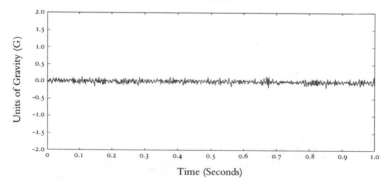

1987 HONDA VFR700F2

Idle Seat Vibration — Fast Fourier Transform (FFT)

x-Axis

γ-Axis

z-Axis

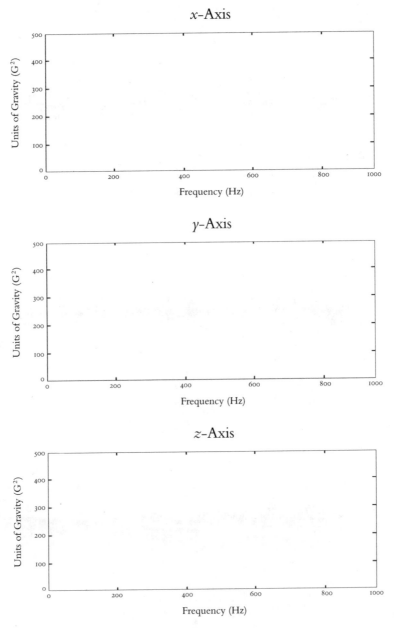

1987 HONDA VFR700F2
Idle Footpeg Vibration — Transducer Data

x-Axis

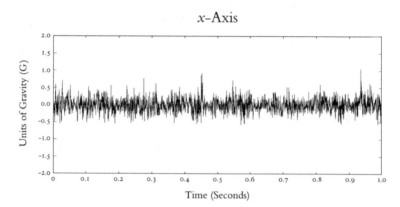

y-Axis

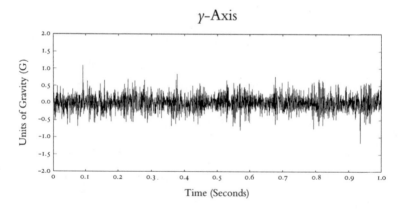

z-Axis

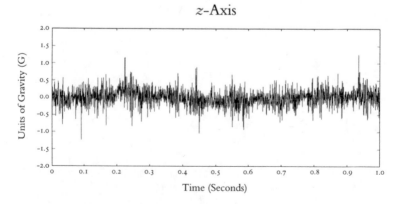

1987 HONDA VFR700F2

Idle Footpeg Vibration — Fast Fourier Transform (FFT)

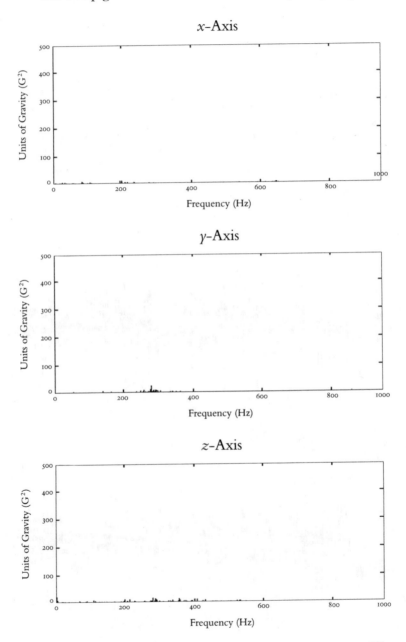

x-Axis

y-Axis

z-Axis

1968 TRIUMPH TR6C
Idle Handlebar Vibration — Transducer Data

x-Axis

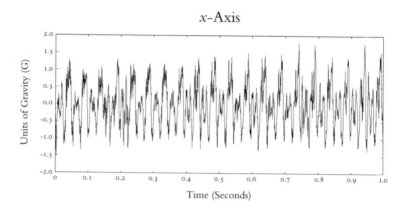

Time (Seconds)

y-Axis

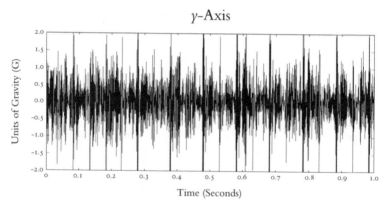

Time (Seconds)

z-Axis

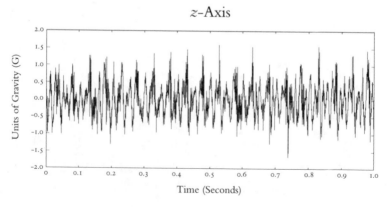

Time (Seconds)

1968 TRIUMPH TR6C

Idle Handlebar Vibration — Fast Fourier Transform (FFT)

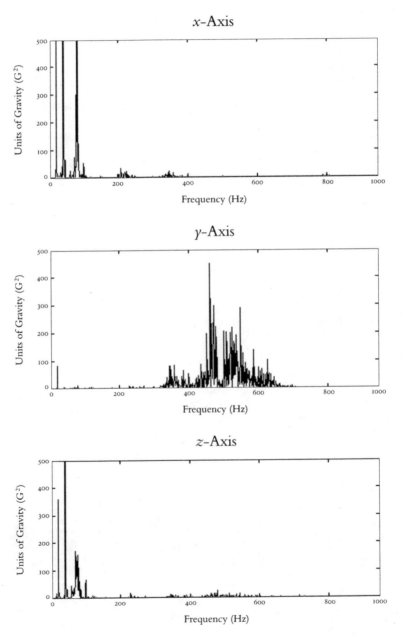

1968 TRIUMPH TR6C

Idle Seat Vibration — Transducer Data

x-Axis

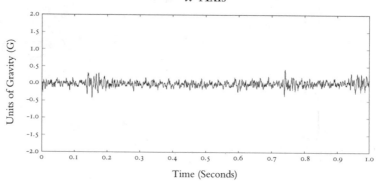

Time (Seconds)

y-Axis

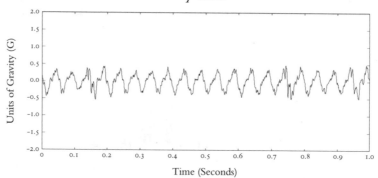

Time (Seconds)

z-Axis

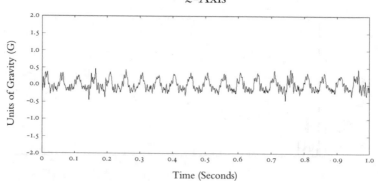

Time (Seconds)

1968 TRIUMPH TR6C

Idle Seat Vibration — Fast Fourier Transform (FFT)

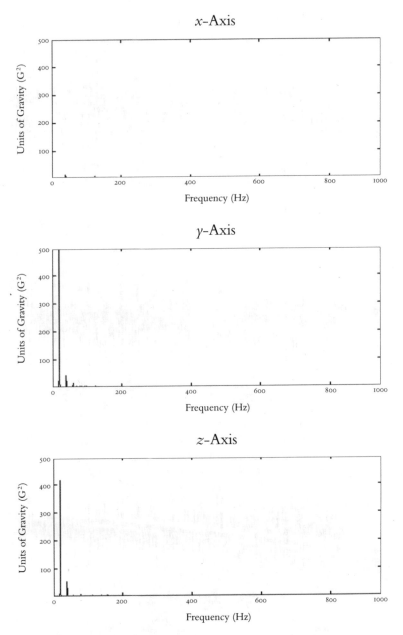

1968 TRIUMPH TR6C
Idle Footpeg Vibration — Transducer Data

x-Axis

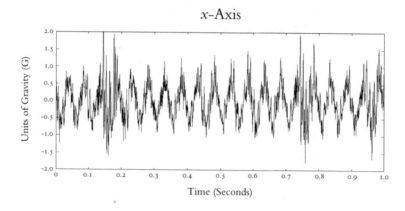

y-Axis

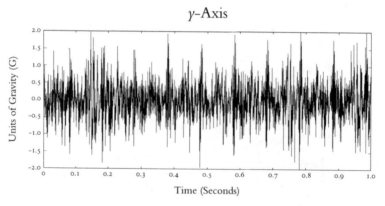

z-Axis

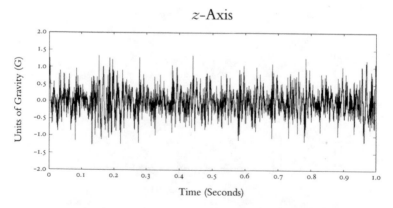

1968 TRIUMPH TR6C

Idle Footpeg Vibration — Fast Fourier Transform (FFT)

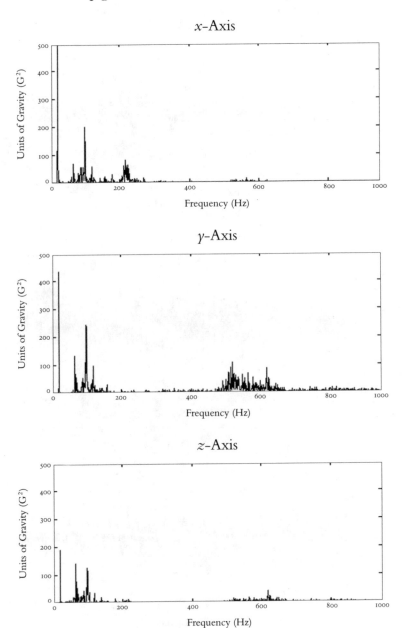

x-Axis

y-Axis

z-Axis

1959 VELOCETTE VENOM

Idle Handlebar Vibration — Transducer Data

x-Axis

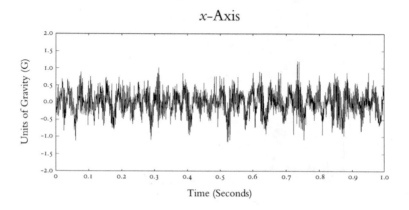

y-Axis

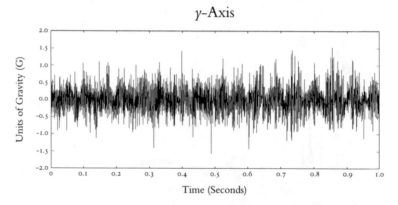

z-Axis

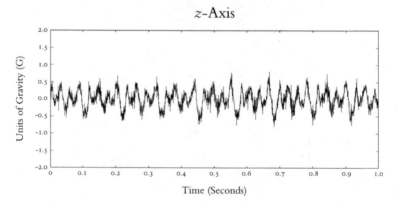

1959 VELOCETTE VENOM

Idle Handlebar Vibration — Fast Fourier Transform (FFT)

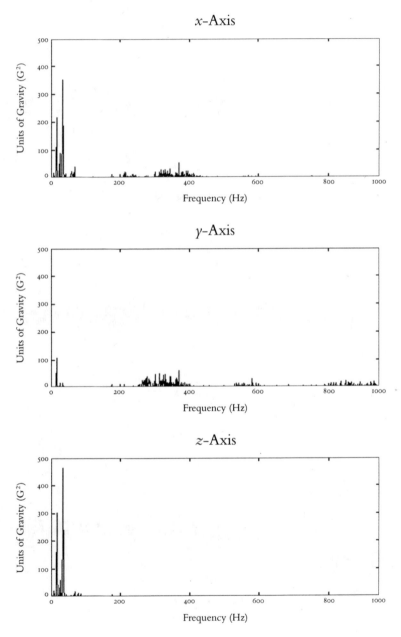

x-Axis

y-Axis

z-Axis

1959 VELOCETTE VENOM

Idle Seat Vibration — Transducer Data

x-Axis

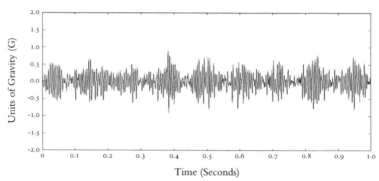

y-Axis

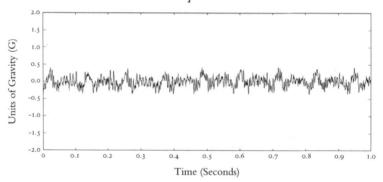

z-Axis

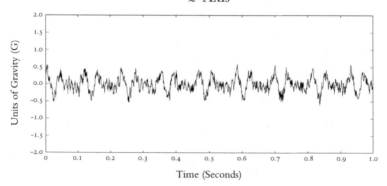

1959 VELOCETTE VENOM

Idle Seat Vibration — Fast Fourier Transform (FFT)

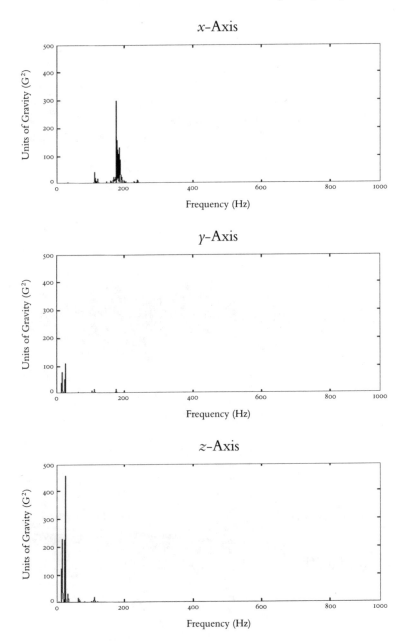

x-Axis

y-Axis

z-Axis

1959 VELOCETTE VENOM

Idle Footpeg Vibration — Transducer Data

x-Axis

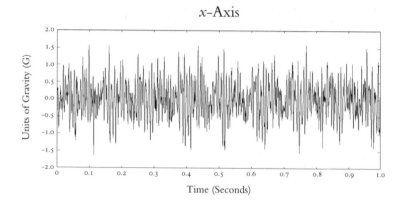

y-Axis

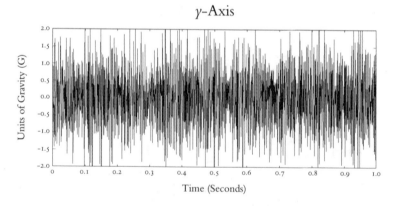

z-Axis

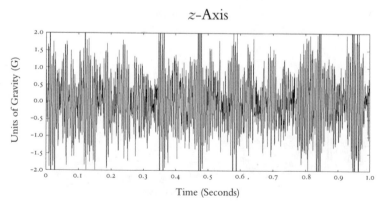

1959 VELOCETTE VENOM

Idle Footpeg Vibration — Fast Fourier Transform (FFT)

x-Axis

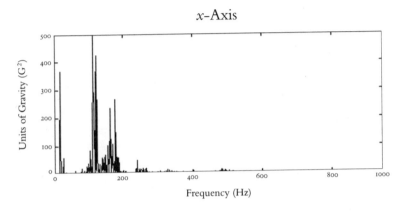

y-Axis

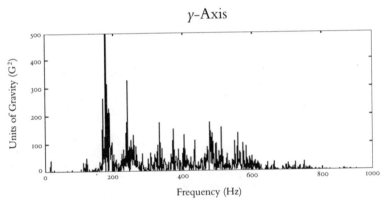

z-Axis

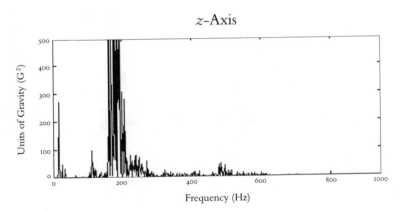

STANFORD UNIVERSITY
VIBRATION STUDY
Acceleration Vibration

OVERALL MOTORCYCLE COMPARISON

Acceleration Handlebar Vibration — Root Mean Square (RMS)

x-Axis

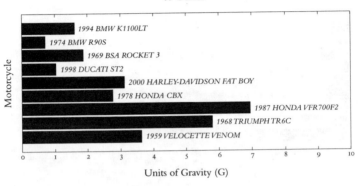

Units of Gravity (G)

y-Axis

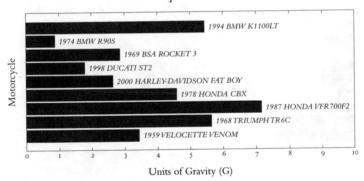

Units of Gravity (G)

z-Axis

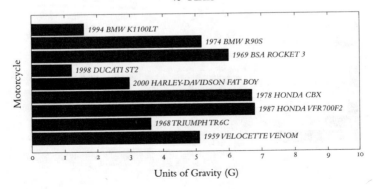

Units of Gravity (G)

OVERALL MOTORCYCLE COMPARISON
Acceleration Seat Vibration — Root Mean Square (RMS)

x-Axis

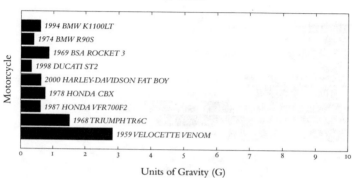

Units of Gravity (G)

y-Axis

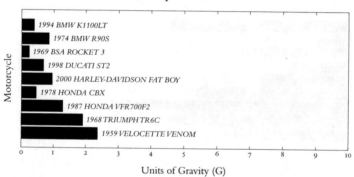

Units of Gravity (G)

z-Axis

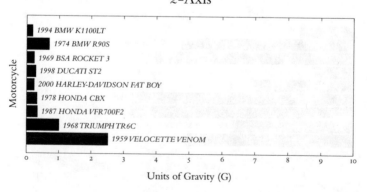

Units of Gravity (G)

OVERALL MOTORCYCLE COMPARISON
Acceleration Footpeg Vibration — Root Mean Square (RMS)

x-Axis

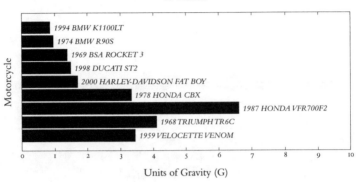

Units of Gravity (G)

y-Axis

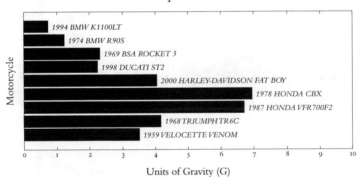

Units of Gravity (G)

z-Axis

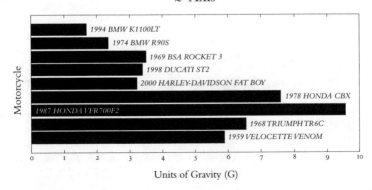

Units of Gravity (G)

1994 BMW K1100LT

Acceleration Handlebar Vibration — Transducer Data

x-Axis

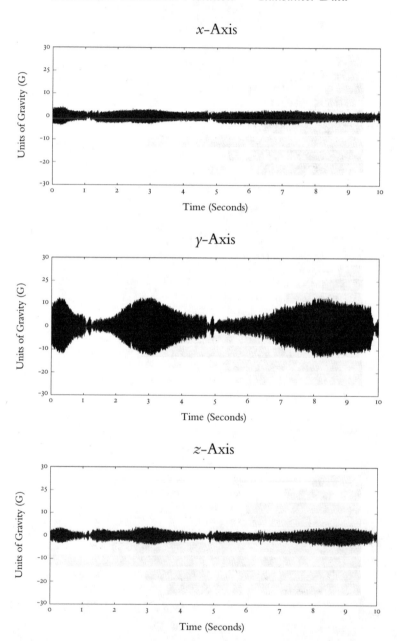

y-Axis

z-Axis

1994 BMW K1100LT

Acceleration Handlebar Vibration — Fast Fourier Transform (FFT)

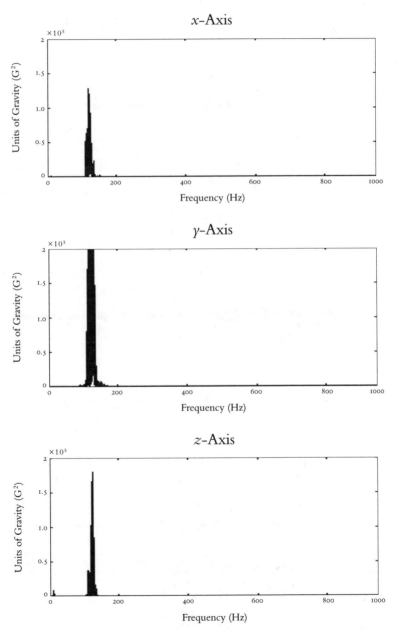

1994 BMW K1100LT

Acceleration Seat Vibration — Transducer Data

x-Axis

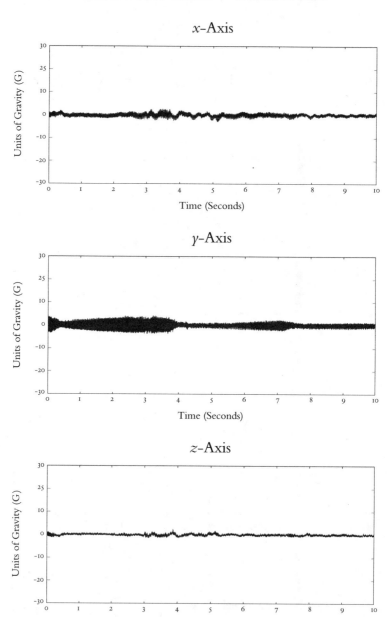

y-Axis

z-Axis

1994 BMW K1100LT

Acceleration Seat Vibration — Fast Fourier Transform (FFT)

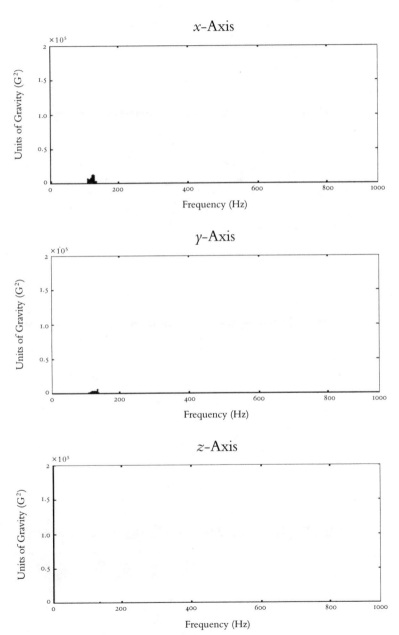

1994 BMW K1100LT

Acceleration Footpeg Vibration — Transducer Data

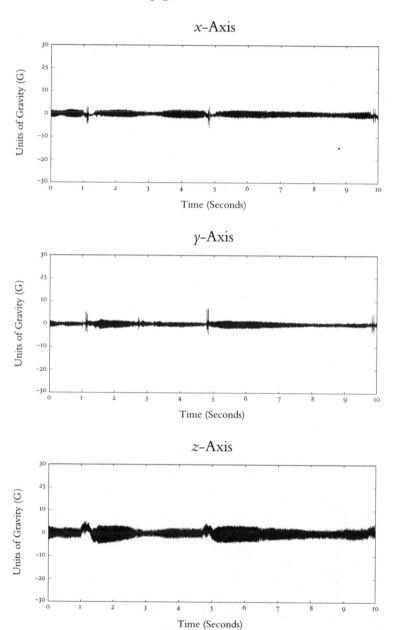

x-Axis

γ-Axis

z-Axis

1994 BMW K1100LT

Acceleration Footpeg Vibration — Fast Fourier Transform (FFT)

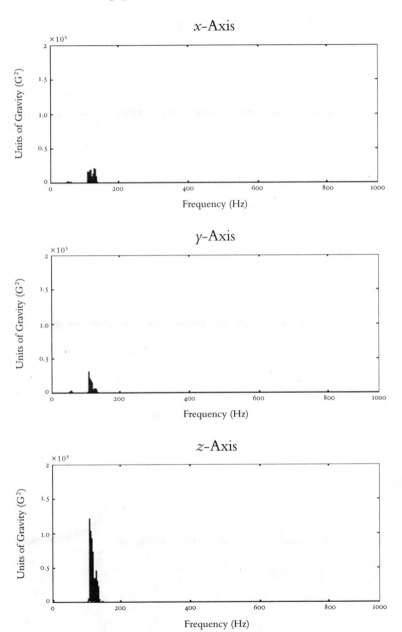

1974 BMW R90S

Acceleration Handlebar Vibration — Transducer Data

x-Axis

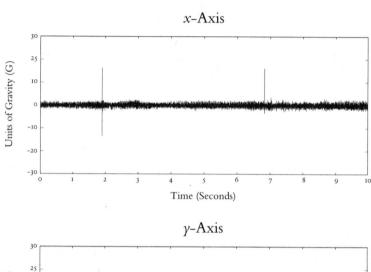

y-Axis

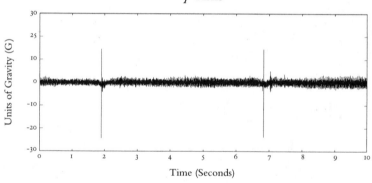

z-Axis

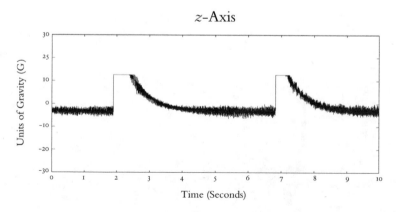

1974 BMW R90S

Acceleration Handlebar Vibration — Fast Fourier Transform (FFT)

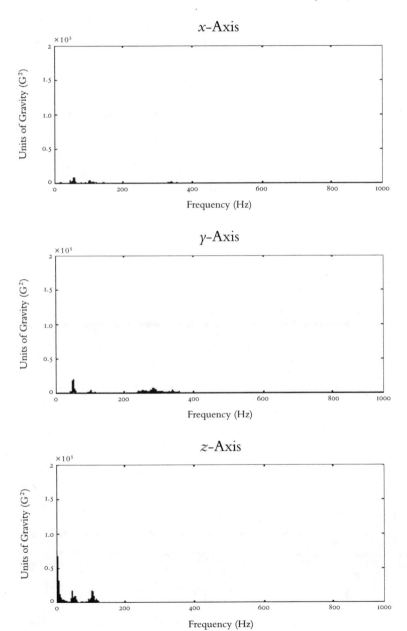

1974 BMW R90S

Acceleration Seat Vibration — Transducer Data

x-Axis

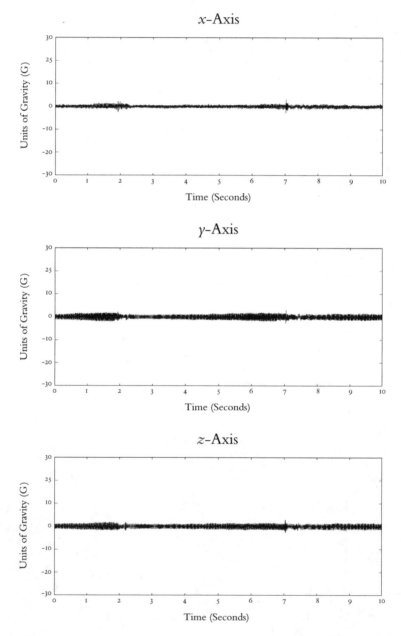

y-Axis

z-Axis

1974 BMW R90S

Acceleration Seat Vibration — Fast Fourier Transform (FFT)

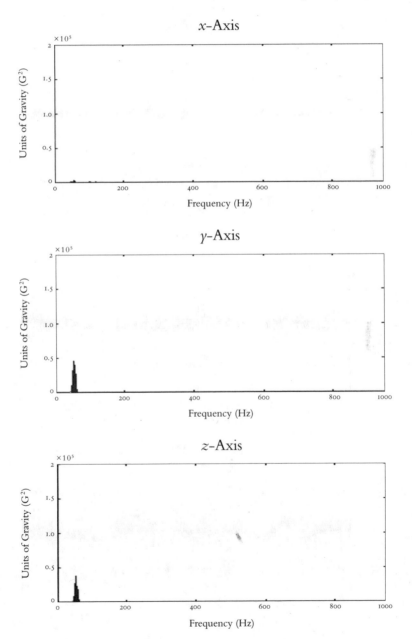

1974 BMW R90S

Acceleration Footpeg Vibration — Transducer Data

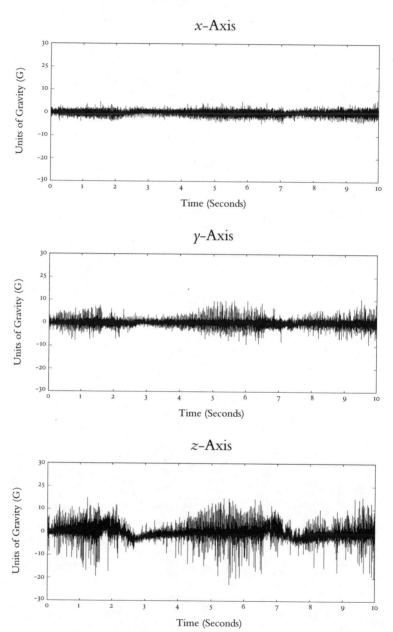

x-Axis

y-Axis

z-Axis

1974 BMW R90S

Acceleration Footpeg Vibration — Fast Fourier Transform (FFT)

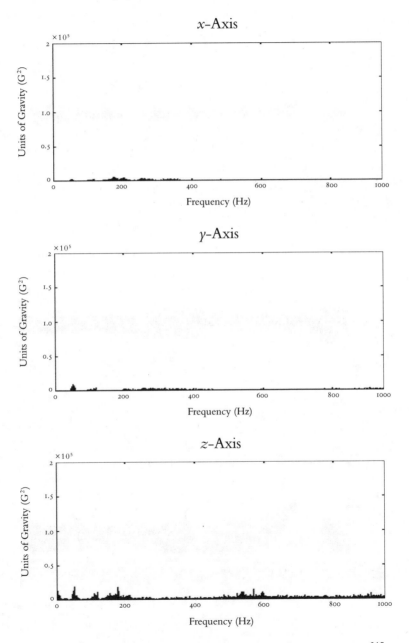

1969 BSA ROCKET 3

Acceleration Handlebar Vibration — Transducer Data

x-Axis

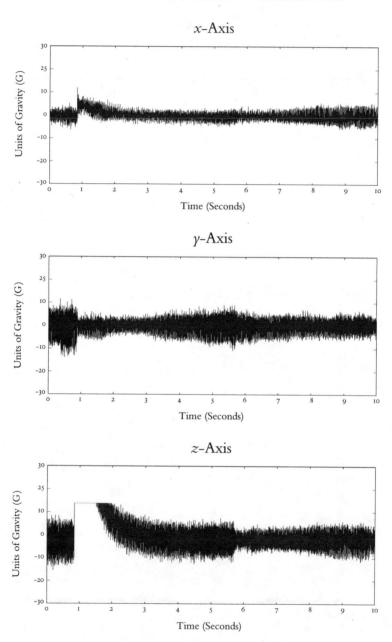

y-Axis

z-Axis

1969 BSA ROCKET 3

Acceleration Handlebar Vibration — Fast Fourier Transform (FFT)

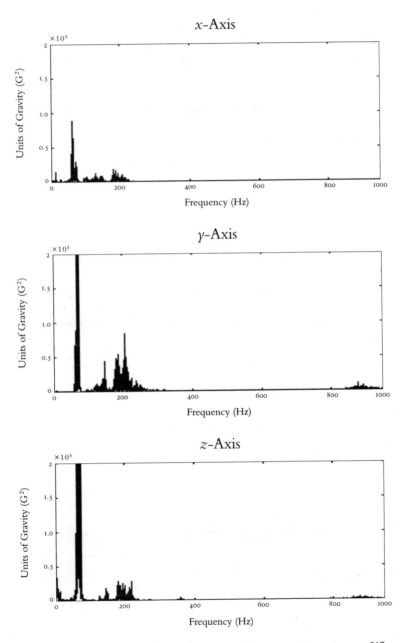

1969 BSA ROCKET 3

Acceleration Seat Vibration — Transducer Data

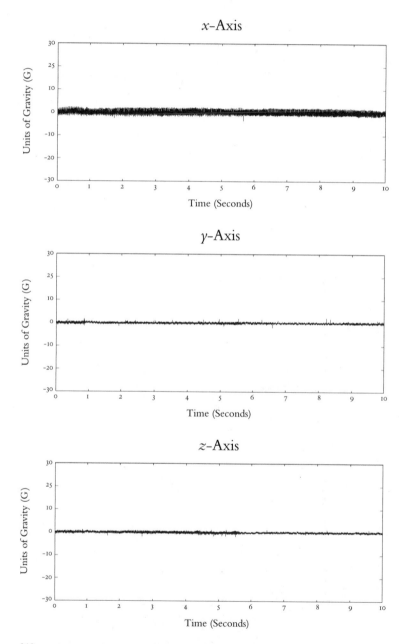

x-Axis

y-Axis

z-Axis

1969 BSA ROCKET 3

Acceleration Seat Vibration — Fast Fourier Transform (FFT)

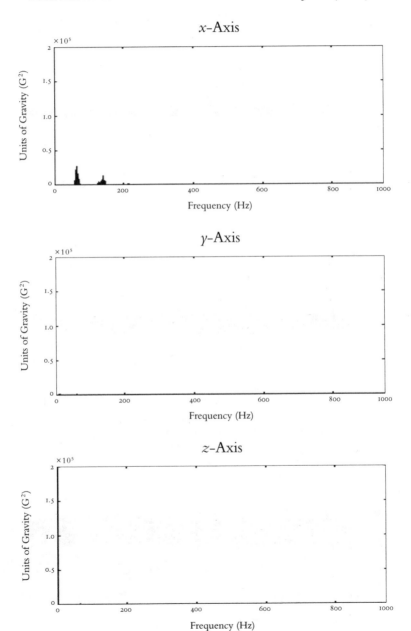

1969 BSA ROCKET 3

Acceleration Footpeg Vibration — Transducer Data

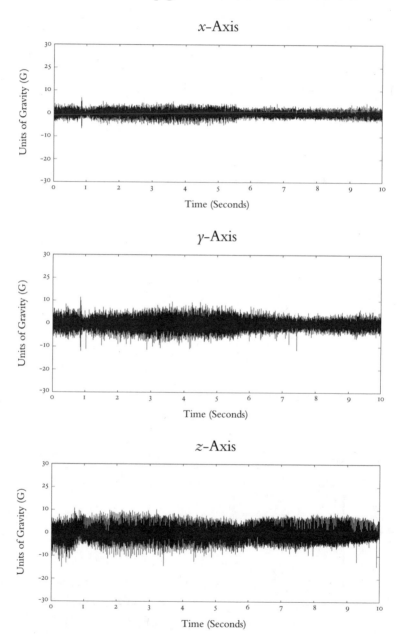

1969 BSA ROCKET 3

Acceleration Footpeg Vibration — Fast Fourier Transform (FFT)

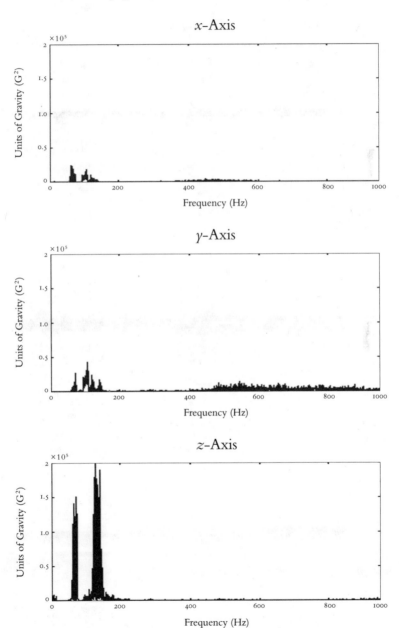

1998 DUCATI ST2

Acceleration Handlebar Vibration — Transducer Data

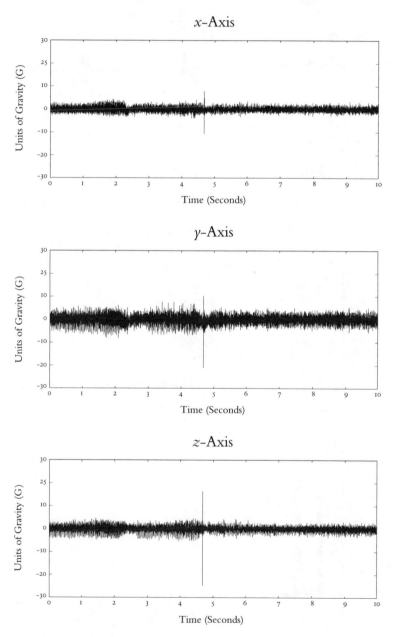

1998 DUCATI ST2

Acceleration Handlebar Vibration — Fast Fourier Transform (FFT)

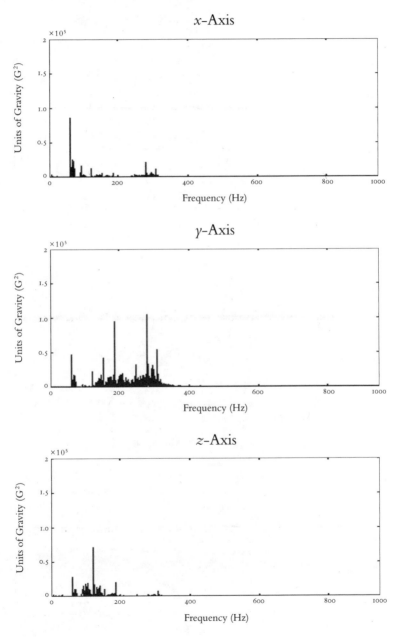

x-Axis

y-Axis

z-Axis

1998 DUCATI ST2

Acceleration Seat Vibration — Transducer Data

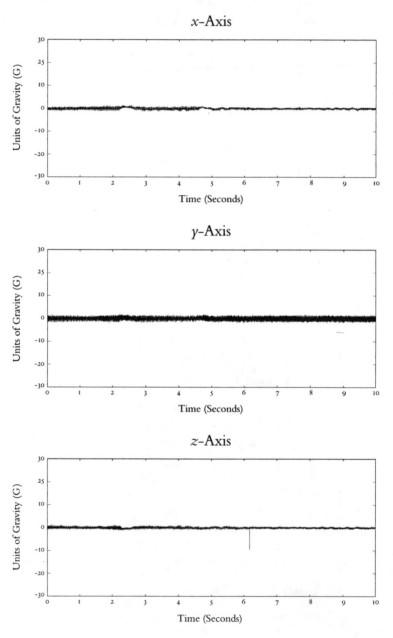

x-Axis

y-Axis

z-Axis

1998 DUCATI ST2

Acceleration Seat Vibration — Fast Fourier Transform (FFT)

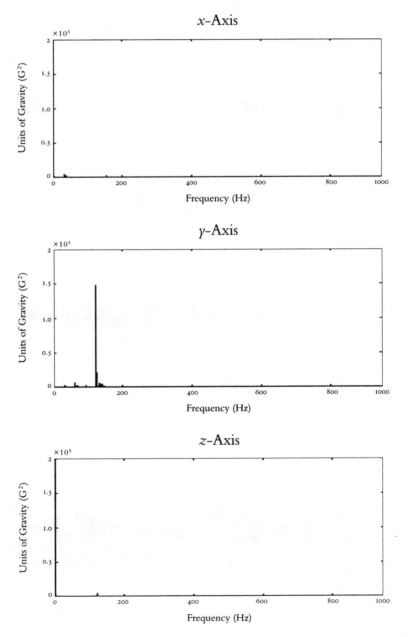

1998 DUCATI ST2

Acceleration Footpeg Vibration — Transducer Data

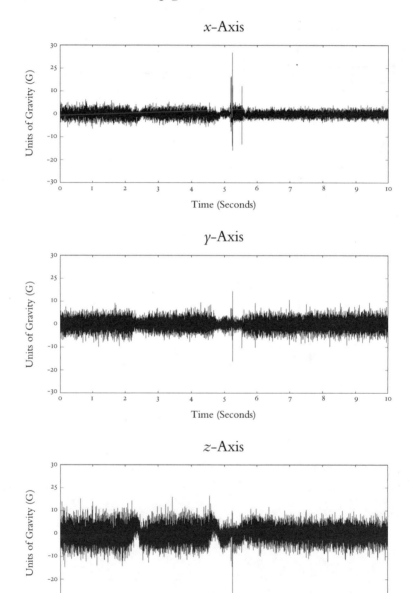

1998 DUCATI ST2

Acceleration Footpeg Vibration — Fast Fourier Transform (FFT)

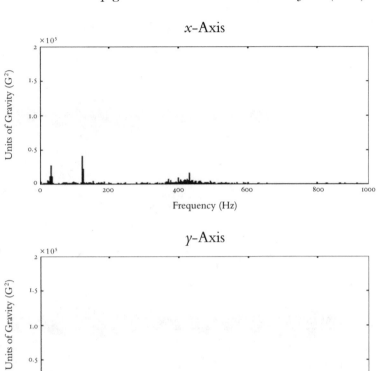

x-Axis

y-Axis

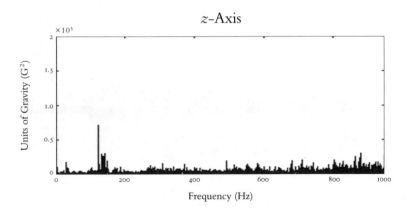

z-Axis

2000 HARLEY-DAVIDSON FAT BOY

Acceleration Handlebar Vibration — Transducer Data

x-Axis

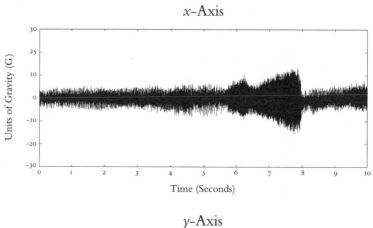

y-Axis

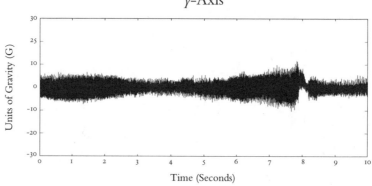

z-Axis

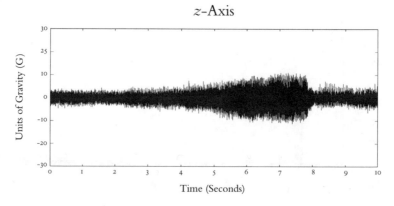

2000 HARLEY-DAVIDSON FAT BOY

Acceleration Handlebar Vibration — Fast Fourier Transform (FFT)

x-Axis

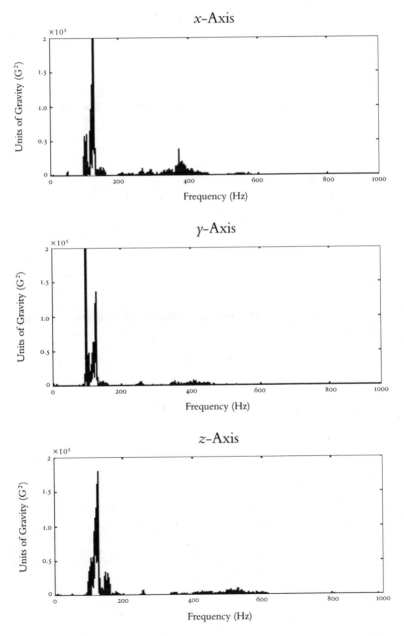

y-Axis

z-Axis

2000 HARLEY-DAVIDSON FAT BOY

Acceleration Seat Vibration — Transducer Data

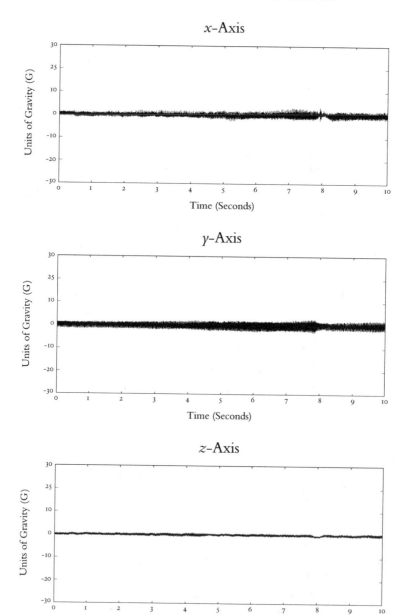

2000 HARLEY-DAVIDSON FAT BOY

Acceleration Seat Vibration — Fast Fourier Transform (FFT)

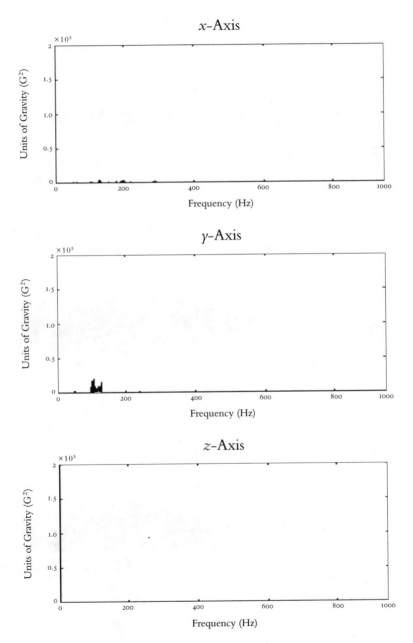

2000 HARLEY-DAVIDSON FAT BOY

Acceleration Footpeg Vibration — Transducer Data

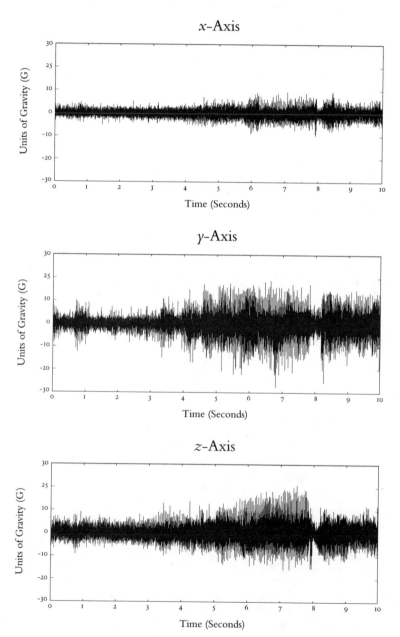

2000 HARLEY-DAVIDSON FAT BOY

Acceleration Footpeg Vibration — Fast Fourier Transform (FFT)

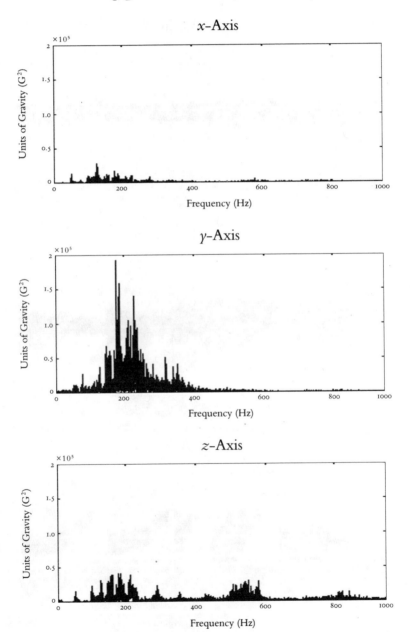

1978 HONDA CBX

Acceleration Handlebar Vibration — Transducer Data

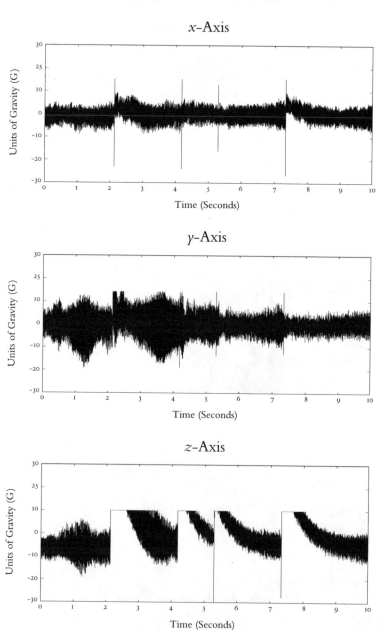

x-Axis

y-Axis

z-Axis

1978 HONDA CBX

Acceleration Handlebar Vibration — Fast Fourier Transform (FFT)

x-Axis

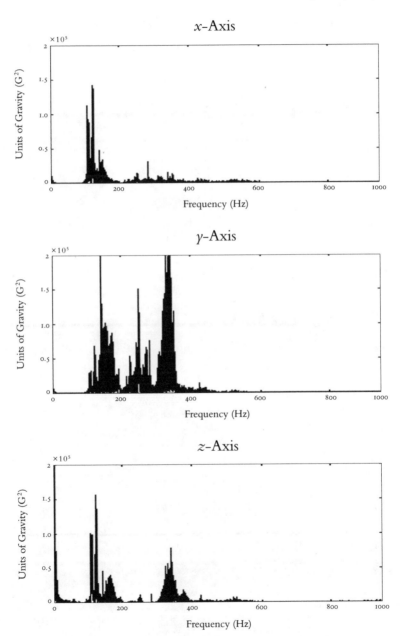

y-Axis

z-Axis

1978 HONDA CBX

Acceleration Seat Vibration — Transducer Data

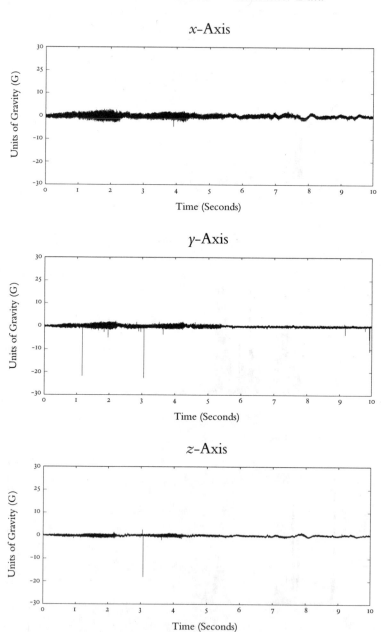

x-Axis

y-Axis

z-Axis

1978 HONDA CBX

Acceleration Seat Vibration — Fast Fourier Transform (FFT)

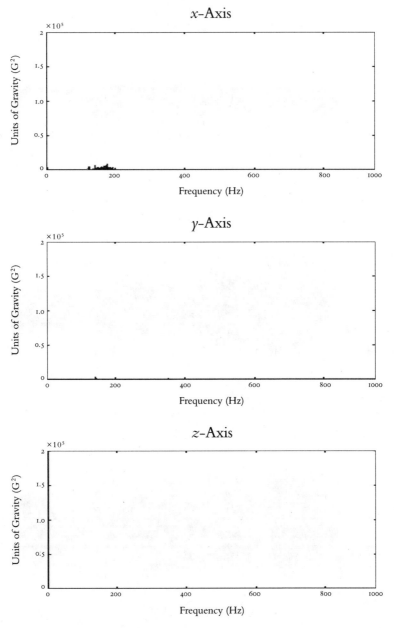

1978 HONDA CBX

Acceleration Footpeg Vibration — Transducer Data

x-Axis

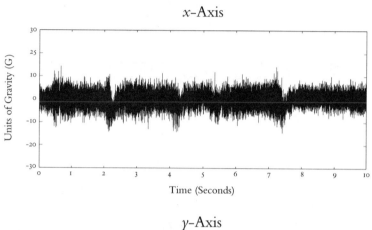

Time (Seconds)

γ-Axis

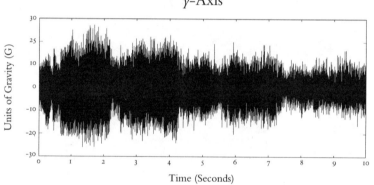

Time (Seconds)

z-Axis

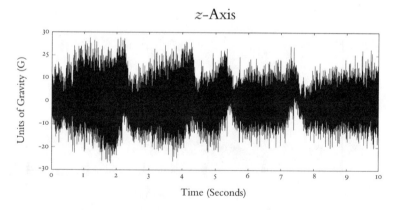

Time (Seconds)

1978 HONDA CBX

Acceleration Footpeg Vibration — Fast Fourier Transform (FFT)

x-Axis

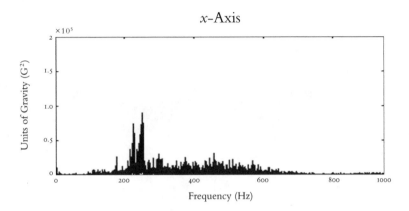

γ-Axis

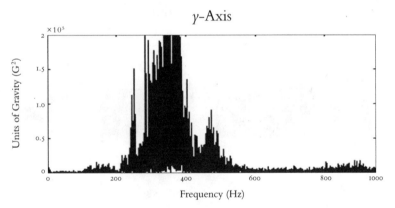

z-Axis

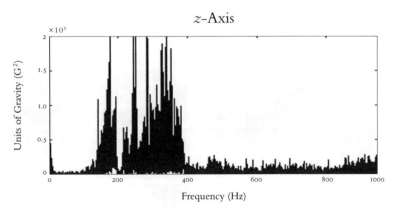

1987 HONDA VFR700F2

Acceleration Handlebar Vibration — Transducer Data

x-Axis

y-Axis

z-Axis

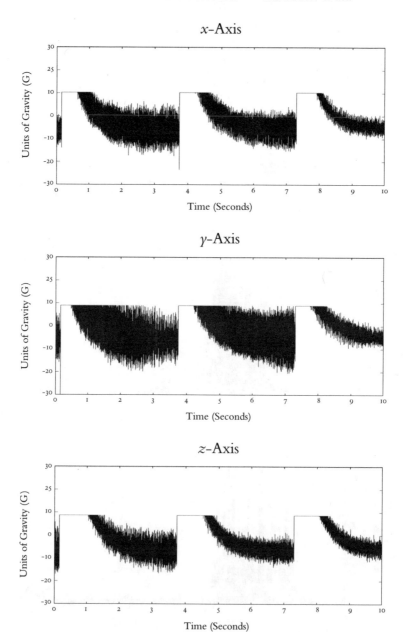

1987 HONDA VFR700F2

Acceleration Handlebar Vibration — Fast Fourier Transform (FFT)

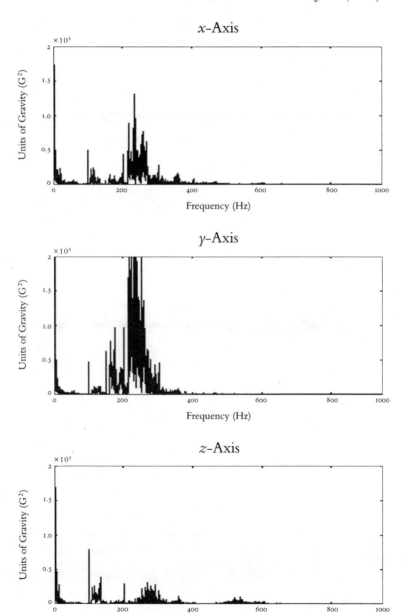

1987 HONDA VFR700F2

Acceleration Seat Vibration — Transducer Data

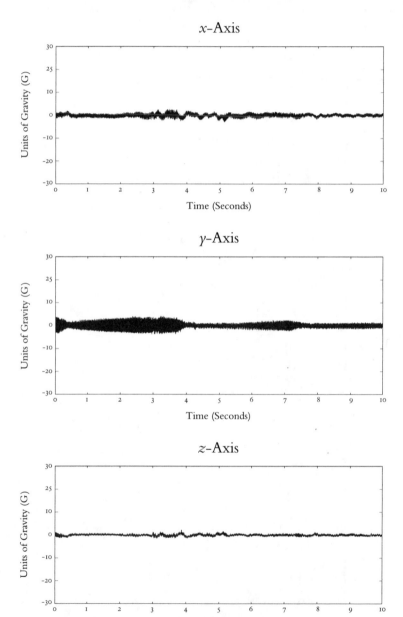

x-Axis

y-Axis

z-Axis

1987 HONDA VFR700F2

Acceleration Seat Vibration — Fast Fourier Transform (FFT)

x-Axis

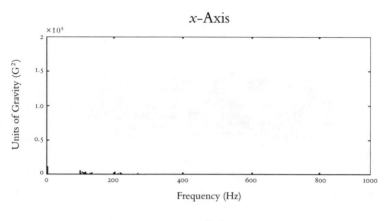

y-Axis

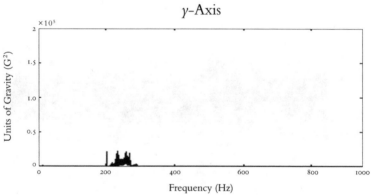

z-Axis

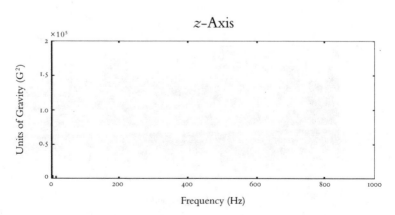

1987 HONDA VFR700F2

Acceleration Footpeg Vibration — Transducer Data

x-Axis

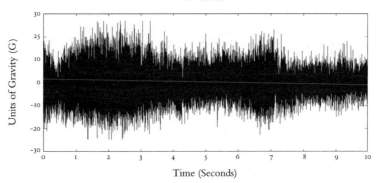

y-Axis

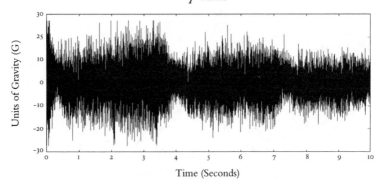

z-Axis

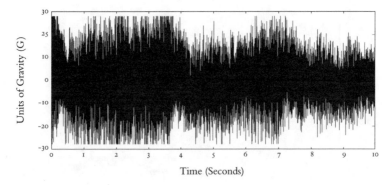

1987 HONDA VFR700F2

Acceleration Footpeg Vibration — Fast Fourier Transform (FFT)

x-Axis

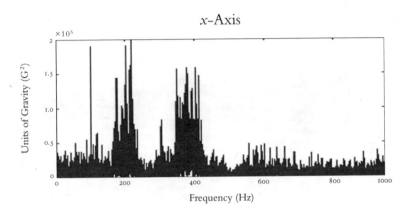

y-Axis

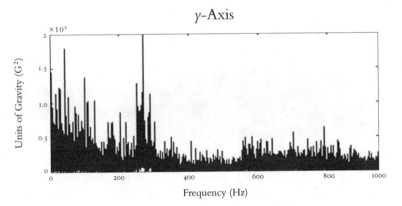

z-Axis

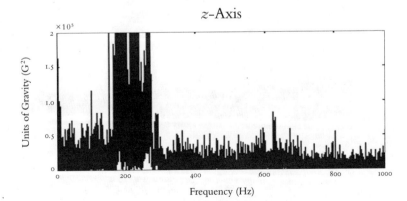

1968 TRIUMPH TR6C

Acceleration Handlebar Vibration — Transducer Data

x-Axis

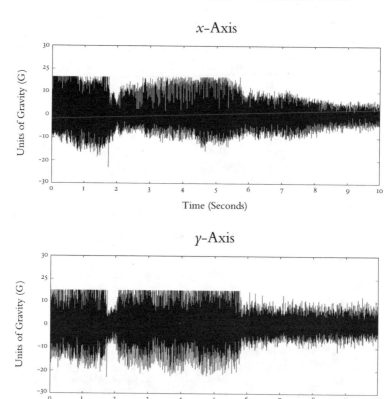

y-Axis

z-Axis

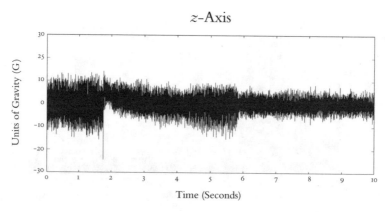

1968 TRIUMPH TR6C

Acceleration Handlebar Vibration — Fast Fourier Transform (FFT)

x-Axis

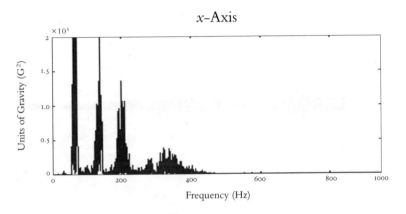

y-Axis

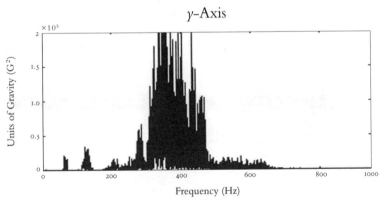

z-Axis

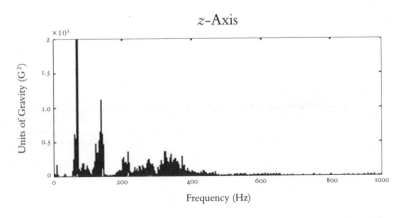

1968 TRIUMPH TR6C

Acceleration Seat Vibration — Transducer Data

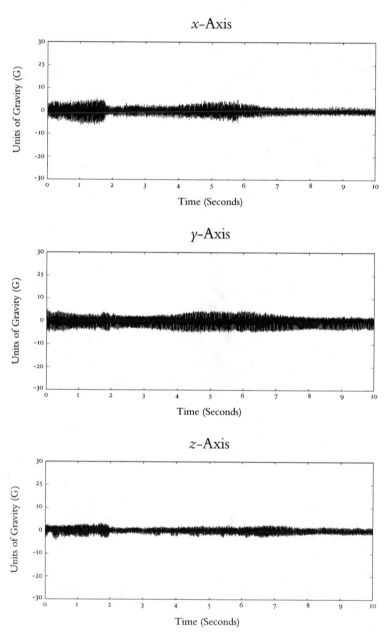

1968 TRIUMPH TR6C

Acceleration Seat Vibration — Fast Fourier Transform (FFT)

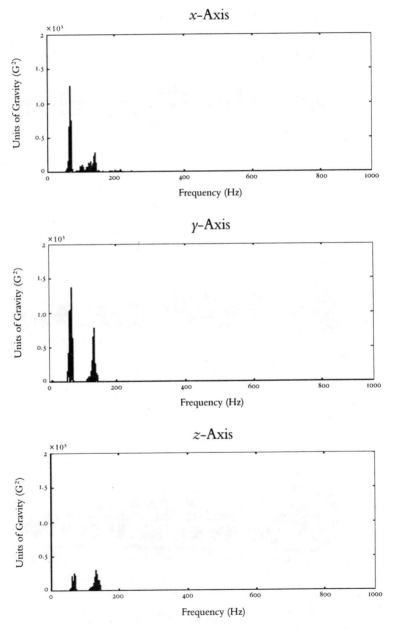

1968 TRIUMPH TR6C

Acceleration FootpegVibration — Transducer Data

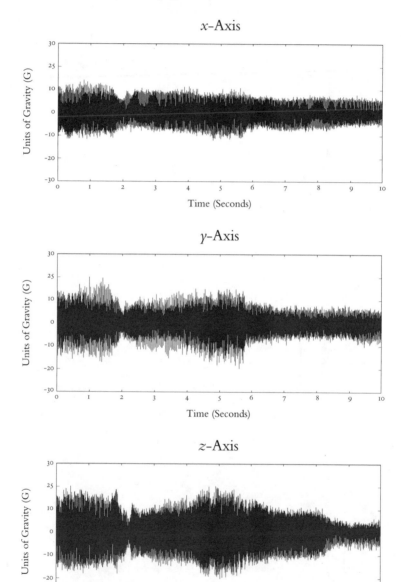

1968 TRIUMPH TR6C

Acceleration Footpeg Vibration — Fast Fourier Transform (FFT)

x-Axis

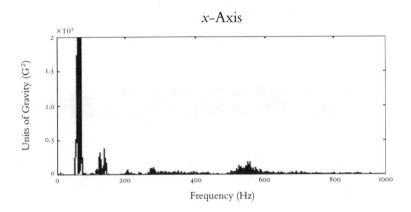

y-Axis

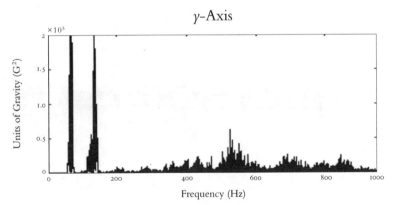

z-Axis

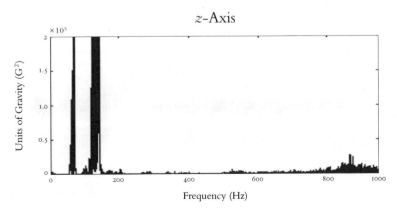

1959 VELOCETTE VENOM

Acceleration Handlebar Vibration — Transducer Data

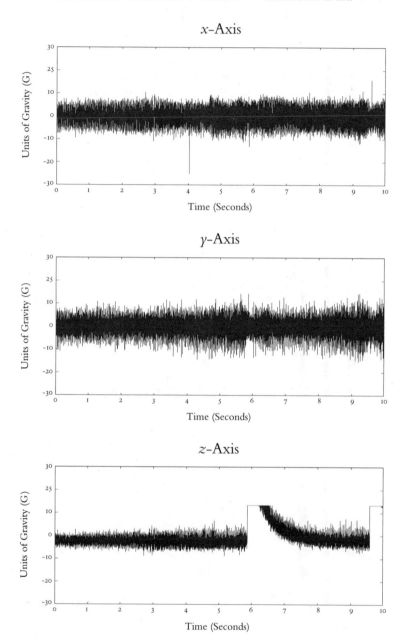

1959 VELOCETTE VENOM

Acceleration Handlebar Vibration — Fast Fourier Transform (FFT)

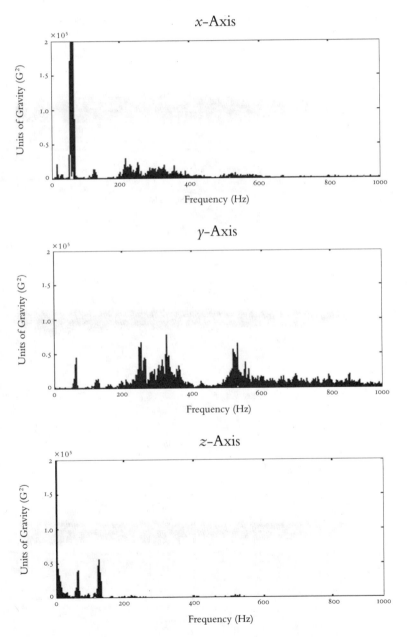

1959 VELOCETTE VENOM
Acceleration Seat Vibration — Transducer Data

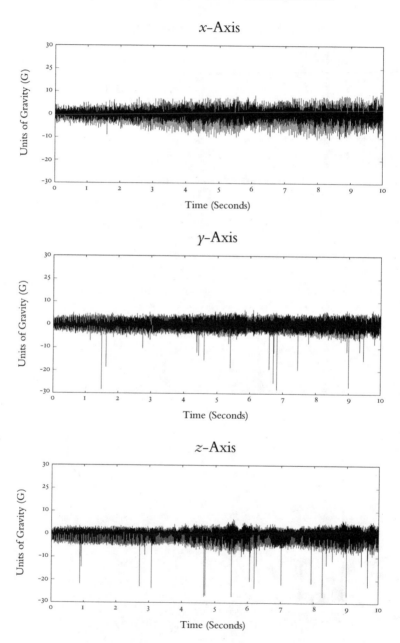

x-Axis

y-Axis

z-Axis

1959 VELOCETTE VENOM

Acceleration Seat Vibration — Fast Fourier Transform (FFT)

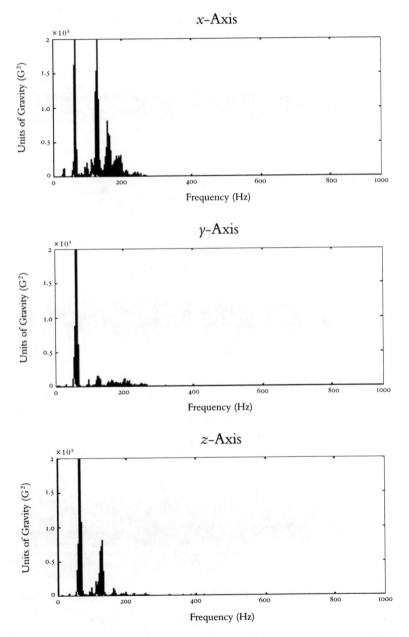

1959 VELOCETTE VENOM

Acceleration Footpeg Vibration — Transducer Data

x-Axis

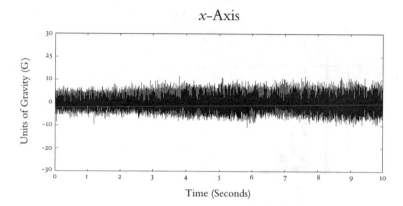

y-Axis

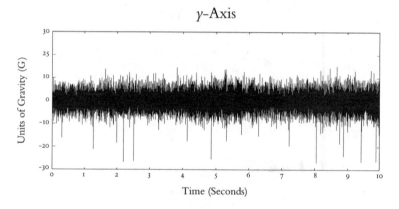

z-Axis

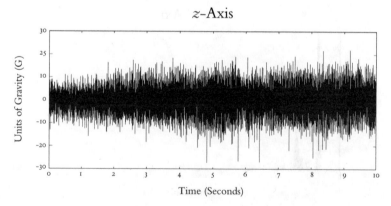

1959 VELOCETTE VENOM

Acceleration Footpeg Vibration — Fast Fourier Transform (FFT)

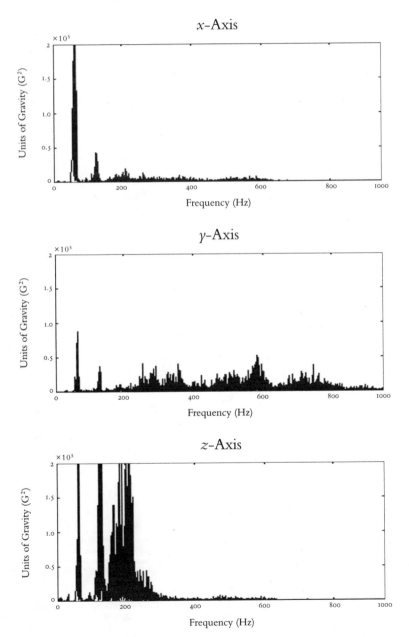

STANFORD UNIVERSITY
VIBRATION STUDY

60mph Vibration

OVERALL MOTORCYCLE COMPARISON

60mph Handlebar Vibration — Root Mean Square (RMS)

x-Axis

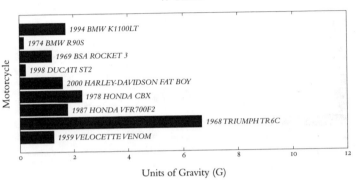

Units of Gravity (G)

γ-Axis

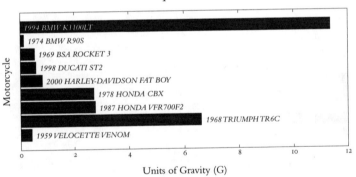

Units of Gravity (G)

z-Axis

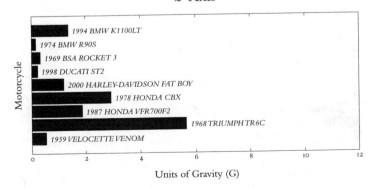

Units of Gravity (G)

OVERALL MOTORCYCLE COMPARISON

60mph Seat Vibration — Root Mean Square (RMS)

x-Axis

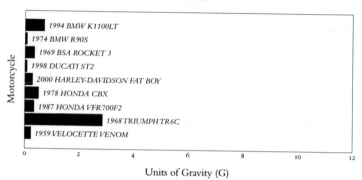

Units of Gravity (G)

y-Axis

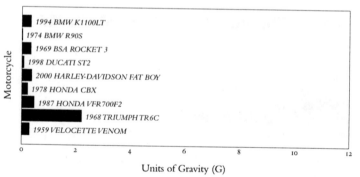

Units of Gravity (G)

z-Axis

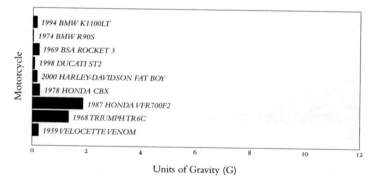

Units of Gravity (G)

OVERALL MOTORCYCLE COMPARISON
60mph Footpeg Vibration — Root Mean Square (RMS)

x-Axis

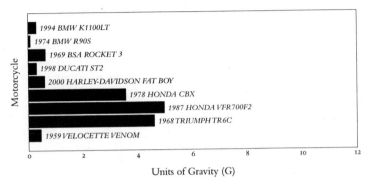

Units of Gravity (G)

y-Axis

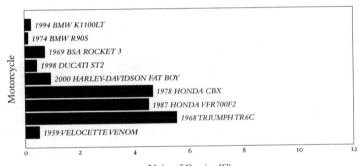

Units of Gravity (G)

z-Axis

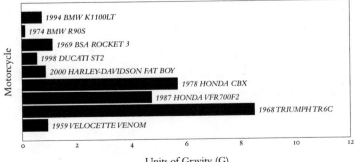

Units of Gravity (G)

1994 BMW K1100LT

60mph Handlebar Vibration — Transducer Data

x-Axis

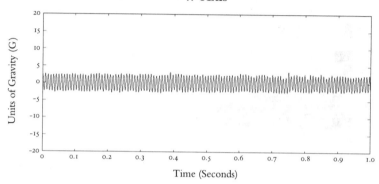

Time (Seconds)

y-Axis

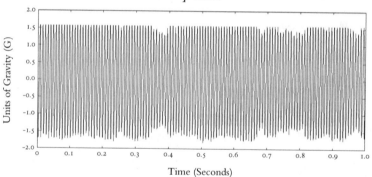

Time (Seconds)

z-Axis

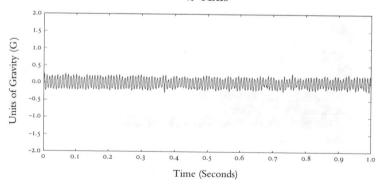

Time (Seconds)

1994 BMW K1100LT

60mph Handlebar Vibration — Fast Fourier Transform (FFT)

x-Axis

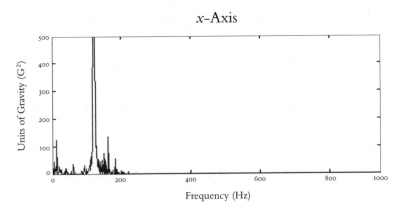

y-Axis

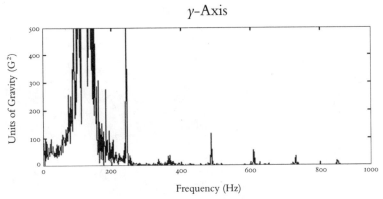

z-Axis

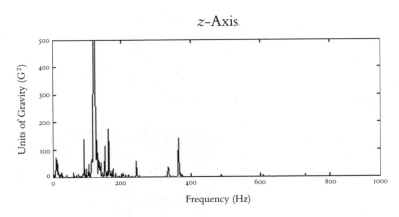

1994 BMW K1100LT

60mph Seat Vibration — Transducer Data

x-Axis

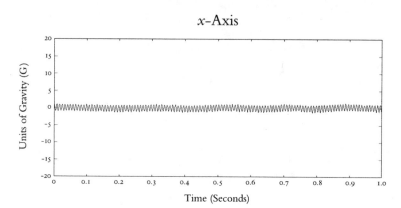

y-Axis

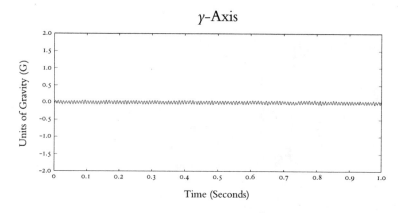

z-Axis

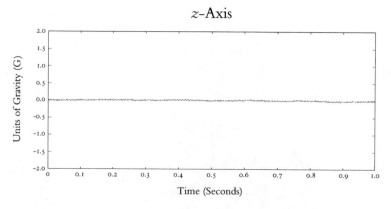

1994 BMW K1100LT

60mph Seat Vibration — Fast Fourier Transform (FFT)

x-Axis

y-Axis

z-Axis

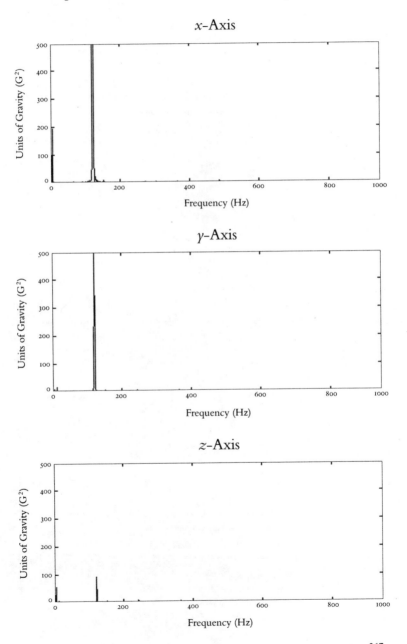

1994 BMW K1100LT

60mph Footpeg Vibration — Transducer Data

x-Axis

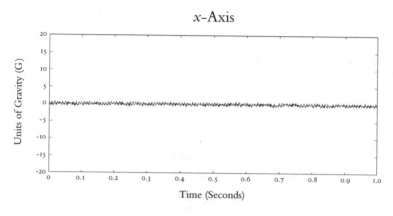

y-Axis

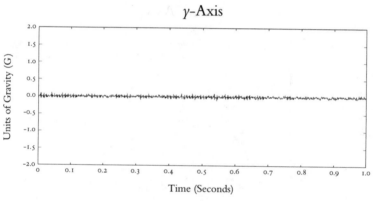

z-Axis

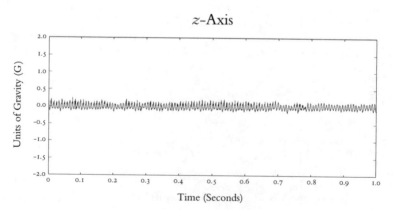

1994 BMW K1100LT

60mph Footpeg Vibration — Fast Fourier Transform (FFT)

x-Axis

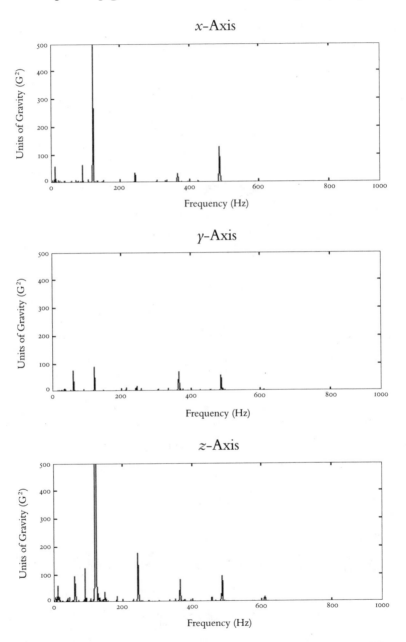

y-Axis

z-Axis

1974 BMW R90S

60mph Handlebar Vibration — Transducer Data

x-Axis

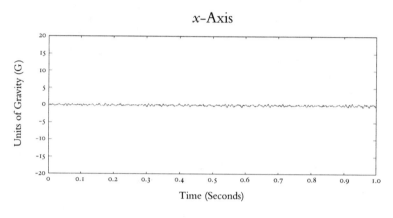

y-Axis

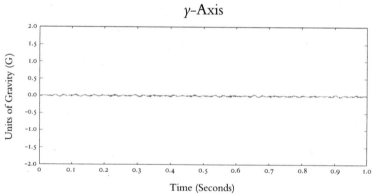

z-Axis

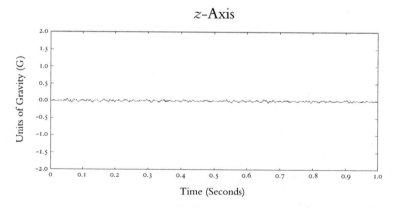

1974 BMW R90S

60mph Handlebar Vibration — Fast Fourier Transform (FFT)

x-Axis

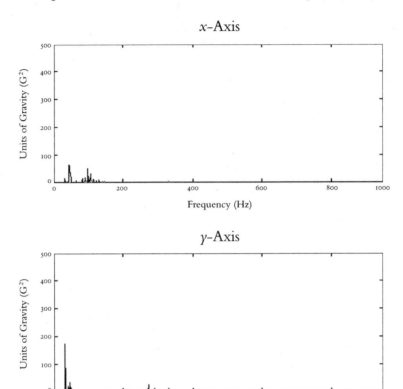

γ-Axis

z-Axis

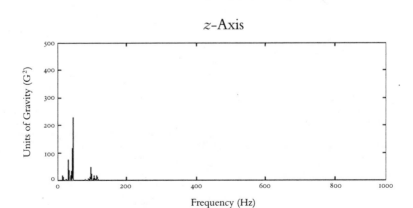

1974 BMW R90S

60mph Seat Vibration — Transducer Data

x-Axis

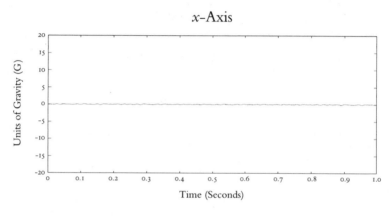

Units of Gravity (G)

Time (Seconds)

y-Axis

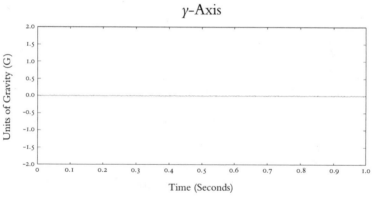

Units of Gravity (G)

Time (Seconds)

z-Axis

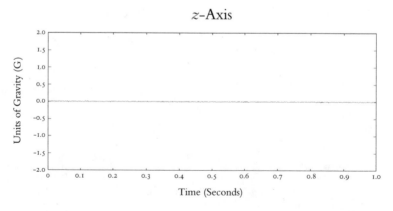

Units of Gravity (G)

Time (Seconds)

1974 BMW R90S

60mph Seat Vibration — Fast Fourier Transform (FFT)

x-Axis

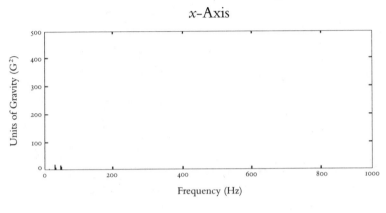

y-Axis

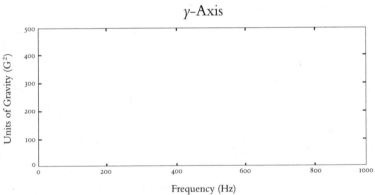

z-Axis

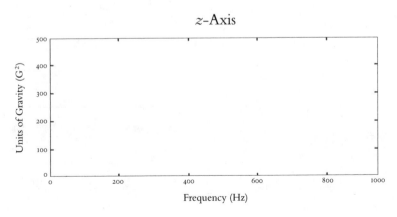

1974 BMW R90S

60mph Footpeg Vibration — Transducer Data

x-Axis

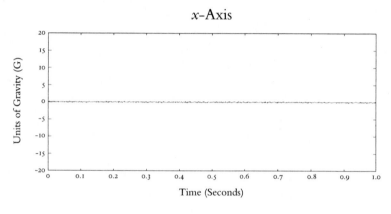

y-Axis

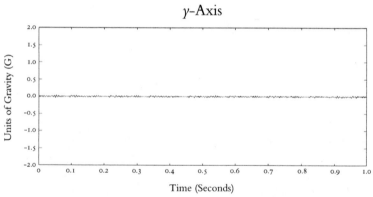

z-Axis

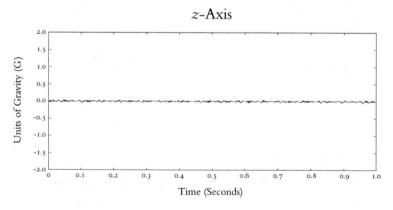

1974 BMW R90S

60mph Footpeg Vibration — Fast Fourier Transform (FFT)

x-Axis

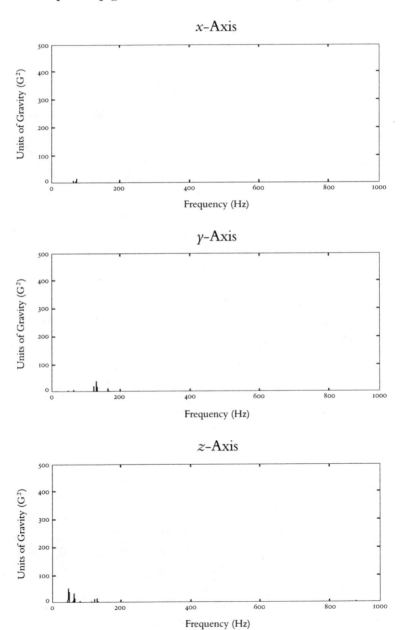

γ-Axis

z-Axis

1969 BSA ROCKET 3

60mph Handlebar Vibration — Transducer Data

x-Axis

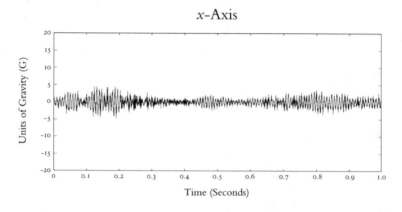

y-Axis

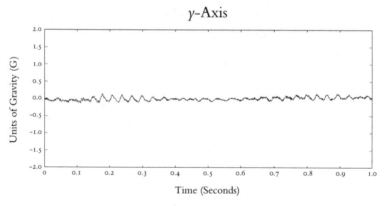

z-Axis

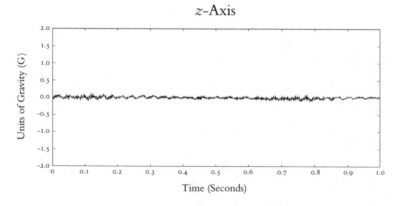

1969 BSA ROCKET 3

60mph Handlebar Vibration — Fast Fourier Transform (FFT)

x-Axis

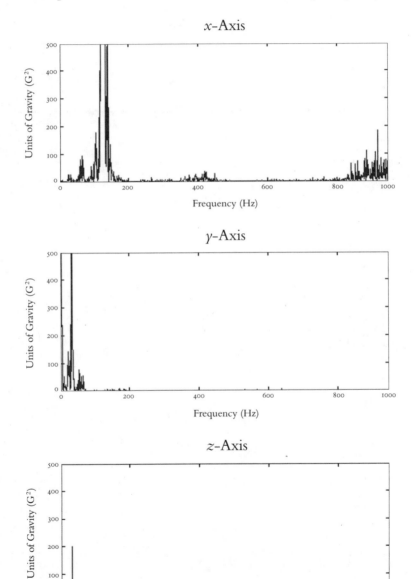

y-Axis

z-Axis

1969 BSA ROCKET 3

60mph Seat Vibration — Transducer Data

x-Axis

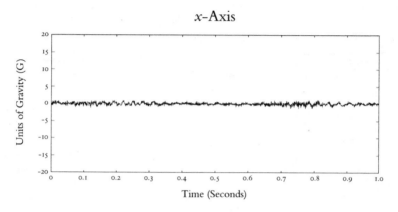

γ-Axis

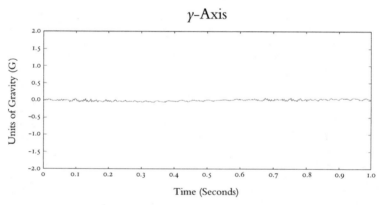

z-Axis

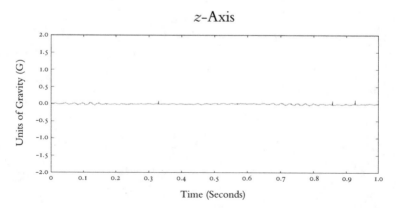

1969 BSA ROCKET 3

60mph Seat Vibration — Fast Fourier Transform (FFT)

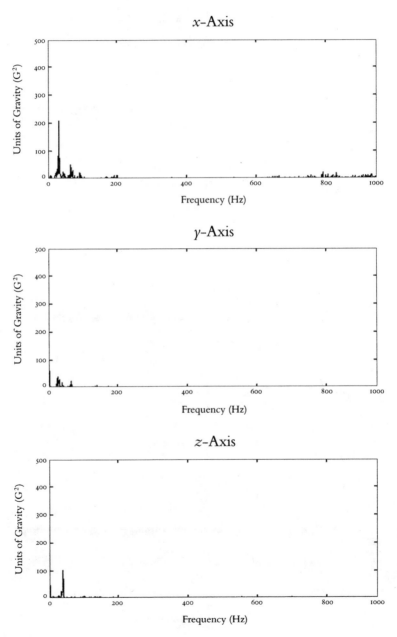

x-Axis

y-Axis

z-Axis

1969 BSA ROCKET 3

60mph Footpeg Vibration — Transducer Data

x-Axis

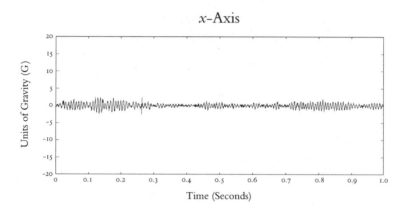

Time (Seconds)

y-Axis

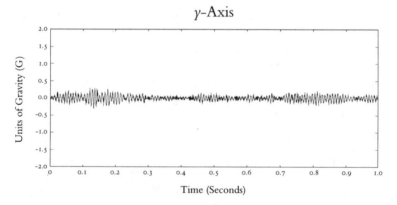

Time (Seconds)

z-Axis

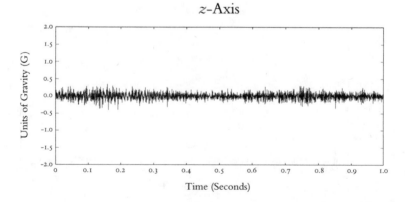

Time (Seconds)

1969 BSA ROCKET 3

60mph Footpeg Vibration — Fast Fourier Transform (FFT)

x-Axis

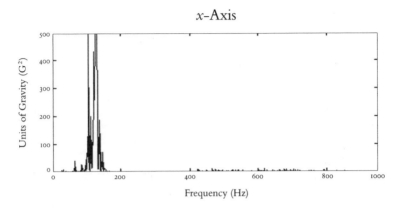

y-Axis

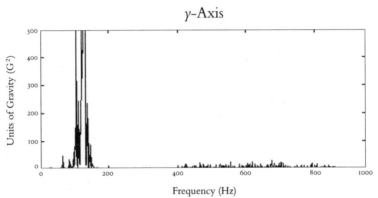

z-Axis

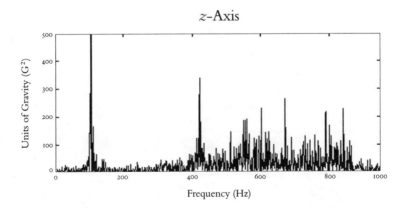

1998 DUCATI ST2

60mph Handlebar Vibration — Transducer Data

x-Axis

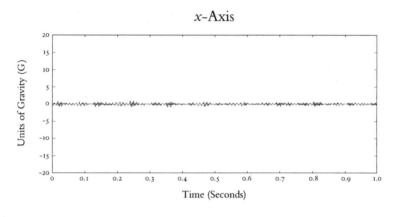

Time (Seconds)

y-Axis

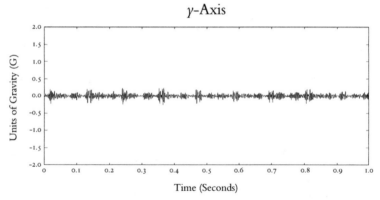

Time (Seconds)

z-Axis

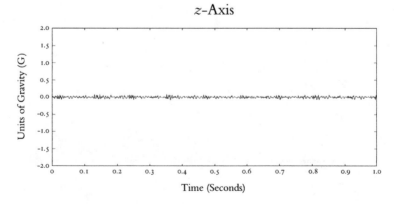

Time (Seconds)

1998 DUCATI ST2
60mph Handlebar Vibration — Fast Fourier Transform (FFT)

x-Axis

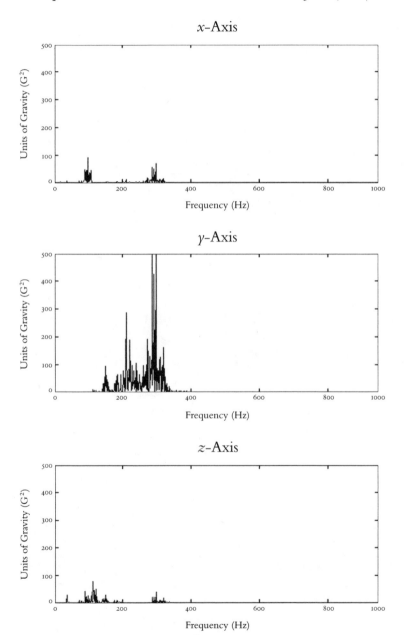

y-Axis

z-Axis

1998 DUCATI ST2

60mph Seat Vibration — Transducer Data

x-Axis

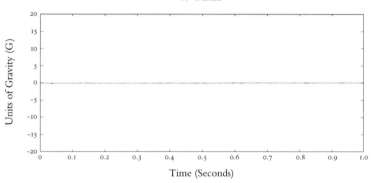

y-Axis

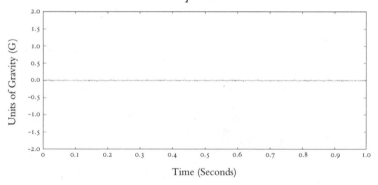

z-Axis

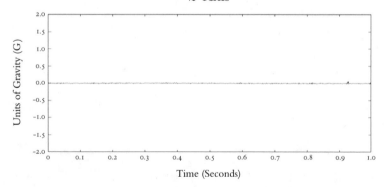

1998 DUCATI ST2

60mph Seat Vibration — Fast Fourier Transform (FFT)

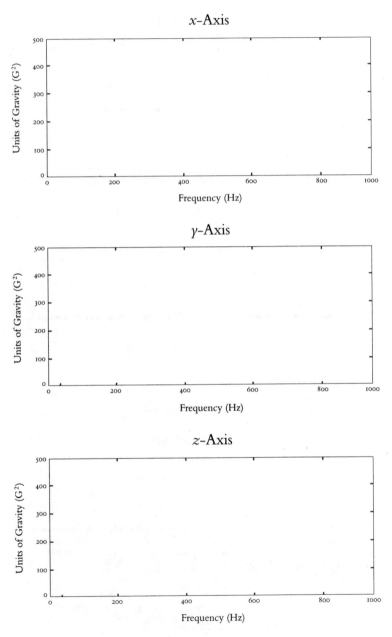

1998 DUCATI ST2

60mph Footpeg Vibration — Transducer Data

x-Axis

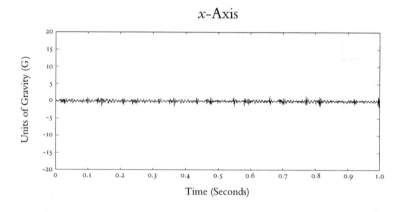

y-Axis

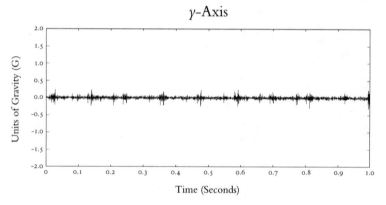

z-Axis

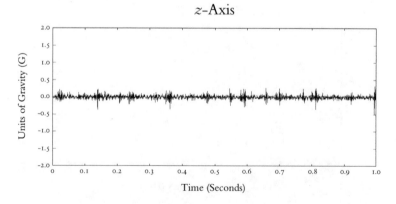

1998 DUCATI ST2

60mph Footpeg Vibration — Fast Fourier Transform (FFT)

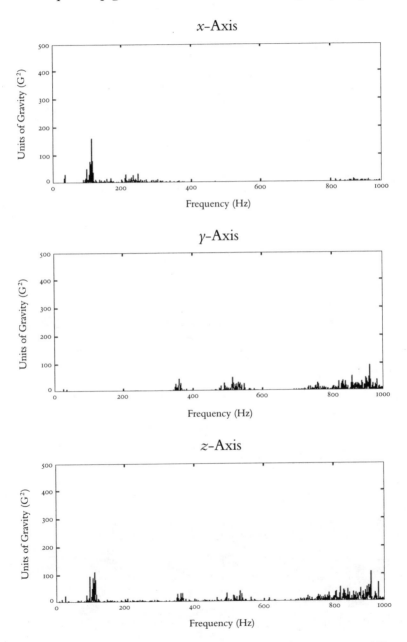

2000 HARLEY-DAVIDSON FAT BOY

60mph Handlebar Vibration — Transducer Data

x-Axis

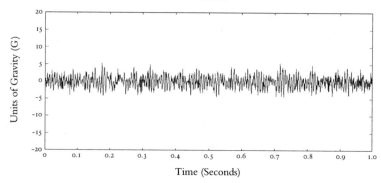

y-Axis

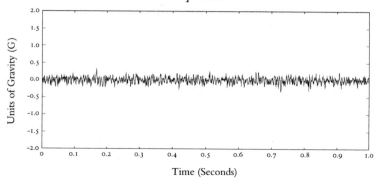

z-Axis

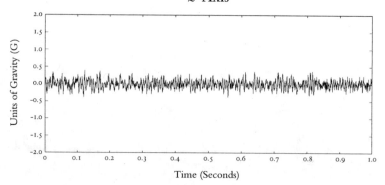

2000 HARLEY-DAVIDSON FAT BOY
60mph Handlebar Vibration — Fast Fourier Transform (FFT)

x-Axis

y-Axis

z-Axis

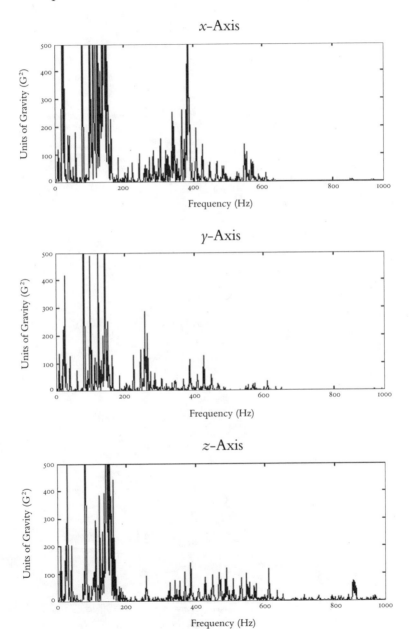

2000 HARLEY-DAVIDSON FAT BOY

60mph Seat Vibration — Transducer Data

x-Axis

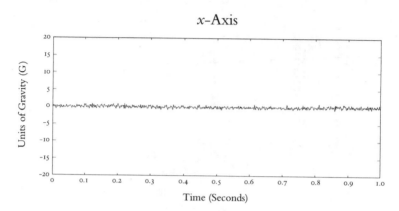

y-Axis

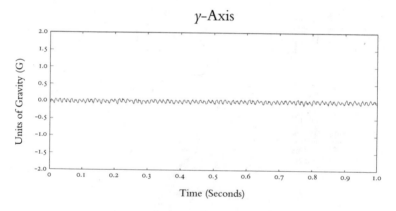

z-Axis

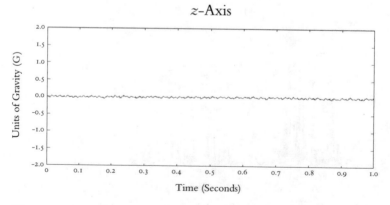

2000 HARLEY-DAVIDSON FAT BOY

60mph Seat Vibration — Fast Fourier Transform (FFT)

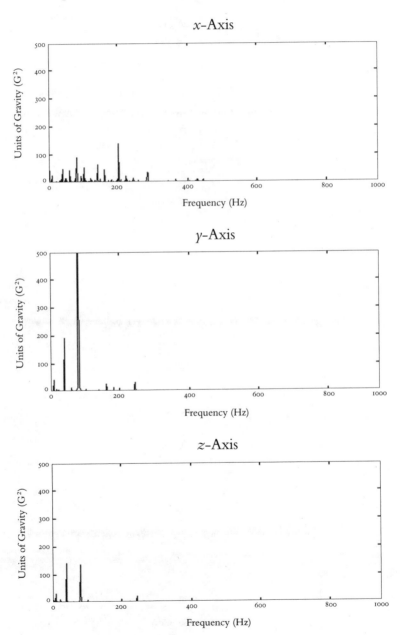

2000 HARLEY-DAVIDSON FAT BOY
60mph Footpeg Vibration — Transducer Data

x-Axis

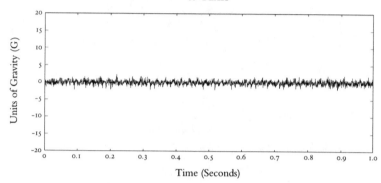

y-Axis

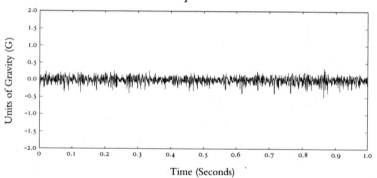

z-Axis

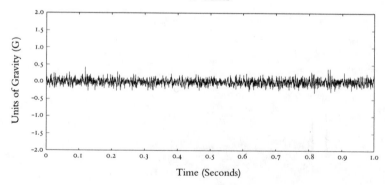

2000 HARLEY-DAVIDSON FAT BOY

60mph Footpeg Vibration — Fast Fourier Transform (FFT)

x-Axis

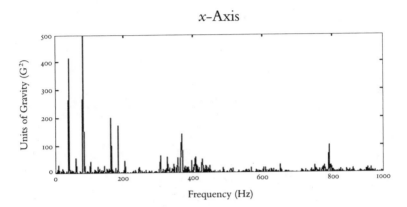

y-Axis

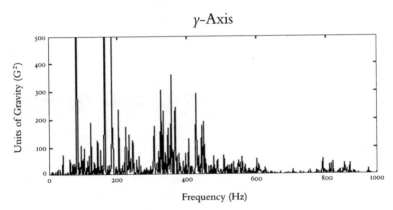

z-Axis

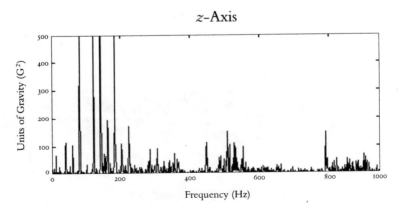

1978 HONDA CBX

60mph Handlebar Vibration — Transducer Data

x-Axis

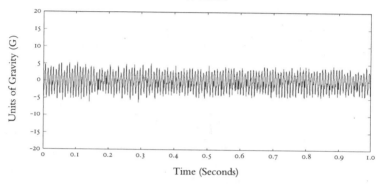

y-Axis

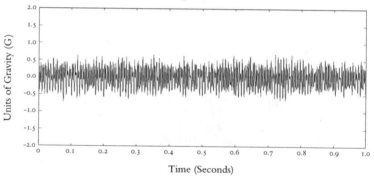

z-Axis

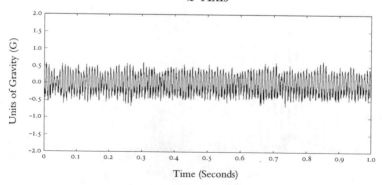

1978 HONDA CBX

60mph Handlebar Vibration — Fast Fourier Transform (FFT)

x-Axis

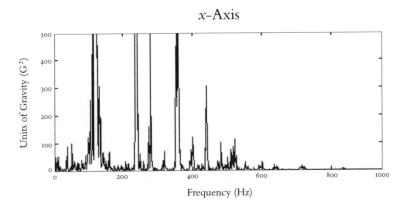

γ-Axis

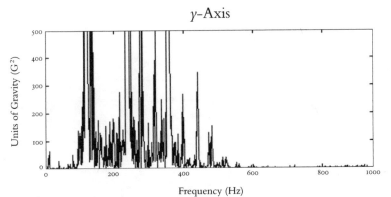

z-Axis

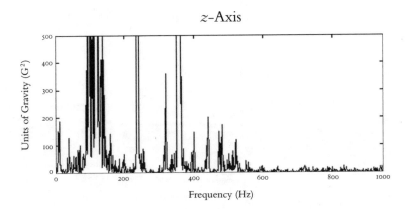

1978 HONDA CBX
60mph Seat Vibration — Transducer Data

x-Axis

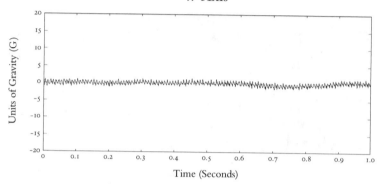

y-Axis

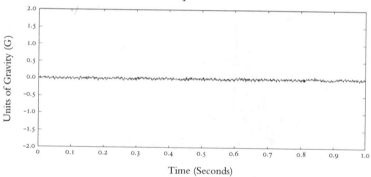

z-Axis

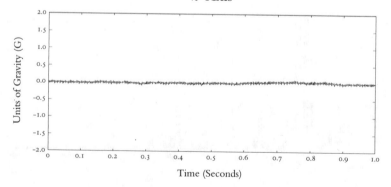

1978 HONDA CBX

60mph Seat Vibration — Fast Fourier Transform (FFT)

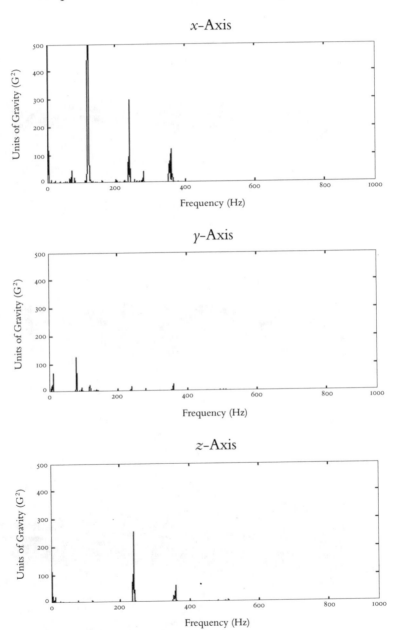

x-Axis

y-Axis

z-Axis

1978 HONDA CBX

60mph Footpeg Vibration — Transducer Data

x-Axis

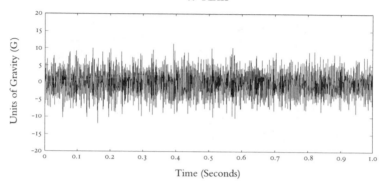

Time (Seconds)

y-Axis

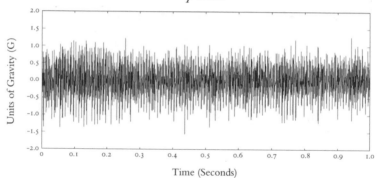

Time (Seconds)

z-Axis

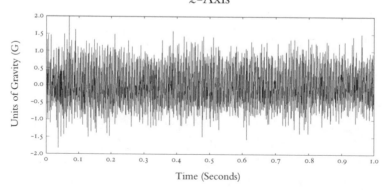

Time (Seconds)

1978 HONDA CBX

60mph Footpeg Vibration — Fast Fourier Transform (FFT)

x-Axis

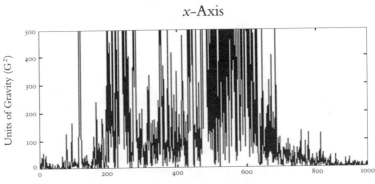

y-Axis

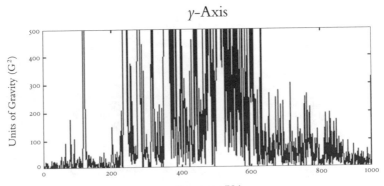

z-Axis

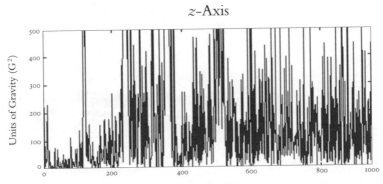

1987 HONDA VFR700F2

60mph Handlebar Vibration — Transducer Data

x-Axis

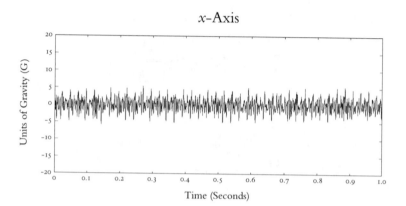

y-Axis

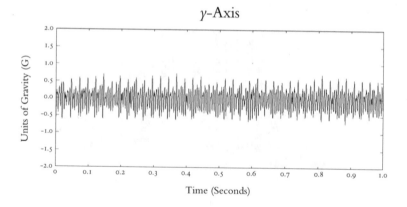

z-Axis

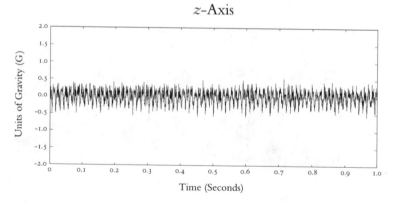

1987 HONDA VFR700F2

60mph Handlebar Vibration — Fast Fourier Transform (FFT)

x-Axis

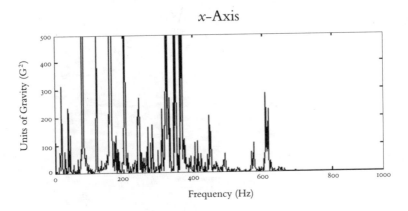

y-Axis

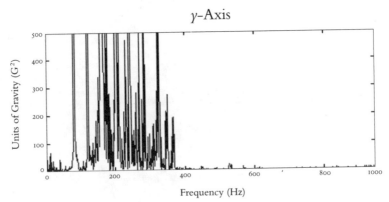

z-Axis

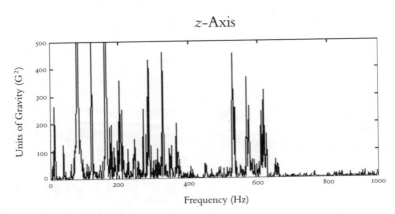

1987 HONDA VFR700F2
60mph Seat Vibration — Transducer Data

x-Axis

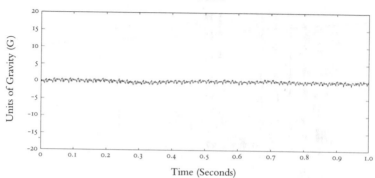

y-Axis

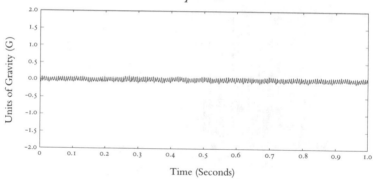

z-Axis

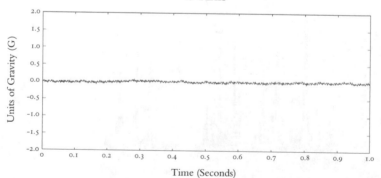

1987 HONDA VFR700F2

60mph Seat Vibration — Fast Fourier Transform (FFT)

x-Axis

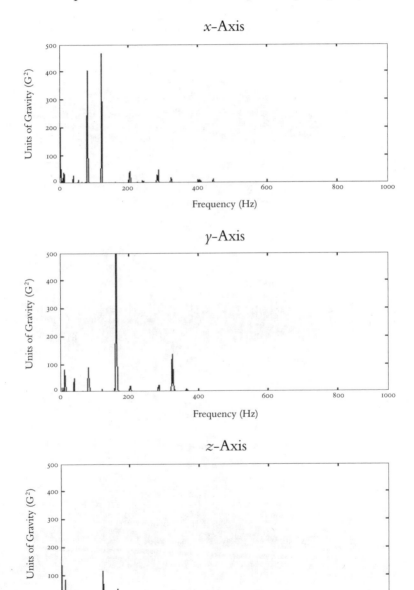

y-Axis

z-Axis

1987 HONDA VFR700F2

60mph Footpeg Vibration — Transducer Data

x-Axis

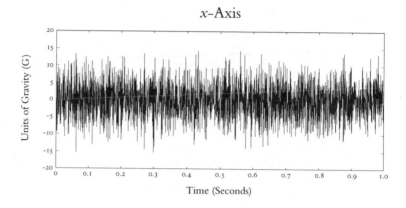

γ-Axis

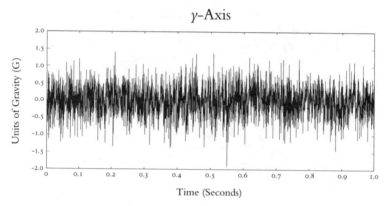

z-Axis

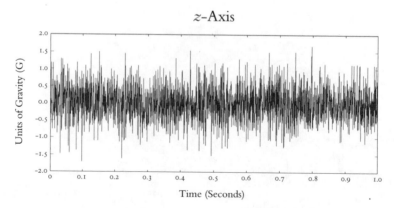

1987 HONDA VFR700F2

60mph Footpeg Vibration — Fast Fourier Transform (FFT)

x-Axis

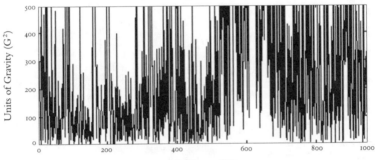

Frequency (Hz)

y-Axis

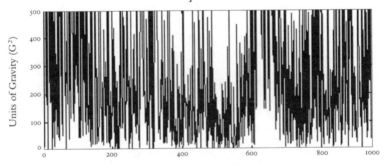

Frequency (Hz)

z-Axis

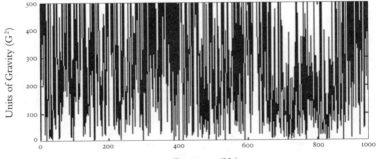

Frequency (Hz)

1968 TRIUMPH TR6C

60mph Handlebar Vibration — Transducer Data

x-Axis

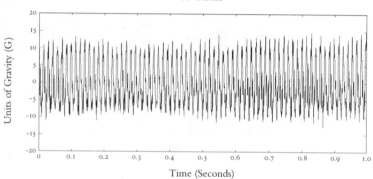

y-Axis

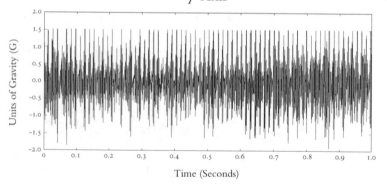

z-Axis

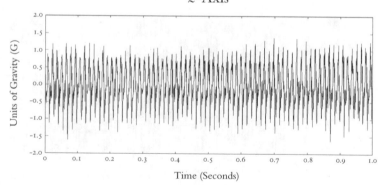

1968 TRIUMPH TR6C

60mph Handlebar Vibration — Fast Fourier Transform (FFT)

x-Axis

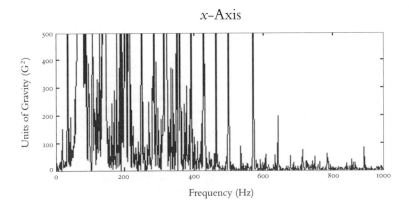

y-Axis

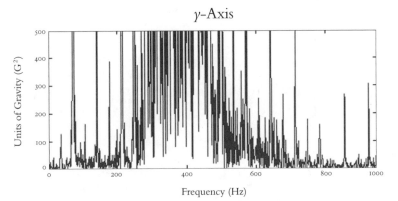

z-Axis

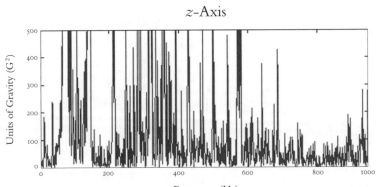

1968 TRIUMPH TR6C

60mph Seat Vibration — Transducer Data

x-Axis

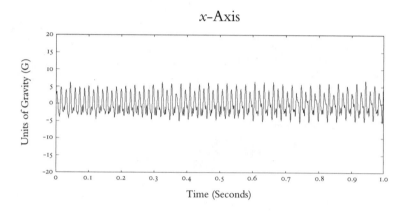

y-Axis

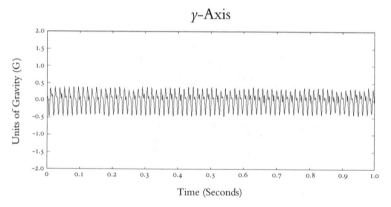

z-Axis

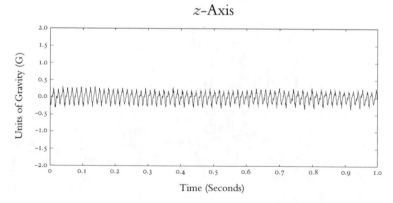

1968 TRIUMPH TR6C

60mph Seat Vibration — Fast Fourier Transform (FFT)

x-Axis

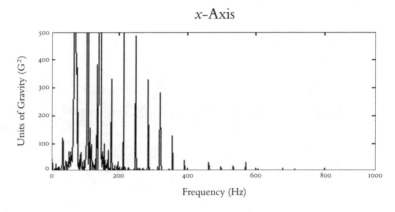

γ-Axis

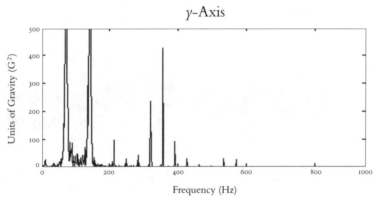

z-Axis

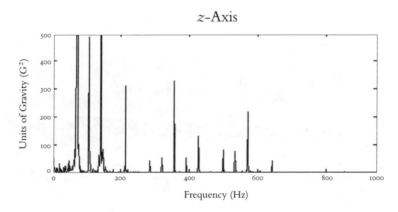

1968 TRIUMPH TR6C

60mph Footpeg Vibration — Transducer Data

x-Axis

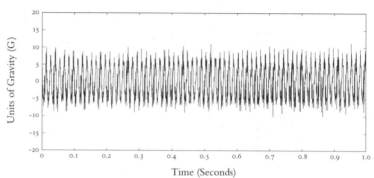

y-Axis

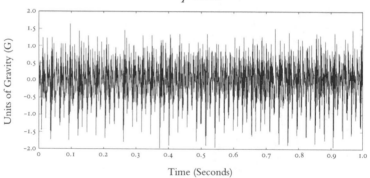

z-Axis

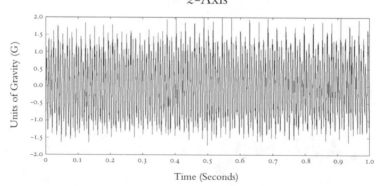

1968 TRIUMPH TR6C

60mph Footpeg Vibration — Fast Fourier Transform (FFT)

x-Axis

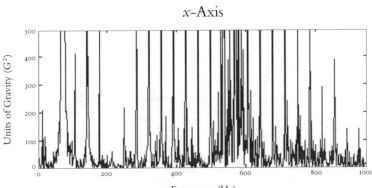

y-Axis

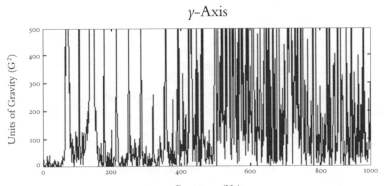

z-Axis

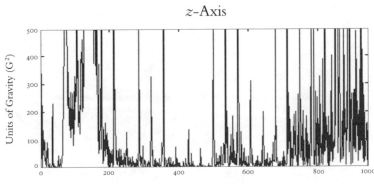

1959 VELOCETTE VENOM
60mph Handlebar Vibration — Transducer Data

x-Axis

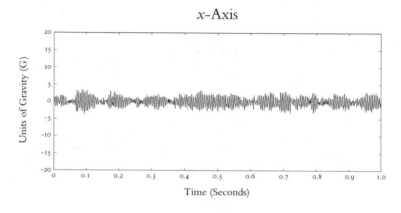

y-Axis

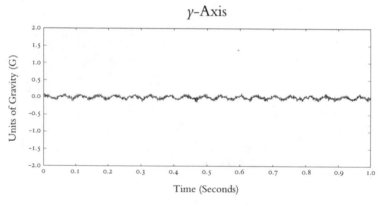

z-Axis

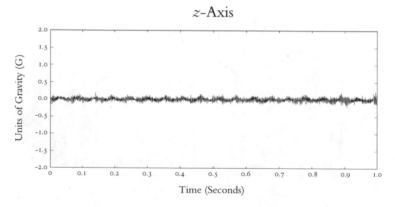

1959 VELOCETTE VENOM

60mph Handlebar Vibration — Fast Fourier Transform (FFT)

x-Axis

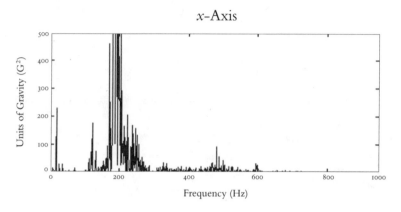

y-Axis

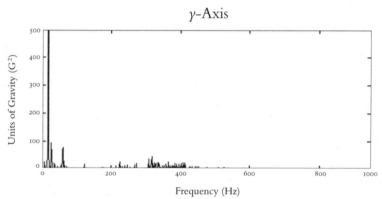

z-Axis

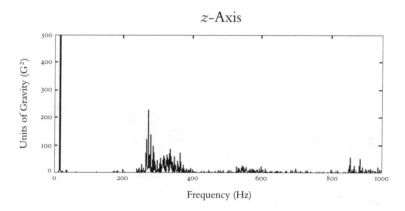

1959 VELOCETTE VENOM

60mph Seat Vibration — Transducer Data

x-Axis

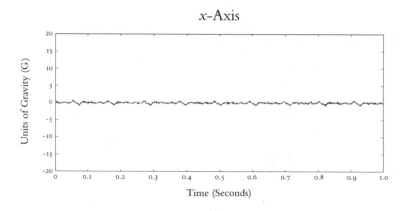

Time (Seconds)

y-Axis

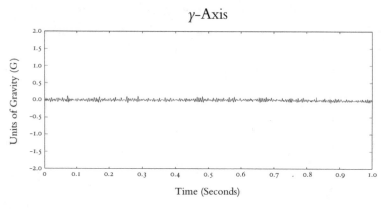

Time (Seconds)

z-Axis

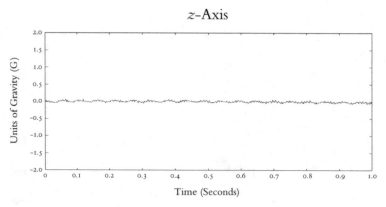

Time (Seconds)

1959 VELOCETTE VENOM

60mph Seat Vibration — Fast Fourier Transform (FFT)

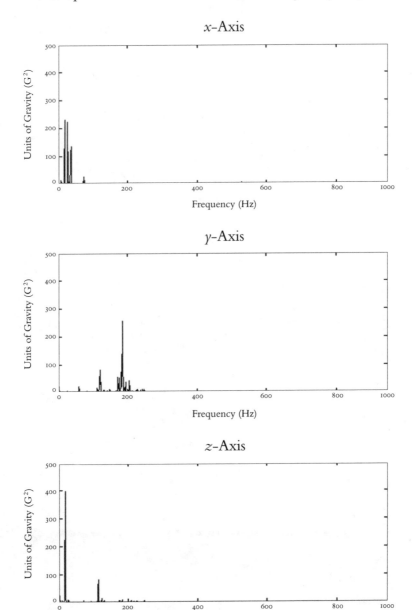

1959 VELOCETTE VENOM

60mph Footpeg Vibration — Transducer Data

x-Axis

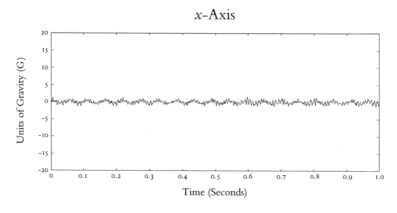

Time (Seconds)

y-Axis

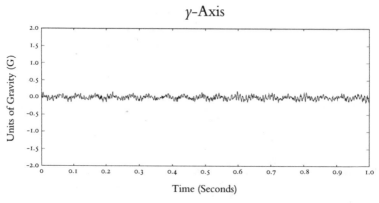

Time (Seconds)

z-Axis

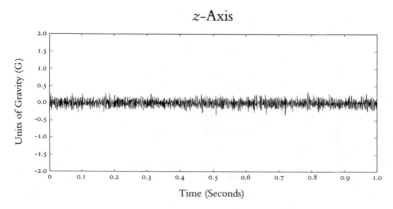

Time (Seconds)

1959 VELOCETTE VENOM

60mph Footpeg Vibration — Fast Fourier Transform (FFT)

x-Axis

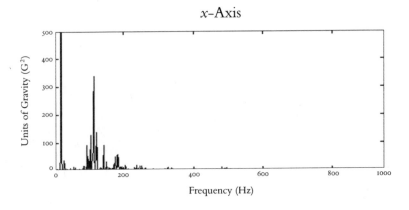

γ-Axis

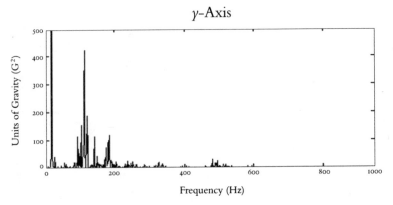

z-Axis

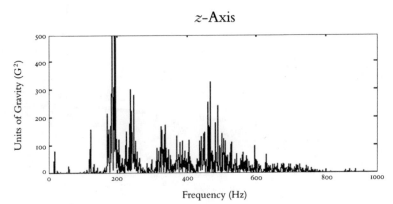